RESPONDING TO SYSTEMIC HUMAN RIGHTS VIOLATIONS

RESPONDING TO SYSTEMIC HUMAN RIGHTS VIOLATIONS

An Analysis of 'Pilot Judgments' of the European Court of Human Rights and their Impact at National Level

Philip LEACH
Helen HARDMAN
Svetlana STEPHENSON
Brad K. BLITZ

intersentia
Antwerp – Oxford – Portland

Distribution for the UK:
Hart Publishing Ltd.
16C Worcester Place
Oxford OX1 2JW
UK
Tel.: +44 1865 51 75 30
Email: mail@hartpub.co.uk

Distribution for the USA and Canada:
International Specialized Book Services
920 NE 58th Ave Suite 300
Portland, OR 97213
USA
Tel.: +1 800 944 6190 (toll free)
Tel.: +1 503 287 3093
Email: info@isbs.com

Distribution for Austria:
Neuer Wissenschaftlicher Verlag
Argentinierstraße 42/6
1040 Wien
Austria
Tel.: +43 1 535 61 03 24
Email: office@nwv.at

Distribution for other countries:
Intersentia Publishers
Groenstraat 31
2640 Mortsel
Belgium
Tel.: +32 3 680 15 50
Email: mail@intersentia.be

Responding to Systemic Human Rights Violations. An Analysis of 'Pilot Judgments' of the European Court of Human Rights and their Impact at National Level
Philip Leach, Helen Hardman, Svetlana Stephenson and Brad K. Blitz

Cover Artwork: Mary Leach

ISBN 978-94-000-0041-4
D/2010/7849/59
NUR 828

CONTENTS

ACKNOWLEDGEMENTS

We would like to thank Aruna Dudhia (Manager of the Human Rights and Social Justice Research Institute at London Metropolitan University) for her administrative support and logistical assistance throughout the duration of this project. Our thanks also to Oksana Popova (at the European Human Rights Advocacy Centre) for her assistance with the Ukrainian interviews and for translating documents from Ukrainian into English.

Our thanks to the following for transcribing interviews: Eleanor Bindman, Silvia Dominici, Delia Midamba, Ida Ogoudikpe, Vladimir Puscalau, Martin Ridley and Elizabeth Sheehan. We are grateful to Damian Pietrzak for translating our consent form into Polish, and to Maite Van Regemorter for translating our consent form and questionnaire into French.

We would like to thank Federica Arisco, Ivana Bartoletti and Silvia Dominici both for their research assistance and for translating documents from Italian into English.

We are very grateful to the members of our advisory group: Constantin Cojocariu (Interights), Andrew Drzemczewski (Head of the Secretariat, Committee on Legal Affairs & Human Rights, Parliamentary Assembly of the Council of Europe), Catharina Harby (AIRE Centre), Jill Heine (Amnesty International), Rob Linham (Ministry of Justice, UK Government) and Linos-Alexander Sicilianos (University of Athens). Very many thanks also to Professor Bill Bowring (Birkbeck College, University of London) and to Costas Paraskeva for their valuable comments on draft sections of the report.

In Strasbourg we received much needed support and assistance from Erik Fribergh (Registrar of the European Court of Human Rights), Michael O'Boyle (Deputy Registrar of the European Court) and from Gail Fitzpatrick (in the Deputy Registrar's Office) for which we are extremely grateful. Many thanks also to Jakub Wołąsiewicz, the Polish Government Agent, whose vision resulted in a seminar being held in Warsaw while we were there in May 2009 (held in conjunction with the Ministry of Foreign Affairs and kindly hosted by the National School of Public Administration in Warsaw).

We would also like to express our thanks to all our interviewees and respondents for generously giving their time in order to assist us with this research.

INTRODUCTION

The focus of this work is an evaluation of the European Court of Human Rights' pilot judgment procedure, which is applied in relation to wide-scale human rights violations – those which can affect many thousands of people. Such violations sometimes occur because of deficiencies in a state's legislation, but more frequently they are caused by a diverse range of factors, including a state's poor administrative practice, the prevalent judicial and legal cultures, budgetary deficits and an absence of sufficient political will to resolve the issue. As a response to these widespread 'structural', or even 'endemic' defects, in 2004, the European Court began to issue 'pilot judgments', the aim of which was not only to exert further pressure on national authorities to tackle these problems, but also to stop the European Court itself being inundated with the same type of cases.[1]

The identification of systemic deficiencies is not of course a new phenomenon for the European Court. Indeed, since pronouncing on some of its earliest cases, such as the 1968 judgment in the *Belgian Linguistic* case,[2] the Court has frequently highlighted legislative faults. The Court has also on occasion found states liable for a 'practice' that is considered to be incompatible with the European Convention on Human Rights,[3] and has even permitted challenges to legislation by complainants to whom it may not in fact have been applied (*almost* on the basis of an '*actio popularis*').[4]

Where, however, the Court has broken new ground with its 'pilot judgment procedure', which has been fashioned out of its own case law and is underpinned

1 Speaking in September 2009, Erik Fribergh, the Registrar of the European Court, stated that 'repetitive' cases accounted for more than 50% of the total judgments delivered by the Court since its inception. See: Erik Fribergh, *Bringing Rights Home or How to deal with repetitive applications in the future*, Round Table, Bled, Slovenia, 21–22.9.09, para. 6. Fribergh advocates moving to a system whereby once the Court has identified a systemic violation, the burden should then shift to the respondent state and the Committee of Ministers, and all similar repetitive cases would be 'repatriated' back to the national level. This would require an amendment to the European Convention on Human Rights.

2 Case *Relating To Certain Aspects of the Laws on the Use of Languages in Education in Belgium v Belgium*, Nos. 1474/62, 1677/62, 1691/62, 1769/63, 1994/63, 2126/64, 23.7.68 (finding a 1963 law on the use of languages in education to be in breach of Article 14 of the European Convention on Human Rights taken together with Article 2 of Protocol No. 1).

3 See, for example, *Bottazzi v Italy*, No. 34884/97, 28.7.99 (as regards the right to a trial within a reasonable time).

4 See, for example, *Klass v Germany*, No. 5029/71, 6.9.78 (relating to legislation which permitted surveillance of mail and telecommunications).

by the principle of subsidiarity, is both in its diagnosis of the causes of systemic human rights violations, and the extent to which it is prepared to direct states to legislate (or take other steps) to resolve them. To a certain extent the procedure also signals a move closer to acknowledging the *collective* nature of some human rights issues.[5] Such judicial innovation raises fundamental questions for both states and victims of human rights violations. It appears to change the relationship between the Council of Europe's supra-national Court and its 47 constituent states, and between the pre-eminent judicial and political entities within the Council of Europe – the European Court and the Committee of Ministers.

The purpose of this body of research has therefore been to analyse and critically evaluate the novel pilot judgment procedure of the European Court, as a response to systemic human rights violations. By examining the nature and context of these judgments, and by assessing to what extent they have led to changes at the national level, we have sought to identify the principal strengths and weaknesses of the procedure, and to make recommendations for reform. Furthermore, by focusing in particular on the ways in which the national authorities have responded to the Strasbourg Court, we have also sought to place renewed emphasis on the importance of the effective *domestic* application of the European Convention on Human Rights.

FRAMING RESEARCH QUESTIONS

A helpful paradigm from the international law literature explains non-compliance with international agreements as being the result of a lack of public pressure, more complex problems which may not be solved through simple legislative change, and the international court over-reaching its powers.[6] Concerning the first factor, in our research we have examined to what extent there is evidence of public pressure in favour of compliance within the respondent state (including that exerted by civil society, the legislature and judiciary). Issues we address in our case studies, therefore, include:

---

5 Indeed, the President of the European Court, Jean-Paul Costa, has recently called for the consideration of 'class actions' and 'collective applications'. See: *Memorandum of the President of the European Court of Human Rights to the States with a view to preparing the Interlaken Conference*, 3 July 2009, p. 7, available at: http://www.coe.int/t/dc/files/themes/protocole14bis/03072009_Memo_Interlaken_anglais.pdf.

6 Condorelli, Luigi (1987), 'L'autorité de la decision des juridictions international permanentes' in SFDI *La juridiction internationale permanente* Colloque de Lyon, Paris, pp. 287–89 [as cited in Letizia Seminara (2009), *Les effets des arrêts de la Cour interaméricaine des droits de l'homme*, Droit et Justice Collection 85, Bruylant, p. 301].

- How has the Government responded to the Court's judgments?
- How does Parliament undertake the legislative process in order to enact laws compatible with the European Convention on Human Rights?
- What pressure is there from civil society that judgments be enforced?
- What awareness is there of the Convention among the general public?

We consider national Parliamentary involvement and oversight to be critical to the effective implementation of the European Convention standards and European Court judgments.[7] As Drzemczewski and Gaughan argue, "national Parliaments may be able in specific instances more effectively than the Committee of Ministers, to identify the social or political problems underlying a violation and understand the measures required to prevent the recurrence of similar infringements". They also conclude that "to enable parliament to effectively supervise the government's response to an adverse decision of the Court, there must exist a procedure through which parliament is promptly and systematically informed of such judgments and the measures implemented in the execution thereof".[8] There are some examples of highly rigorous and effective scrutiny by parliamentary bodies, such as the monitoring carried out by the parliamentary Joint Committee on Human Rights in the UK.[9] However, the available evidence does not suggest that many national Parliaments are in fact sufficiently engaged.[10] Based on a study of nine Council of Europe states, the JURISTRAS project concluded in 2009 that parliaments

---

[7] See, for example: Joint Committee on Human Rights (JCHR): *Enhancing Parliament's role in relation to human rights judgments*, HL Paper 85, HC 455, 26 March 2010, paras. 13–17. http://www.publications.parliament.uk.pa/jt200910/jtselect/jtrights/85/85.pdf.

[8] Andrew Drzemczewski and James Gaughan (forthcoming), 'Implementing Strasbourg Court Judgments: the Parliamentary Dimension' in *Wolfgang Benedek, Wolfram Karl and Anja Mihr (eds.), European Yearbook on Human Rights 2010*, Vol. II , European Academic Press, pp. 247–258.

[9] See, for example: Joint Committee on Human Rights (JCHR): *Monitoring the Government's Response to Human Rights Judgments: Annual Report 2008*, HL Paper 173, HC 1078, 31 October 2008 http://www.publications.parliament.uk/pa/jt200708/jtselect/jtrights/173/17302.htm. The JCHR has, for example, called on the Ministry of Justice in the UK to adopt a central coordinating role in Government to ensure the effective implementation of adverse human rights judgments and to create a database on the implementation of outstanding European Court judgments (see para. 6 of its Annual Report 2008).

[10] See, for example: Parliamentary Assembly of the Council of Europe. Committee on Legal Affairs and Human Rights, *The role of national parliaments in verifying state obligations to comply with the European Convention on Human Rights, including Strasbourg Court judgments: an overview*, in *Stockholm Colloquy: 'Towards stronger implementation of the European Convention on Human Rights at national level'*, 9–10 June 2008, AS/Jur (2008) 32 rev, 23 June 2008; Parliamentary Assembly of the Council of Europe. Committee on Legal Affairs and Human Rights (CLAHR) (2009), *Implementation of judgments of the European Court of Human Rights*, Christos Pourgourides, AS/Jur (2009) 36 31 August 2009, available at: http://assembly.coe.int/CommitteeDocs/2009/ejdoc36ADD_2009.pdf; Andrew Drzemczewski and James Gaughan (forthcoming), 'Implementing Strasbourg Court Judgments: the Parliamentary Dimension' in *Wolfgang Benedek, Wolfram Karl and Anja Mihr (eds.), European Yearbook on Human Rights 2010*, Vol. II, European Academic Press, pp. 247–258.

> "... do not have an active or decisive role in monitoring [European Court judgments] and assessing their implications for national laws and policies, neither in promoting requisite reforms. While relevant parliamentary committees and representatives are in principle informed (or must be informed) about ECtHR judgments against their country, a relatively small number of deputies who are interested in human rights issues have knowledge about the latter. Discussion and debates relating to Strasbourg Court case law are for most part scant and rarely become the subject of discussions in parliament and in deliberations about draft legislation."[11]

Our research also assesses, in the event of non-implementation of the Court's judgments, to what extent this is by design on the part of the state, or the result of a confluence of factors beyond the state's control.[12]

The ratification of human rights conventions has been explained by political scientists as being motivated by the executive's expectation that membership will reduce political uncertainty by locking in certain conditions which are likely to protect them against radical regime change by future governments.[13] For example in the case of the newer Council of Europe member states from central or eastern Europe, this might be a return to the *status quo ante* of socialism or some other form of authoritarian regime. So, ratification denotes some normative commitment on the part of the executive, at the time of signing, to democracy and therefore to the human rights regime that has developed in postwar Europe. This suggests that states would, in principle, be *willing* to comply with the ideals enshrined in the Convention, and most theories for states' non-compliance with international agreements are based on this premise.

Both international law and political science view states' compliance as most often occurring as the result of a 'coincidence of interests' between the state and the relevant international organisation.[14] In other words, the state would in any event have acted as such, regardless of their being bound to do so by the international agreement. This interpretation is underpinned by an assumption that states

---

11 Dia Anagnostou and Alina Mungiu-Pippidi (2009), *Why Do States Implement Differently the European Court of Human Rights Judgments? The Case Law on Civil Liberties and the Rights of Minorities*, JURISTRAS Project, April 2009, pp. 22–23, available at: http://www.juristras.eliamep.gr/wp-content/uploads/2009/09/why-do-states-implement-differently-the-european-court-ofhuman.pdf.

12 Corinne Amat (Head of Division, Department for the Execution of Judgments of the European Court of Human Rights) has made the point that, although there may well be sufficient political will to co-operate, more often there are other more complex domestic reasons for states' failure to implement European Court judgments: Seminar hosted by the Equality and Human Rights Commission and Matrix Chambers, *Making Strasbourg work: The Execution of Judgments of the European Court of Human Rights*, London, 7 October 2009.

13 Andrew Moravcsik (2000), 'The Origins of Human Rights Regimes: Democratic delegation in Postwar Europe' *International Organization* v.54, no. 2, pp. 217–52.

14 Jack Goldsmith and Eric A. Posner (2005), *The Limits of International Law*, OUP, p. 39.

generally do comply and that mechanisms of 'enforcement' have played little part in achieving this.[15] Chayes and Chayes go further in attributing non-compliance to faulty architecture in the treaty itself, rather than a wilful act on the state's part not to comply.[16]

In her comparison of states' responses within the Inter-American and European human rights systems, Letizia Seminara has argued that non-compliance is the result of 'voluntary' or 'involuntary' resistance. 'Voluntary' resistance denotes a conscious decision on the part of the state not to execute a judgment, and is justified by the state invoking 'higher reasons', which may in reality serve the purposes of particular interest groups.[17] In the case of 'involuntary resistance', there is political will to implement the judgment, but the state is simply not able to bring about the required changes. In this respect Seminara cites the case of *Scordino v Italy* (which we discuss in chapter 4) and argues that the problem of the excessive length of legal proceedings is the result of a fundamental dysfunction in the domestic system, so that "the achievement of the intended goal is beyond the means of the judicial system itself". This therefore leads us to question in what circumstances the pilot judgment procedure is most appropriately applied: whether certain violations (where simple legislative change will bring about the desired effect) lend themselves better to the application of the procedure than those where the violation is the result of a more fundamental, and widespread, judicial or administrative practice.

RESEARCH METHODOLOGY

Funded by the Leverhulme Trust, this research has been carried out by an interdisciplinary team from the Human Rights and Social Justice Research Institute at London Metropolitan University, bringing together perspectives from law, sociology and political science.

The first stage of the research involved an analytical study of the available literature relating to European Court pilot judgments, including academic commentaries, Council of Europe reports and resolutions and NGO reports.

The second stage comprised an investigation and critical assessment of the pilot judgment procedure, and the measures taken at the national level by way of response to the Court's delivery of pilot judgments. The research team carried out

---

15 Harold Hongju Koh (1997), 'Review essay: Why do Nations obey International Law?' *Yale Law Journal* v.106, pp. 2599–2659, p. 2603.

16 Chayes and Chayes 1993, p. 183 as cited in Michael Byers (2006), *Custom, power and the power of rules: international relations and customary international law*, CUP.

17 Letizia Seminara (2009), *Les effets des arrêts de la Cour interaméricaine des droits de l'homme*, Bruylant, pp. 303–9.

semi-structured interviews in Strasbourg with representatives of various Council of Europe entities: the European Court of Human Rights (Judges, Registrars and Court Registry lawyers), the Department for the Execution of Judgments of the European Court of Human Rights, the Parliamentary Assembly (Committee on Legal Affairs and Human Rights) and the Office of the Commissioner for Human Rights. Interviews with Government representatives were also conducted in Strasbourg.

These interviews focused on the methodology that has been adopted by the Council of Europe, and by the respondent states, in respect of the implementation of pilot judgments. Key themes included the following: how the Council of Europe has liaised with state bodies; what are the perceived benefits of the pilot judgment process; what problems have been encountered and how they have been overcome; what are the most effective levers for change; whether a common methodology can be said to be emerging; and what are currently the key concerns about the process.

Case Studies: Poland, Slovenia and Italy

Studies were then conducted in respect of three Council of Europe countries which had been the subject of the pilot judgment procedure: Poland, Slovenia and Italy.[18] Members of the research team travelled to Warsaw (May 2009), Ljubljana (June 2009), Rome and Milan (June 2009), to conduct semi-structured interviews with a range of interlocutors, including: Government Ministers and civil servants, members of parliament, ombudspersons, the judiciary and practising lawyers, Council of Europe officials, academics, and civil society representatives.

The primary aims of these interviews were to establish what steps had been taken following the publication of the pilot judgments; to find out what problems had arisen; and to assess the adequacy and sufficiency of the measures taken. We sought to ascertain what are the key obstacles to implementation in each country (in terms, *inter alia*, of the legislative, administrative and budgetary constraints, and the complexity of the issues addressed by the pilot judgments). The interviews were also intended to take into account the particular national context (legal,

---

[18] Each country had already been the subject of either a 'full' pilot judgment or a 'quasi-pilot' judgment (these terms are defined in Chapter one). A further 'quasi-pilot' judgment had been issued in the case of *Xenides-Arestis v Turkey*, a case concerning property rights of Greek Cypriots in the 'Turkish Republic of Northern Cyprus'. We decided however not to focus on investigating the *Xenides-Arestis* case, as the issues arising from it are inextricably linked to the international resolution of the status of northern Cyprus. The application of the pilot judgment procedure to Poland, Slovenia and Italy, however, concerned matters which are purely 'domestic', and therefore it was considered to be more fruitful to carry out study visits in order to investigate the proposed research questions in respect of those three countries. Nevertheless, in chapter 5 we do discuss the *Xenides-Arestis* case, as well as a number of other pilot (and quasi-pilot) judgments which were published by the Court during the course of this research.

political, economic and social), by considering the attitudes of the political elite to the role of the European Court of Human Rights, the nature and extent of the tensions and sensitivities which arise (including perceptions of national sovereignty) and how the role and functions of the Court (and the other Council of Europe bodies) could be developed in order to ensure the optimum national engagement and co-operation.

In Warsaw we also held a seminar, on 14–15 May 2009, in conjunction with the Polish Ministry of Foreign Affairs (hosted by the National School of Public Administration) to discuss pilot judgments. The seminar was attended by representatives from Government, the Council of Europe and civil society. The papers from that seminar were separately published in 2009.[19]

Expert Advisory Group

The research has benefitted from the advice and assistance of an Expert Advisory Group comprising representatives from Government, the Council of Europe, civil society and the academy:

- Constantin Cojocariu (Lawyer, Interights);
- Andrew Drzemczewski (Head of the Secretariat, Committee on Legal Affairs & Human Rights, Parliamentary Assembly of the Council of Europe);
- Catharina Harby (Lawyer, AIRE Centre);
- Jill Heine (Amnesty International);
- Rob Linham (Head of Litigation, Legislation and Council of Europe, Human Rights Division, Ministry of Justice (UK Government));
- Linos-Alexander Sicilianos (Associate Professor of Law, National and Kapodistrian University of Athens; former member, DH-PR Committee, Council of Europe).

THE HUMAN RIGHTS AND SOCIAL JUSTICE RESEARCH INSTITUTE, LONDON METROPOLITAN UNIVERSITY[20]

The Human Rights and Social Justice Research Institute was created in 2003 to facilitate multidisciplinary research, policy analysis, training, teaching and consultancy. The Research Institute brings together academics and practitioners from a range of disciplines including law, social policy, sociology, politics, health policy and philosophy.

---

19 Wołąsiewicz, Jakub (ed.) (2009), *Pilot Judgment Procedure in the European Court of Human Rights and the development of Human Rights standards and procedures: Third informal seminar for government agents and other institutions, Warsaw, 14–15 May*, Kontrast.

20 http://www.londonmet.ac.uk/research-units/hrsj/.

The Research Institute has been awarded four Economic and Social Research Council grants and has conducted training and consultancy projects for various bodies, including the Council of Europe, the OSCE, the Foreign & Commonwealth Office and the British Council. In 2006-2007 the Research Institute was commissioned by the Council of Europe to research and report on the implementation of the recommendations of the Committee for the Prevention of Torture (CPT) in respect of three countries: Albania, Georgia and Moldova. In 2009 the Research Institute published a report (funded by the Nuffield Foundation) on the fact-finding function of the European Court.[21] In 2008-2010, the Research Institute has been commissioned by the Equality and Human Rights Commission to carry out three research projects on the implementation of the Human Rights Act by public authorities in the UK,[22] and on the process for developing a Bill of Rights in the UK.

THE STRUCTURE OF THIS REPORT

In Chapter one, we consider the origins and objectives of the pilot judgment procedure, and propose a typology comprising three tiers: 'full' pilot judgments, 'quasi-pilot' judgments and other judgments addressing systemic issues. We define each category and give examples. We discuss how the procedure has developed, how it is currently applied and analyse some of the principal questions arising from the application of the procedure.

In Chapters two, three and four, we consider the application of the pilot judgment procedure *vis-à-vis* Poland, Slovenia and Italy. Chapter five considers pilot and quasi-pilot judgments relating to other states, including Russia, Ukraine, Moldova, Bosnia and Turkey. Finally, Chapter six draws together our conclusions and recommendations.

NOTE ON TRANSLITERATION

We have adopted the Library of Congress system to transliterate Cyrillic references into the Roman alphabet.

---

21 Philip Leach, Costas Paraskeva and Gordana Uzelac (2009), *International Human Rights and Fact-Finding – An analysis of the fact-finding missions conducted by the European Commission and Court of Human Rights*, Human Rights & Social Justice Research Institute, London Metropolitan University, February 2009.

22 *Human Rights in Britain since the Human Rights Act 1998: A Critical Review*, 2008 (co-authored with Jenny Watson & Alice Donald), and *Evaluating the Impact of Selected Cases under the Human Rights Act on public service provision*, 2009 (co-authored with Jenny Watson, Alice Donald & Liz Mottershaw).

CHAPTER 1

THE PILOT JUDGMENT PROCEDURE

Responding to states' failure to resolve systemic human rights violations

1.1. THE ORIGINS OF THE PROCEDURE: THE COURT'S BACKLOG AND STATES' FAILURE TO IMPLEMENT COURT JUDGMENTS

The need for a more effective mechanism in order to handle structural or systemic cases has become increasingly urgent as a large backlog of pending cases has accumulated at the Court. Following the enlargement of the Council of Europe during the 1990s, the Court's workload proliferated, with thousands of cases coming from the newer member states. There was a realisation that the Court had to place much more emphasis on tackling what Luzius Wildhaber, the former President of the Court, described as "structural dysfunction in the operation of legal systems".[1]

The idea for such a mechanism was conceived in 2000, following an audit which identified a sharp increase in the number of repetitive cases coming to the Court.[2] In the early 2000s, there were suggestions that these repetitive cases should be dealt with in a different way. According to Michael O'Boyle, the Deputy Registrar of the Court, there was an understanding that what was needed was a procedure

---

1 Luzius Wildhaber (2002), 'A Constitutional Future for the European Court of Human Rights?' *Human Rights Law Journal* 23, pp. 161–165, p. 164. As well as the perennial problem of the excessive length of domestic court proceedings, he cited other examples from Turkey (State Security Court composition; delays in payment; expropriations; expulsion from the army), the United Kingdom (court martial cases; poll tax; widowers' benefits) and Spain (cases arising out of the Spanish rapeseed oil affair).

2 *The Council of Europe's European Convention on Human Rights and the European Union's Charter of Fundamental Rights: Judges' Symposium - Luxembourg - 16 September 2002. Remarks by Ambassador Justin Harman*, 16.9.02. http://www.coe.int/T/e/com/files/events/2002-09-Symposium-Judges/harman.asp.

"that focused less on giving individual justice ... and more on the systemic and structural problems which were at the root of repetitive cases".[3]

In its *Position Paper* of September 2003, the Court proposed the introduction of a 'pilot-judgment' procedure to be applied in 'clone' cases dealing with systemic breakdown. It was suggested that a pilot judgment would trigger an accelerated execution procedure before the Committee of Ministers which would require the state not only to eliminate future violations, but also to provide domestic redress with retroactive effect. Individual applications raising the same issue would be frozen in anticipation of their being resolved through the new domestic remedial process, but they could be re-opened if domestic resolution was not provided within a reasonable time.[4]

In May 2004, as part of a package of reform measures, in order to improve the execution of Court judgments, the Committee of Ministers of the Council of Europe adopted a resolution calling on the Court to identify in its judgments any underlying systemic problems in Council of Europe states, and the sources of any such problems.[5] Thus the Committee of Ministers sought to tackle the phenomenon of 'repetitive' or 'clone' cases – that a high proportion of judgments delivered by the Court concern similar cases which are directly the consequence of a structural or systemic situation in the member state. The Committee of Ministers invited the Court:

> "as far as possible, to identify, in its judgments finding a violation of the Convention, what it considers to be an underlying systemic problem and the source of this problem, in particular when it is likely to give rise to numerous applications, so as to assist states in finding the appropriate solution and the Committee of Ministers in supervising the execution of judgments"

and

> "to specially notify any judgment containing indications of the existence of a systemic problem and of the source of this problem not only to the state concerned and to the Committee of Ministers, but also to the Parliamentary Assembly, to

---

3 Interview with Michael O'Boyle, Strasbourg, 25.3.09.

4 Steering Committee for Human Rights (CDDH). *Position Paper of the European Court of Human Rights on proposals for reform of the European Convention on Human Rights and other measures as set out in the report of the Steering Committee for Human Rights of 4 April 2003* (CDDH(2003)006 final) paras. 43–46. http://www.coe.int/t/e/human_rights/cddh/3._committees/07.%20other%20committees%20and%20working%20groups/archives/06.%20guaranteeing%20human%20rights%20(cddh-gdr)/01.%20working%20documents/2003/2003_024_en.asp#TopOfPage.

5 Committee of Ministers (2004), RES (2004)3 *Resolution on judgments revealing an underlying systemic problem adopted by the Committee of Ministers on 12 May 2004 at its 114th Session* https://wcd.coe.int/ViewDoc.jsp?id=743257&Lang=fr.

the Secretary General of the Council of Europe and to the Council of Europe Commissioner for Human Rights, and to highlight such judgments in an appropriate manner in the database of the Court."[6]

However, even before the adoption of this resolution, a blueprint for the procedure had evidently already been devised by the Court,[7] which proposed that one case, which could be considered representative of a widespread or systemic problem, be singled out. The Court would then identify explicitly the cause of the violation and make recommendations in the judgment as to the appropriate 'general measures' to be taken. It was then intended that the remainder of the clone cases would be 'repatriated' on the understanding that the respondent state should find a holistic solution to the problem.[8] The development of this procedure arguably constituted quite a significant departure for the Court in that it entailed prescribing to states more precisely in what way domestic legislation did not comply with the Convention, and directing respondent governments to amend the relevant legislation.[9] The intention was to reduce the Court's burden in having to repeat the same type of judgment many times over.

Following the application of the pilot judgment procedure for the first time, in the case of *Broniowski v Poland* in 2004, the Group of Wise Persons advocated in its 2006 report to the Committee of Ministers that the Court "use the pilot judgment procedure as far as possible in the future."[10] In 2006 the Committee of Ministers amended its procedural rules to give priority to the supervision of those cases where a systemic violation had been identified.[11] The President of the Court, Jean-

---

6 Committee of Ministers (2004), RES (2004)3 *Resolution on judgments revealing an underlying systemic problem adopted by the Committee of Ministers on 12 May 2004 at its 114th Session* https://wcd.coe.int/ViewDoc.jsp?id=743257&Lang=fr See also Committee of Ministers (2004), Rec (2004)6 *Recommendation of the Committee of Ministers to member states on the improvement of domestic remedies (adopted by the Committee of Ministers on 12 May 2004, at its 114th Session)* https://wcd.coe.int/ViewDoc.jsp?Ref=Rec(2004)6&Language=lanEnglish&Site=CM&BackColorInternet=C3C3C3&BackColorIntranet=EDB021&BackColorLogged=F5D383 (and paras. 13–19 of the Appendix).

7 Interview with Judge Lech Garlicki, Strasbourg, 25.03.09.

8 Erik Fribergh (2008), 'Pilot judgments from the Court's perspective' *Stockholm Colloquy, 9–10 June 2008.*

9 See also: Philip Leach (2005), 'Beyond the Bug River: a new dawn for redress before the European Court of Human Rights?' *European Human Rights Law Review* 2, pp. 148–164.

10 Committee of Ministers (2006), CM(2006)203. *Report of the Group of Wise Persons to the Committee of Ministers, 15 November 2006, 979bis Meeting*, para. 105 https://wcd.coe.int/ViewDoc.jsp?id=1063779&BackColorInternet=9999CC&BackColorIntranet=FFBB55&BackColorLogged=FFAC75.

11 Committee of Ministers (2006), 116th Session of the Committee of Ministers (Strasbourg, 18–19 May 2006), *Rules of the Committee of Ministers for the supervision of the execution of judgments and of the terms of friendly settlements (Adopted by the Committee of Ministers on 10 May 2006 at the 964th meeting of the Ministers' Deputies)*, Rule 4, para. 1. https://wcd.coe.int/ViewDoc.jsp?Ref=CM(2006)90&Language=lanEnglish&Site=COE&BackColorInternet=9999CC&BackColorIntranet=FFBB55&BackColorLogged=FFAC75.

Paul Costa, affirmed the Wise Persons' recommendation at the Council of Europe Colloquy in San Marino in 2007 and stated that the Court would "continue to look into the possibilities offered by this procedure and the context in which it should be implemented."[12]

Although a number of statements from Council of Europe institutions referring to the pilot judgment procedure have been issued since 2007, they have been fairly open-ended. An information note published by the Court Registrar in 2009 provides guidance on the application of the procedure, but the emphasis on its adaptability clearly signalled that the procedure is still evolving:

> "The Court has used the procedure flexibly since it delivered the first pilot judgment in 2004. It is not every category of repetitive case that will be suitable for a pilot-judgment procedure and not every pilot judgment will lead to an adjournment of cases, especially where the systemic problem touches on the most fundamental rights of the person under the Convention."[13]

In the lead-up to the Interlaken Conference in February 2010, the Secretary General of the Council of Europe proposed that

> "[t]he Court's innovative pilot judgment and similar procedures represent a very welcome development and should, if at all possible, now be made more transparent and systematic, if necessary by codification in the Convention, or in a future Statute of the Court, the better to ensure their effective operation in future."[14]

This recognition that the procedure is neither sufficiently transparent, nor systematically applied, reflects the fact that there is a good deal of confusion as to what the procedure entails and the circumstances in which it will be used. A number of our respondents within the Court felt that the procedure should be better defined in the Rules of the Court, because of questions about the legality of the procedure.[15] In view of these uncertainties, the following section proposes a working definition of the procedure, in order to facilitate our identification of pilot judgments that have been issued to date. In the chapters that follow, we then

---

12 Jean-Paul Costa (2007), 'Comments on the Wise Persons' Report from the perspective of the European Court of Human Rights' in *"Future developments of the European Court of Human Rights in the light of the Wise Persons' Report", San Marino*, 22.3.07, pp. 34–43. http://www.coe.int/t/e/human_rights/cddh/1._publications/SanMarino_en.pdf (last accessed 8.4.10).

13 European Court of Human Rights (2009), *The Pilot Judgment Procedure: information note issued by the Registrar.* http://www.echr.coe.int/NR/rdonlyres/DF4E8456-77B3-4E67-8944-B908143A7E2C/0/Information_Note_on_the_PJP_for_Website.pdf.

14 Council of Europe. Secretary General (2009), *Contribution of the Secretary General of the Council of Europe to the preparation of the Interlaken Ministerial Conference*, SG/Inf(2009)20, para. 20. https://wcd.coe.int/ViewDoc.jsp?id=1571667&Site=COE.

15 Interview with Santiago Quesada, Court Registry, Strasbourg, 26.3.09.

seek to evaluate how states have responded to these judgments, and the efficacy of the procedure in solving systemic human rights violations.

1.2. THE PURPOSE OF THE PILOT JUDGMENT PROCEDURE AND THE DEFINING ELEMENTS OF A PILOT JUDGMENT

Interviewees in Strasbourg were consistent as to the predominant functions served by the pilot judgment procedure, but we heard a number of differing emphases. The Court Registrar, Erik Fribergh, stressed that the main purpose of the procedure is to secure the future enforcement of the Court's judgment by inducing states to find a remedy to a systemic violation:

> "It's a question, in my view, of enforcing the first judgment: proper implementation, execution of the first judgment."[16]

Michael O'Boyle, the Deputy Registrar of the Court, explained that the intention was "to focus in on the reasons why [repetitive] cases have been brought in the first place and encourage the state to do something about providing a remedy".[17] John Darcy, from the Court Registry, characterised the procedure as a form of 'judicial management'.[18] A number of our respondents stressed the need for the procedure to be both flexible and adaptable.

One Judge at the European Court explained that the procedure was designed to serve three important interests: the interests of the state in enabling it to resolve a systemic problem at the national level; the interests of the applicant in providing a rapid form of redress; and the interests of the European Court itself in easing its burden.[19]

Judge Zupančič suggested that the pilot judgment procedure would not have been necessary if the Court's judgments were binding *erga omnes*:

> "It's a question of making sure that a particular state ... takes seriously what has been decided in one case by this Court ... The difference between us in Strasbourg and a constitutional court of a particular country ... lies in the fact that they are the top of the internal, domestic legal pyramid, which is hierarchically structured so the lower courts must of necessity follow the guidelines of the constitutional court or the supreme court. We ... in Strasbourg ... [are the] ... tip of the pyramid

16 Interview with Erik Fribergh, Court Registry, Strasbourg, 25.3.09.
17 Interview with Michael O'Boyle, Strasbourg, 25.3.09.
18 Interview with John Darcy, Strasbourg, 26.3.09.
19 Interview with a Judge of the European Court, Strasbourg, 26.3.09.

without a pyramid ... and given that we are dealing with 47 different countries, it is clear that the [European Court's] message would be interpreted differently in different countries."[20]

Judge Zupančič acknowledged that some countries took Strasbourg judgments more seriously than others (for example, he argued that common law countries were used to legal precedents as a source of law), but his primary proposition was that the pilot judgment procedure compensated for the fact that the Court's judgments were not in practice binding on the states.

In its second pilot judgment, *Hutten-Czapska v Poland,* the Court explained that the aim of the procedure was "to facilitate the most speedy and effective resolution of a dysfunction affecting the protection of the Convention right in question in the national legal order". Furthermore, it was "primarily designed to assist the Contracting States in fulfilling their role in the Convention system by resolving such problems at national level, thereby securing to the persons concerned their Convention rights and freedoms as required by Article 1 of the Convention, offering to them more rapid redress". [21] In its more recent decisions (such as *Olaru and others v Moldova*), the Court has explicitly recognised that the procedure therefore aims to implement the principle of subsidiarity. It has also emphasised that the Court's role of ensuring that states comply with the Convention "is not necessarily best achieved by repeating the same findings in large series of cases".

In the course of carrying out this research, it quickly became clear that identifying 'pilot judgments', or defining them, was the subject of some confusion.[22] Therefore, in seeking to achieve greater clarity, we have adopted a typology comprising three tiers of cases (which are defined in the following sections). In summary, in the first tier are the 'full' pilot judgments – those that are expressly identified as pilot cases by the Court itself in the judgment. At the time of carrying out interviews in Strasbourg in March 2009, there was clear agreement about which judgments constituted the first tier: *Broniowski v Poland*, *Hutten-Czapska v Poland* and

20 Interview with Judge Zupančič, Strasbourg, 26.3.09.

21 *Hutten-Czapska v Poland,* No. 35014/97, 19 June 2006, para. 234.

22 Indeed, the Court itself has not always been clear and consistent about this. For example, the judgment in *Doğan v. Turkey,* Nos. 8803-8811/02, 8813/02 and 8815-8819/02, 29.6.04 (concerning the applicants' forced eviction from their homes) was not defined by the Court as a pilot judgment, but in the later admissibility decision in *İçyer v. Turkey,* No. 18888/02, dec. 12.1.06 the Court referred to *Doğan* as a 'pilot judgment' (paras. 73 & 94). The Committee of Ministers uses the term 'leading cases' to mean "cases which reveal a possible new systemic/ general problem in a respondent state and which thus require the adoption of new general measures" – a category which includes pilot judgments. See: Committee of Ministers (2009), *Supervision of the execution of judgments of the European Court of Human Rights, 2nd annual report 2008*, p. 31, available at: https://wcd.coe.int/com.instranet.InstraServlet?command=com.instranet.CmdBlobGet&InstranetImage=1221103&SecMode=1&DocId=1393816&Usage=2.

Burdov v Russia (No. 2). In the next section we have identified a number of common distinguishing features which such judgments share.

Our second tier of cases we characterise as 'quasi-pilot judgments'. These are cases which concern systemic problems and in which the Court refers to the provision contained in Article 46(1) of the Convention relating to the binding force of Court judgments (and for that reason they have sometimes been referred to as 'Article 46 judgments'). However, the Court does not itself describe the decision as a pilot judgment as such. It is this group of cases which has caused the greatest uncertainty – are they 'pilot judgments' or not?

We also consider a third tier – other judgments addressing systemic issues (such as, for example, *Bottazzi v Italy*, *Kudła v Poland* and *Belinger v Slovenia*). These are not pilot judgments as such (indeed some of them pre-date the pilot judgment procedure), but were raised with us by some of our interviewees and arguably have been instrumental in the development of the procedure.

Since the pilot judgment procedure is still under development and, at the time of writing, has still not been 'codified' within the Rules of the Court, we have sought to examine a selection of cases from the three tiers, in an attempt to evaluate their implementation and accordingly the effectiveness of the procedure to date, in the context of differing national circumstances.

1.2.1. THE FIRST TIER: 'FULL' PILOT JUDGMENTS

At the time of writing (January 2010), the Court had issued six 'full' pilot judgments – between June 2004 and November 2009. Three of these judgments relate to states of the former Soviet Union (Russia, Moldova and Ukraine), two to Poland and the other to Bosnia and Herzegovina. In each case the right to property (Article 1 of Protocol No. 1) was found to have been violated. The right to a fair hearing (Article 6(1)) was breached in three cases, and the right to an effective domestic remedy (Article 13) was violated in two cases.

We briefly outline the six cases in this section, before analysing their common elements. The cases are: *Broniowski v Poland* (2004),[23] *Hutten-Czapska v Poland* (2006),[24] *Burdov v Russia (No. 2)* (2009),[25] *Olaru and others v Moldova*

---

[23] No. 31443/96, 22.6.04.
[24] No. 35014/97, 19.6.06.
[25] No. 33509/04, 15.1.09.

(2009),[26] *Yuriy Nikolayevich Ivanov v Ukraine* (2009)[27] and *Suljagić v Bosnia and Herzegovina* (2009).[28]

1.2.1.1. Broniowski v Poland

To a large extent the pilot judgment procedure was crafted around the case to which it was first applied: *Broniowski v Poland,*[29] concerning the failure to compensate individuals who had lost land in the course of the Second World War. Although there were just 167 similar cases pending before the European Court by 2004, the Polish Government admitted that the potential applicants could number as many as 80,000.[30] In 1992, Jerzy Broniowski applied to the Cracow District Court for supplementary compensation for his grandmother's property situated in Lviv, Ukraine.[31] At the time his grandmother had owned the property, Lviv was part of Poland. However, following the Ribbentrop-Molotov Pact of 1939, Poland lost portions of territory along its eastern frontier, to the bordering Soviet Republics of Belarus, Lithuania and Ukraine. Polish residents living in these territories, along the Bug River, known as the 'Kresy' regions, mostly abandoned their properties and relocated to Poland. Some compensation for the loss of this property was awarded, but it was established that the amount constituted just 2% of the value of Mr Broniowski's grandmother's property.[32]

In its judgment, the Grand Chamber of the European Court found that Mr Broniowski had a 'right to credit' under Polish legislation (the Land Administration Act 1985), entitling him to claim compensatory property, which had also been recognised by the Supreme and Constitutional Courts. However, in practice his right had been delayed and obstructed by the authorities. Although it recognised the potential financial burden on the state of the 'right to credit', the Court found that the applicant's rights under Article 1 of Protocol No. 1 to the Convention (the right to property) had been violated because the authorities had continuously failed to implement Mr Broniowski's right over many years. As thousands of people were in the same situation, the Court found that the violation "originated in a widespread problem which resulted from a malfunctioning of Polish legislation and administrative practice".[33] In its operative provisions, the Court stipulated that the Government should:

---

26 Nos. 476/07, 22539/05, 17911/08 and 13136/07, 28.7.09.
27 No. 40450/04, 15.10.09.
28 No. 27912/02, 3.11.09.
29 Interview with Judge Lech Garlicki, Strasbourg, 25.3.09.
30 No. 31443/96, 22.6.04, para. 193.
31 No. 31443/96, 22.6.04, para. 21.
32 No. 31443/96, 22.6.04, para. 18.
33 No. 31443/96, 22.6.04, para. 189.

> "through appropriate legal measures and administrative practices, secure the implementation of the property right in question in respect of the remaining Bug River claimants or provide them with equivalent redress in lieu, in accordance with the principles of protection of property rights under Article 1 of Protocol No. 1."[34]

The Court also decided that all similar applications (including future applications) were to be adjourned pending the outcome of *Broniowski* and the adoption of the measures to be taken at the national level.[35] In 2005 a new law was enacted in Poland to provide compensation to the Bug River claimants,[36] on the basis of which the pilot judgment procedure was closed by the Court in September 2008 (as was confirmed by the Committee of Ministers in September 2009).[37] We discuss this case, and the implementation of the 2005 law, further in chapter 2.

This research has established that the Court had a number of concerns in applying the pilot judgment procedure in the *Broniowski* case. Firstly, the Court was reluctant to adjourn the other similar pending cases until there was some evidence that the Polish Government had devised new legislation that would solve the issue holistically.[38] Thus the intention was, at least in part, to protect applicants and ensure that the Polish Government would deliver on its promise. At the same time, the Court delayed the final judgment of the *Broniowski* case until the new domestic remedy came into force, as a means of dissuading other Bug River Region claims from flooding the European Court.[39] In its 2004 judgment, the Court adjourned all other Bug River Region cases, on the understanding that the new legislation, which was expected to solve the violation, would be implemented 'within a reasonable time'.[40] A system was then devised to keep other Bug River Region applicants regularly informed, through pro-forma letters, of the progress of the *Broniowski* case.[41]

---

34 No. 31443/96, 22.6.04, operative provisions, para. 4.

35 No. 31443/96, 22.6.04, para. 198. See also: European Court of Human Rights (2004), *'Bug River' Cases Adjourned*, European Court of Human Rights Press Release, 31 August 2004. http://cmiskp.echr.coe.int/tkp197/view.asp?action=html&documentId=799850&portal=hbkm&source=externalbydocnumber&table=F69A27FD8FB86142BF01C1166DEA398649.

36 Law of 8 July 2005 on the realisation of the right to compensation for property left beyond the present borders of the Polish State (*Ustawa o realizacji prawa do rekompensaty z tytułu pozostawienia nieruchomości poza obecnymi granicami państwa polskiego*).

37 See: *E.G. v Poland (and 175 other Bug River applications)*, No. 50425/99, dec. 23.9.08. See also: Committee of Ministers (2009), *Final Resolution* CM/ResDH(2009)89 *Execution of the judgments of the European Court of Human Rights Broniowski against Poland*, 30 September 2009 http://cmiskp.echr.coe.int/tkp197/view.asp?item=6&portal=hbkm&action=html&highlight=Broniowski&sessionid=50829028&skin=hudoc-en.

38 Interview with Renata Degener, Court Registry, Strasbourg, 26.3.09.

39 Interview with Renata Degener, Court Registry, Strasbourg, 26.3.09.

40 No. 31443/96, 22.06.04, para. 198.

41 Interview with Renata Degener, Court Registry, Strasbourg, 26.3.09.

1.2.1.2. *Hutten-Czapska v Poland*

In the case of *Hutten-Czapska* the Grand Chamber of the Court again found a systemic violation of the right to peaceful enjoyment of property (Article 1 of Protocol 1 to the Convention) – as a consequence of the failure by the Polish state to effectively protect landlords' rights. Legislation protecting tenants' rights prohibited landlords from raising rents above a certain fixed percentage each year and there was no system enabling landlords to recover losses incurred in connection with property maintenance. Although the Court acknowledged that there were not very many similar cases pending before it (only 18), one of them included an application from a landlords' association on behalf of 200 of its members. The Court did note, however, that the violation had wide-reaching consequences for, potentially, some 100,000 landlords and 600,000-900,000 tenants.[42]

In its judgment the Court required the Polish Government to put in place a mechanism that would resolve the systemic problem – one which maintained "a fair balance between the interests of landlords and the general interest of the community" in accordance with Convention standards.[43] As in the case of *Broniowski*, time limits were not stipulated. One interesting element of the case is that the Polish Government contested the application of the pilot judgment procedure.[44] The case itself was resolved by way of a friendly settlement concluded in April 2008.[45] We consider this case further, and its resolution, in Chapter 2.

1.2.1.3. *Burdov v Russia (No. 2)*

In the case of *Burdov (No. 2)* the Court found a systemic violation of the Convention as a result of the non-enforcement of domestic court judgments in Russia. Anatoliy Burdov was engaged in emergency recovery operations following the Chernobyl disaster between 1986 and 1987 and was consequently subjected to extensive radioactive emissions. He was entitled to benefits as a result of his illness, but the state failed to pay them fully and promptly. Since 1997, Mr Burdov had repeatedly sued the state authorities and although the courts had granted his claims, a number of judgments had remained unenforced for various periods of time.[46] The First Section of the Court accordingly found a violation of Article 6 (the right to a fair hearing) and Article 1 of Protocol No. 1 to the Convention (the right to property) – and a breach of Article 13 (the right to an effective remedy).

---

42 *Hutten-Czapska v Poland*, No. 35014/97, 19.6.06, paras. 235–236.
43 *Hutten-Czapska v Poland*, No. 35014/97, 19.6.06, operative provisions, para. 4.
44 *Hutten-Czapska v Poland*, No. 35014/97, 19.6.06, paras. 227–228.
45 *Hutten-Czapska v Poland*, No. 35014/97, 28.4.08.
46 *Burdov v Russia* (No. 2), No. 33509/04, 15.1.09, paras. 6–8.

There were two distinct differences between *Burdov (No. 2)* and the earlier Polish pilot judgments (*Broniowski* and *Hutten-Czapska*). Firstly, Mr Burdov did not belong to an 'identifiable class of citizens' – the problem of the non-implementation of domestic court judgments affected many thousands of people in very different situations. In that sense, the category of people affected was 'open-ended'. Secondly, his case was far from being the first case against Russia relating to the problem of non-enforcement of domestic judgments – indeed there had been 200 such judgments since the first case brought by Mr Burdov himself in 2002. The Russian Judge at the European Court of Human Rights, Anatoly Kovler, suggested to us that the choice of *Burdov (No. 2)* as a pilot judgment was made to remind the Russian Government of the repeated nature of the violation ("like Pavlov's dog").[47] In view of the long history of the problem, the fact that there were another 700 similar cases pending against Russia, and that there was no effective remedy (either preventive or compensatory), the Court expressly identified a "persistent structural dysfunction" and a practice incompatible with the Convention.

Although the Court did not specify that the general measures required a legislative response as such, the Court stipulated in the operative provisions that a remedy must be established to provide redress for the non-enforcement, or delayed enforcement, of domestic judgments. Unlike the previous pilot judgments, the Court in *Burdov (No. 2)* laid down a specific timetable: six months to set up the remedial system and one year within which to provide redress to all applicants in a similar situation whose cases had been lodged before the delivery of the judgment (and which had been communicated to the Government). Furthermore, all other similar newly lodged cases were to be adjourned for a period of one year. This formula was also adopted in the other pilot judgments issued in 2009 in relation to Moldova and Ukraine (both cases concerning the non-enforcement of domestic court decisions) and Bosnia and Herzegovina (relating to inadequate compensation for lost foreign currency savings) (see below).

We discuss the response of the Russian authorities to the *Burdov (No. 2)* case in Chapter 5.

1.2.1.4. Olaru and others v Moldova

This case concerned the non-implementation of legislation granting housing provision for public employees, which local authorities were unable to honour because of a lack of funding. This situation had given rise to numerous cases of public employees applying to local courts to seek compensation. The courts upheld the relevant laws, and required the local authorities to compensate the

47 Interview with Judge Anatoly Kovler, Strasbourg, 26.3.09.

victims accordingly. As the judgments in the applicants' cases had remained unenforced for periods of between three and eleven years, the European Court found violations of both Article 6 of the Convention (the right to a fair hearing) and Article 1 of Protocol No. 1 to the Convention (the right to property). The Court noted that the non-execution of domestic judgments was the main issue being raised in Strasbourg as regards Moldova (there were 300 pending cases) and that about 50% of those concerned social housing.[48]

In its judgment the Court also confirmed that draft legislation, the purpose of which was to abolish social housing provision for various categories of public employees, would solve the problem in the future. This was an unusual step for the Court, in effect, condoning 'levelling down', but it reflected the parlous situation in which local authorities found themselves – simply not having the funding to provide the housing required by the legislation. Indeed the Court noted that the local authorities were forced to choose between operating schools and kindergartens or using their funds to provide housing for judges, police officers and prosecutors.

The operative provisions were similar to those in *Burdov (No. 2)*: a mechanism of redress to be set up within six months; redress to be granted within a year to all victims in the social housing cases (whose applications had already been lodged); and the adjournment for a year of all new similar cases. We discuss *Olaru* further in chapter 5.

1.2.1.5. Yuriy Nikolayevich Ivanov v Ukraine

In the case of *Ivanov*, the Court found a systemic failure as a result of the non-enforcement of domestic court judgments in Ukraine, similar to the situation in *Burdov (No.2)*. Mr. Ivanov's complaints that, following his retirement from the army, he had received neither his retirement payment, nor compensation for his uniform, were upheld by the domestic courts. The failure to implement those decisions for a period of several years led to a finding by the European Court of violations of Articles 6(1) and 13 of the Convention (the right to a fair hearing and an effective remedy), and of Article 1 of Protocol No. 1 to the Convention (the right to property).

The Court noted that the non-enforcement of domestic decisions was the most frequent reason for finding Ukraine to be in violation of the Convention. There had been 300 such judgments in the previous five years, and the systemic nature

---

48 *Olaru and Others v Moldova*, Nos. 476/07, 22539/05, 17911/08 and 13136/07, 15.11.09, paras. 53–54.

of the case was apparent from the fact that there were 1,400 similar cases pending before the Court.[49]

As had happened in *Hutten*-Czapska, the Government objected to the application of the pilot judgment procedure, arguing (unsuccessfully) that as the problem had multiple causes (insufficient budgets; shortcomings in legislation or practice; or omissions by the bailiffs) the case did not concern a systemic problem.

Noting that the Committee of Ministers had already made specific recommendations to the Ukrainian Government about these problems, the Court required the adoption of appropriate legislative and administrative reforms (but without prescribing what form they should take).[50] In the operative provisions, as in the cases of *Burdov (No.2)* and *Olaru*, the Court stipulated that a domestic remedy be introduced within one year, that redress should be granted within a year to all applicants whose cases were pending before the Court, and that all similar cases would be adjourned for a year.[51] The authorities' response to the *Ivanov* case is discussed in chapter 5.

1.2.1.6. Suljagić v Bosnia and Herzegovina

The case brought by Mr. Suljagić concerned the authorities' failure to provide him with adequate compensation for lost foreign currency savings. During the financial crisis of the 1980s in the former Yugoslavia, legislation had been introduced to prevent the withdrawal of hard-currency savings. After the break up of the federation in 1991 and the outbreak of war in Bosnia and Herzegovina, the state incurred large debts and remained unable to compensate individuals for their lost savings.[52] Mr. Suljagić remained entitled under the domestic law to claim his deposit (with interest), and as a result of the defective implementation of the relevant legislation, the Court found a violation of Article 1 of Protocol No.1 to the Convention (the right to property).

The Government objected to the application of the pilot judgment procedure (denying that there had been a violation of the Convention). However, noting that there were already 1,350 similar applications (on behalf of 13,500 applicants), and that the potential number of affected persons could reach nearly one million, the Court found that the violation was systemic and constituted "a serious threat to the future effectiveness of the Convention machinery".[53]

---

49 *Yuriy Nikolayevich Ivanov v Ukraine*, No. 40450/04, 15.10.09, paras. 83–86.
50 *Yuriy Nikolayevich Ivanov v Ukraine*, No. 40450/04, 15.10.09, paras. 91–92.
51 *Yuriy Nikolayevich Ivanov v Ukraine*, No. 40450/04, 15.10.09, operative provisions, paras. 5–7.
52 *Suljagić v Bosnia and Herzegovina*, No. 27912/02, dec. 20.6.06.
53 *Suljagić v Bosnia and Herzegovina*, No. 27912/02, dec. 20.6.06; 3.11.09, para. 63.

In its operative provisions, the Court was rather more prescriptive than it had been in the previous pilot judgments, requiring the Government in such cases to issue the promised government bonds and to pay any outstanding instalments, together with interest, within six months. Other similar, pending cases were adjourned for six months.

1.2.1.7. *The common characteristics of 'full' pilot judgments*

The six cases all share the following features, which we suggest are the criteria that define a 'full' pilot judgment:

(i) the explicit application by the Court of the pilot judgment procedure;

(ii) the identification by the Court of a systemic violation of the Convention;

(iii) general measures are stipulated in the operative part of the judgment in order that the respondent state should resolve the systemic issue (which may be subject to specific time limits).

A pilot judgment *may* also adjourn all other cases arising from the same systemic issue, either for a particular period of time, or, more generally, pending the resolution of the issue by the state (as was in fact the case for each of the six 'full' pilot judgments).

The core systemic problem in these cases is alternatively described by the Court as being 'widespread' (*Broniowski*) or 'structural' (*Olaru*). In three cases, the cause was the 'malfunctioning' of domestic legislation or practice, or the 'deficient implementation' of legislation (*Broniowski*, *Hutten-Czapska* and *Suljagić*). The particular problem of the non-enforcement of domestic court judgments is characterised as being prolonged, recurrent and/or persistent, such that it is found to amount to a 'practice' that is incompatible with the Convention (*Burdov (No. 2)*, *Olaru*, *Ivanov*). The causes may of course be multiple, as the Court recognised in *Ivanov*, noting a 'variety of dysfunctions' in the Ukrainian legal system (insufficient budgetary allocations, bailiffs' omissions and shortcomings in the legislation). The procedure may be applied after an issue has already been monitored over many years by the Committee of Ministers. For example, in *Ivanov*, the Court's apparent frustration with the Ukrainian authorities' "almost complete reluctance to resolve the problems" is made evident.[54] The Court took note, in *Ivanov*, that the Committee of Ministers itself had characterised the issue as a structural problem.[55] In *Suljagić* the Court remarked on the case's 'long

---

54 *Yuriy Nikolayevich Ivanov v Ukraine*, No. 40450/04, 15.10.09, para. 91.
55 *Yuriy Nikolayevich Ivanov v Ukraine*, No. 40450/04, 15.10.09, para. 87.

history' – it had been lodged in 2002, before Bosnia and Herzegovina had ratified the Convention.

The sheer numbers of people affected is evidently an important consideration in applying the pilot judgment procedure, not only because of the implications for the victims, and the state, but also for the Court itself. For example, the fact that nearly 80,000 people were affected by the issue raised by Mr Broniowski was "not only an aggravating factor as regards the State's responsibility under the Convention for an existing or past state of affairs, but also represents a threat to the future effectiveness of the Convention machinery".[56] In some of the cases, notably in the more recent cases of 2009, the respective systemic violation constituted the largest source of cases coming to the Court from that state.[57] In a case like *Broniowski*, the victims are described as "an identifiable class of citizens", because the case concerned a particular problem affecting only the Bug River claimants. As noted above, the procedure has been applied both in the first case of its kind (e.g. *Broniowski*) and after there had already been numerous other similar applications (e.g. *Burdov (No. 2)*). Indeed, as the Court noted in *Hutten-Czapska*:

> "the identification of a 'systemic situation' justifying the application of the pilot-judgment procedure does not necessarily have to be linked to, or based on, a given number of similar applications already pending. In the context of systemic or structural violations the potential inflow of future cases is also an important consideration in terms of preventing the accumulation of repetitive cases on the Court's docket, which hinders the effective processing of other cases giving rise to violations, sometimes serious, of the rights it is responsible for safeguarding."[58]

The stipulation of general measures in the operative part of the judgment, rather than just the body of the judgment, is a very important facet of the process. As one European Court judge told us, "in the case of states it's the operative part that works the magic".[59] The general measures to be introduced must, by definition, provide redress for other victims of the same structural problem. It is this aspect of the pilot judgment procedure which has led the Court away from its traditional focus on individual cases and, arguably, into the realm of class actions. In *Hutten-Czapska* the Court stated that:

---

56 *Broniowski v Poland*, No. 31443/96, 22.6.04, para. 193.

57 As regards Russia (see Chapter 5, Section 5.2.1), Bosnia and Herzegovina (1,350 cases pending; although there is no statement that this constitutes the largest source of violation, the Court states that the violation affects as much as one quarter of the population, (*Suljagić*, para. 63)), Ukraine (*Ivanov*, para.73) and Moldova (*Olaru*, para. 53).

58 *Hutten-Czapska v Poland*, No. 35014/97, 19.6.06, para. 236.

59 Interview with European Court judge, Strasbourg, 26.3.09.

> "One of the fundamental implications of the pilot-judgment procedure is that the Court's assessment of the situation complained of in a 'pilot' case necessarily extends beyond the sole interests of the individual applicant and requires it to examine that case also from the perspective of the general measures that need to be taken in the interest of other potentially affected persons."[60]

The Court clearly acknowledges the scale and complexity of the structural problems faced by the respondent states, and the difficulties they face in implementing the necessary measures, which may require both legislative and administrative steps, and which may involve various authorities at the federal and local levels (as in *Burdov (No. 2)*). The national authorities are therefore generally left to decide precisely what remedial measures are to be taken. However, the Court may put forward proposals or recommendations as to how the state should respond (which are not binding). These may reflect, for example, an earlier decision by a domestic court (as in *Hutten-Czapska*).[61] In *Suljagić* the Court was able to be more prescriptive, in requiring the state to issue government bonds, and pay outstanding instalments, to compensate depositors for lost foreign currency savings, directly in accordance with the applicable domestic legislation, from 2006,[62] which had been reviewed (and approved) by the Constitutional Court.

The Court is also careful to distinguish between its own role and that of the Committee of Ministers: the adequacy of the state's response is to be supervised by the Committee of Ministers. The potential blurring of the respective roles was raised by the Ukrainian Government in the *Ivanov* case, but the Court held that, contrary to their submissions, the application of the pilot judgment procedure "does not run counter to the division of functions between the Convention institutions".[63]

1.2.2. THE SECOND TIER: 'QUASI-PILOT' JUDGMENTS

In addition to the 'full' pilot judgments, the European Court has in recent years been issuing another category of decisions which also highlight systemic violations of the European Convention on Human Rights – variously known as 'quasi-pilot' judgments or 'Article 46 judgments'. As with the full pilot judgment, the Court identifies a widespread or systemic dysfunction in legislation or practice and

---

60 *Hutten-Czapska v Poland*, No. 35014/97, 28.4.08, para. 33.

61 *Hutten-Czapska v Poland*, No. 35014/97, 19.6.06, para. 239.

62 The Old Foreign-Currency Savings Act 2006.

63 *Yuriy Nikolayevich Ivanov v Ukraine*, No. 40450/04, 15.10.09, para. 82. See also *Sejdović v Italy*, No. 56581/00, 1.3.06, paras. 115–118 (as to the Italian Government's arguments in opposition to the application of the pilot judgment procedure).

invokes Article 46 of the Convention to remind the respondent state in question that it is bound to remedy the violation holistically through appropriate means.

These decisions can be distinguished from 'full' pilot judgments for a number of reasons. Firstly, the Court itself does not describe them as pilot judgments. Secondly, although the Court does identify a systemic issue that has arisen and requires the state to take appropriate steps to resolve the problem, it does not go on to prescribe general measures in the operative part of the judgment. There are, however, rare exceptions to this second element. We discuss in chapters 3, 4 and 5 respectively, the judgments in *Lukenda v Slovenia*,[64] *Sejdović v Italy*[65] and *Xenides-Arestis v Turkey*[66] in which the respondent states were required by the operative provisions to take remedial measures. Thirdly, in 'quasi-pilot' judgments, other similar cases are usually not adjourned. Again, the case of *Xenides-Arestis* was an exception to the rule.[67]

One example of an 'Article 46' or 'quasi-pilot' judgment is the case of *Manole and others v Moldova*[68] in which the Court found a systemic violation of the right to freedom of expression (Article 10) on account of the Government's control over the most popular television channel in Moldova. Television coverage of opposition parties was restricted and only limited discussion of certain sensitive issues was allowed, such as human rights violations perpetrated during the Soviet era. According to the Court, these problems had their roots in deficiencies in the legislative framework. By applying Article 46, the Court held therefore that legal reform was required to resolve the issue:

> "... the respondent State is under a legal obligation under Article 46 to take general measures at the earliest opportunity to remedy the situation which gave rise to the violation of Article 10. In the light of the deficiencies found by the Court, these general measures should include legislative reform, to ensure that the legal framework complies with the requirements of Article 10 ..."[69]

The context of this case, and the response of the Moldovan authorities to it, are discussed in chapter 5.

There is now an abundance of such cases. For example, 'quasi-pilot' or 'Article 46' judgments have been issued in respect of the following types of cases: systemic violations of Article 6(1) (the excessive length of proceedings) – *Faimblat v*

64 No. 23032/02, 6.10.05.
65 No. 56581/00, 10.11.04 (Chamber) and 1.03.06 (Grand Chamber).
66 *Xenides-Arestis v Turkey*, No. 46347/99, 22.12.05.
67 *Xenides-Arestis v Turkey*, No. 46347/99, 22.12.05, para. 50.
68 *Manole and others v Moldova*, No. 13936/02, 17.9.09.
69 *Manole and others v Moldova*, No. 13936/02,17.9.09, para 117.

Romania,[70] *Lukenda v Slovenia*,[71] *Ramadhi v Albania*,[72] *Scordino v Italy (No. 1)*;[73] cases concerning Article 6(2) (the right to a fair trial) – *Sejdović v Italy*;[74] and cases relating to Article 1 of Protocol 1 (the right to compensation for expropriated property) – *Driza v Albania*,[75] *Katz v Romania*,[76] *Viaşu v Romania*,[77] and *Xenides-Arestis v Turkey*.[78] Furthermore, Article 46 judgments have also been issued in respect of systemic violations of other fundamental rights, such as Article 5 (poor prison conditions and excessive terms of pre-trial detention) – *Sławomir Musiał v Poland*[79] and *Kauczor v Poland*.[80]

1.2.3. THE THIRD TIER: OTHER JUDGMENTS ADDRESSING SYSTEMIC ISSUES

In this study, we have also included discussion of a 'third tier' of judgments which address systemic (or repetitive) violations of the European Convention on Human Rights. In these judgments, there is no explicit application of Article 46, as such, but the Court notes that the problem which the case raises, is systemic or widespread, and that holistic measures need to be taken to resolve the problem at its root.

To a certain extent the definition of this 'third tier' is rather indeterminate. Moreover, a number of such cases pre-date the development of the pilot judgment procedure, reflecting the fact that in some areas the Court has for a number of years sought to draw more attention to certain recurring problems that were far too frequently being raised before it, and thus demonstrating that they were not being resolved within the domestic system.

As Chapters 2-4 will illustrate, a number of these 'third tier' judgments have been followed by 'full' pilot judgments or Article 46 judgments relating to the same systemic issue in the same state. One example is the 1999 Grand Chamber judgment in *Bottazzi v Italy* which concerned the apparently insoluble problem of the excessive length of domestic legal proceedings in Italy. The Court made it clear that the problem was systemic:

---

70 No. 23066/02, 13.1.09.
71 No. 23032/02, 6.10.05.
72 No. 38222/02, 13.11.07.
73 No. 36813/97, 29.3.06.
74 No. 56581/00, 1.3.06.
75 No. 33771/02, 13.11.07.
76 No. 29739/03, 20.1.09.
77 No. 75951/01, 9.12.08.
78 No. 46347/99, 22.12.05.
79 No. 28300/06, 20.1.09.
80 No. 45219/06, 3.2.09.

> "The frequency with which violations are found shows that there is an accumulation of identical breaches which are sufficiently numerous to amount not merely to isolated incidents. Such breaches reflect a continuing situation that has not yet been remedied and in respect of which litigants have no domestic remedy. This accumulation of breaches accordingly constitutes a practice that is incompatible with the Convention."[81]

Bottazzi was subsequently followed by the quasi-pilot Grand Chamber judgment of *Scordino v Italy (No. 1)* in 2006,[82] which we discuss in chapter 4.

Another example of a 'third tier' case is the judgment in *Kudła v Poland*,[83] concerning the right to a trial within a reasonable time (in which the Court, for the first time, also found a violation of the right to an effective remedy - Article 13 - in conjunction with Article 6(1)). Of particular interest in that case, is that the Court was responding to large numbers of length of proceedings cases from various Council of Europe states, not just from Poland:

> "In the Court's view, the time has come to review its case-law in the light of the continuing accumulation of applications before it in which the only, or principal, allegation is that of a failure to ensure a hearing within a reasonable time in breach of Article 6 § 1."[84]

Other cases which have systemic, or at least 'recurrent', elements and which accordingly could be considered to fall into our 'third tier' include: *Krawczak v Poland*,[85] *Robert Lesjak v Slovenia*,[86] *Šilih v Slovenia*[87] and *Matko v Slovenia*.[88] We consider the Polish cases in chapter 2 and the Slovenian cases in chapter 3.

A further reason for including certain cases within our 'third tier' is that governments have responded to them *as if* the Court had issued a quasi-pilot judgment identifying a systemic issue that required holistic resolution. A number of cases have been treated by the respondent Government as raising a systemic issue, even though the judgment itself does not characterise the issue as being structural. Examples include *Šilih v Slovenia* and *Matko v Slovenia* (see chapter 3) and *Saadi v Italy* (see chapter 4).

---

81 *Bottazzi v Italy*, No. 34884/97, 28.7.99, para. 22 (the Grand Chamber also referred to more than 1,400 European Commission reports resulting in a Committee of Ministers' resolution finding Italy in violation of Article 6(1) for the same reason).

82 *Scordino v Italy No.1*, No. 36813/97, 29.03.06.

83 *Kudła v Poland*, No. 30210/96, 26.10.00.

84 *Kudła v Poland*, No. 30210/96, 26.10.00, para. 148.

85 No. 40387/06, 8.4.08.

86 No. 33946/03, 13.7.09.

87 No. 71463/01, 9.4.09.

88 No. 43393/98, 2.11.06.

We also discuss the question why some cases concerning systemic problems are selected as pilot judgments (or 'quasi-pilot' judgments), and others are not, in section 1.4.1 below.

1.2.4. QUESTIONS ARISING FROM THE INITIAL APPLICATION OF THE PILOT JUDGMENT PROCEDURE

The early evolution of the procedure around the *Broniowski* case led to questions being raised as to the most appropriate context in which the procedure should be applied – should it only be utilised in 'class action' cases comparable to *Broniowski*, where there was an 'identifiable class of citizens'?[89] Indeed, Court Registry lawyer Renata Degener described *Broniowski* as a 'clear-cut situation': there was a large number of potential applicants and a 'clearly defined dysfunction'.[90] Pierre-Henri Imbert, the former Director General of Human Rights of the Council of Europe, described the procedure in 2004 as one which was designed for "judgments revealing a problem – whether systemic or specific – affecting a category or class of persons."[91] According to Imbert, this distinction has consequences for the enforcement of the judgments in such cases: solving a 'truly systemic' problem will usually be more difficult and time-consuming than a 'specific problem'.[92] As we discuss in chapters 3, 4 and 5, the application of the procedure, since 2004, to endemic problems in Slovenia, Italy, Russia and Ukraine has indeed proved to have been somewhat problematic. Others have questioned the utility of issuing pilot judgments in the context of inter-state political conflict.[93] We have also heard divergent views as to the suitability of the pilot judgment procedure to cases arising from armed conflict.[94] As we discuss in chapter 5, the Court has consulted

---

89 Interview with Judge Lech Garlicki, Strasbourg, 25.3.09.

90 Interview with Renata Degener, Court Registry, Strasbourg, 26.3.09.

91 Pierre Henri Imbert (2004), "Follow-up of the Committee of Ministers' Recommendations on the implementation of the Convention at the domestic level and the Declaration on 'Ensuring the effectiveness of the implementation of the European Convention on Human Rights at national and European levels'", Speech by M. Pierre-Henri Imbert, *High Level Seminar on Reform of the European Human Rights System*, 18.10.04, Oslo, Norway. The UK Government has described these cases as "issue-specific class actions" – see: *Pilot Judgments – Categorisation of Cases*, UK Government Paper produced at the request of the Reflection Group (DH-S-GDR), 2008, paras. 16–17 (unpublished – on file with the authors).

92 *Ibid.* See also: Philip Leach (2005), 'Beyond the Bug River: a new dawn for redress before the European Court of Human Rights?' *European Human Rights Law Review* 2, pp. 148–164.

93 See, e.g., Andrea Gattini (2007), 'Mass claims at the European Court of Human Rights' in *Stephan Breitenmoser ed. Human Rights, Democracy and the Rule of Law: Liber Amicorum Luzius Wildhaber, Nomos*, pp. 271–294, p. 282, commenting on the *Xenides-Arestis* judgment.

94 One former judge suggested to us that the pilot judgment procedure could be applied in respect of the Chechen cases (and could have been applied *vis-à-vis* the Kurdish cases): interview with former European Court judge, 6.5.09. The UK Government has suggested that cases relating to 'the quality of an investigation into allegations of torture' or, what it calls, 'public controversy cases' (including those relating to the resort to lethal force or torture) are not suitable for the

the parties about its application in cases related to the conflict between Georgia and Russia in August 2008.

Even more fundamental questions were raised as to the circumstances in which pilot judgments should be issued by the Court. Judge Lech Garlicki suggested that the legal basis of pilot judgments remained "relatively fragile and certain circumspection in resorting to that procedure may be in order" and that "an inflation of pilot judgments would be counterproductive".[95]

Concerns were also expressed that although the procedure had been approved by the Committee of Ministers, it was not reflected in the text of the Convention itself. Judge Zagrebelsky, in a partly dissenting opinion in *Hutten-Czapska,*[96] suggested on the one hand that the arguments set out by the Committee of Ministers in its 2004 resolution and recommendation[97] addressed to governments, were "undoubtedly of much importance and must be taken into account by the ECtHR with a view to ensuring that the reasons given in its judgments are as clear as possible". On the other hand, he argued that the "fact that the proposals to which the European Court of Human Rights refers ... were not included in the recent Protocol No. 14 amending the ECHR" cannot be overlooked. Similarly, Judge Kovler expressed his concerns during his interview with us that "we now have new competencies which are not restrained by the Convention and by our rules".[98]

The notion of adjourning other similar cases in the wake of a pilot judgment has also sparked controversy. Some respondents stressed the importance of the adjournment of all other clone cases pending at the Court – and that these cases are thus 'repatriated' for the respondent government to resolve.[99] The Court's 2003 position paper on the reform of the Court had defined the procedure as including the adjournment of cases, which would then be referred back to the state following the introduction of a remedy by the state authorities "within a reasonable time". In the event that there was an insufficient response it was envisaged that the

application of the pilot judgment procedure. See: *Pilot Judgments – Categorisation of Cases*, UK Government Paper produced at the request of the Reflection Group (DH-S-GDR), 2008, paras. 10–11 (unpublished – on file with the authors).

95 Lech Garlicki (2007), 'Broniowski and After: On the Dual Nature of Pilot Judgments' in *Lucius Caflisch ed. (et al.) Liber amicorum Luzius Wildhaber: Human Rights, Strasbourg views, N.P. Engel*, pp. 177–192, p. 191.

96 *Hutten-Czapska v Poland*, No. 35014/97, 19.6.06.

97 Committee of Ministers (2004), Resolution Res (2004) 3 and Recommendation Rec (2004) 6 of 12 May 2004.

98 Interview with Judge Anatoly Kovler, Strasbourg, 26.3.09.

99 Interview with Section Registrar, Strasbourg, 25.3.09.

Court would reserve the right to re-open the adjourned applications.[100] Thus, the rationale behind adjourning cases stems from the notion of 'subsidiarity', whereby respondent states should themselves find solutions to make their system 'Convention-compliant'.[101] Section Registrar Santiago Quesada suggested that the process of adjournment requires the Court's trust in the respondent state effecting the measures promised to resolve the issue; hence for other cases to be frozen the Court needs to be satisfied that the respondent government will deliver what is needed.[102] Another Section Registrar told us that, in some cases, adjournment is therefore not appropriate. Similarly, cases in which a person's safety or well-being are at stake should also not be adjourned.[103] Renata Degener, the Court Registry lawyer, also stressed that it would not always be necessary to adjourn other similar cases.[104]

Some commentators have suggested that there are potential weaknesses and shortcomings arising from the application of the pilot judgment procedure, and in particular as a consequence of the adjournment of cases of similarly situated applicants. Could it leave the remaining applicants in an uncertain position and vulnerable to long delays whilst a resolution is agreed upon and implemented?[105] Furthermore, if all other related cases are frozen, will there be a risk that this procedure delays rather than speeds up the full implementation of the Convention?[106] Lambert-Abdelgawad has alluded to the risk that individuals who have previously submitted their cases to Strasbourg will have to revert to the domestic courts, where they cannot be assured of obtaining effective redress. If

---

100 Steering Committee for Human Rights (CDDH). *Position Paper of the European Court of Human Rights on proposals for reform of the European Convention on Human Rights and other measures as set out in the report of the Steering Committee for Human Rights of 4 April 2003* (CDDH(2003)006 final), para 43. http://www.coe.int/t/e/human_rights/cddh/3._committees/07.%20other%20committees%20and%20working%20groups/archives/06.%20guaranteeing%20human%20rights%20(cddh-gdr)/01.%20working%20documents/2003/2003_024_en.asp#TopOfPage.

101 Interview with Section Registrar, Strasbourg, 25.3.09.

102 Interview with Santiago Quesada, Court Registry, Strasbourg, 26.3.09.

103 Interview with Section Registrar, Strasbourg, 25.3.09. Santiago Quesada gave the example of prison over-crowding cases: interview with Santiago Quesada, Court Registry, Strasbourg, 26.03.09.

104 Interview with Renata Degener, Court Registry, Strasbourg, 26.3.09.

105 Philip Leach (2005), 'Beyond the Bug River: a new dawn for redress before the European Court of Human Rights?' *European Human Rights Law Review* 2, pp. 148–164, p. 162. See also: *Report of the Group of Wise Persons*, SAGES(2006) 06 EN Def., Council of Europe, 10 November 2006, para. 105. https://wcd.coe.int/ViewDoc.jsp?id=1063779&Site=COE&BackColorInternet=DBDCF2&BackColorIntranet=FDC864&BackColorLogged=FDC864.

106 Parliamentary Assembly of the Council of Europe. Committee on Legal Affairs and Human Rights (CLAHR) (2006), *Implementation of Judgments of the ECtHR, Report, Committee on Legal Affairs and Human Rights, Rapporteur: Mr Erik Jurgens, Netherlands, Socialist Group*, Doc. 11020, 18 September 2006 http://assembly.coe.int/Main.asp?link=/Documents/WorkingDocs/Doc06/EDOC11020.htm.

this happens, she has argued, they will have to go back to the European Court once again, thus extending considerably the length of such proceedings.[107]

Further questions were raised by civil society representatives – how could the Committee of Ministers ensure not only the rapid execution of pilot judgments, but also guarantee that their manner of implementation genuinely afforded an effective remedy for similarly situated persons?[108] Lambert-Abdelgawad has called for monitoring of the measures taken by member states in implementing pilot judgments.[109]

Other commentators sought to analyse the broader implications of the procedure. The reforms adopted in May 2004 can be characterised as an attempt to spread the burden of solving the problem of the backlog of cases across the various 'players' within the Council of Europe system (*i.e.* the Court, the Committee of Ministers and member states). The former President of the Court, Luzius Wildhaber, has argued that "faced with a structural situation, the European Court is in effect saying to the respondent states and to the Committee of Ministers that they too must play their role and assume their responsibilities".[110] Lagoutte, however, has argued that pilot judgments are not a solution to all of the problems of the European human rights protection system. Therefore, she has suggested that the jurisprudence needs to be developed and refined in order to be fully accepted by the member states.[111] Colandrea has characterised pilot judgments as being 'future-oriented' and as representing the Court's 'persuasive function'.[112]

---

107 Elisabeth Lambert-Abdelgawad (2005), 'Le protocole 14 et l'exécution des arrêts de la Cour européenne des droits de l'homme' in *Gérard Cohen-Jonathan, et Jean-François Flauss, La Réforme du système de contrôle contentieux de la Convention européenne des droits de l'homme*, Droit et Justice, Vol. 61, Bruylant, pp. 79–114, p. 102.

108 NGO Comments on the Group of Wise Persons' Report, January 2007, p. 11.

109 Elisabeth Lambert-Abdelgawad (2005), 'Le protocole 14 et l'exécution des arrêts de la Cour européenne des droits de l'homme' in *Gérard Cohen-Jonathan, et Jean-François Flauss, La Réforme du système de contrôle contentieux de la Convention européenne des droits de l'homme*, Droit et Justice, Vol. 61, Bruylant, pp. 79–114, p. 102.

110 Luzius Wildhaber (2004), 'Consequences for the ECtHR of Protocol No. 14 and the Resolution on Judgments Revealing an Underlying Systemic Problem- Practical Steps of Implementation and Challenges' in *Applying and Supervising the ECHR-Reform of the European Human Rights System, Proceedings of the high-level seminar*, Oslo, 18 October 2004, pp. 23–32, p. 26 http://www.coe.int/T/E/Human_rights/prot14e.asp; http://www.coe.int/t/e/human_rights/1reformeurhrsystem_e.pdf.

111 Stéphanie Lagoutte (2007), 'The Future of the European Human Rights Control System: Fighting With its Back to the Wall' in *Stéphanie Lagoutte, Hans-Otto Sano, Peter Scharff Smith, Human Rights in Turmoil, Facing Threats, Consolidating Achievements, Martinus Nijhoff Publishers*, pp. 25–48, p. 39.

112 Valerio Colandrea (2007), 'On the Power of the European Court of Human Rights to order Specific Non-monetary Measures: Some Remarks in Light of the Assanidze, Broniowski and Sejdovic Cases' *Human Rights Law Review* 2, pp. 409–410.

1.3. SECURING STATES' COMPLIANCE WITH THE EUROPEAN CONVENTION

The legal and social science literature suggests that a managerial, non-confrontational approach may be the most effective way to secure states' compliance with international law. This is because resorting to 'enforcement' in this context, through invoking the 'rule of law', "can lead to conflict between an ... international legal order and state sovereignty or constitutional democracy".[113] According to this premise, the optimal way for an international organisation to secure compliance is to treat the matter as a problem for cooperative resolution, through managerial methods, rather than resorting to the application of sanctions and determining the matter as one to be solved through 'enforcement'. This would appear to be borne out by the experience of the European Court, as, according to the Court Registrar, Erik Fribergh, there are real doubts about the effectiveness of the process for the supervision of the enforcement of Court judgments, and the need for the pilot judgment procedure is indicative of this:

> "I would ... say that the pilot judgment procedure is an indication that the system doesn't work ... the idea with the whole system should be that the Court delivers one judgment and then that judgment should be properly enforced and executed by the state and supervised by the Committee of Ministers ..."
>
> "Concerning non-enforcement of domestic judgments in Russia, the Court first delivered the Burdov judgment in 2002. Thereafter the Court has delivered 200 similar judgments. The Court still has some 1,000 similar cases on its docket and chose to apply a pilot judgment procedure in the *Burdov (No. 2)* case. In that judgment it said to the Government 'you introduce a remedy and take care of the other pending cases'. But ... it shouldn't be necessary for the Court to have done that ... after 200 judgments, ... if ... the Committee of Ministers are not able to understand what is necessary ... then it doesn't work very well ..."[114]

There are, additionally, concerns that the selective way in which the Committee of Ministers enforces Court judgments indicates that the process has become overly politicised. Erik Fribergh suggested to us that:

> "Enforcement of judgments ... is ... of course ... partly political but also [a] judicial procedure and I think it has become too much a political procedure. The judicial aspect of it is ensured in a sense by the Secretariat ... [which] ... is doing a fantastic job, but it's very difficult when you get into political trouble ... there is

113 Gianluigi Palombella (2009), 'The rule of law beyond the state: failures, promises and theory' *International Journal of Constitutional Law* 7:3, pp. 442–467, p. 442. See also the literature referred to in the Introduction ('Framing Research Questions').

114 Interview with Erik Fribergh, Court Registry, Strasbourg, 25.3.09.

> this phenomenon: if you're not too hard [on] my country, I will not be too hard on your country the next time ..."[115]

Increasing the Court's authority to allow it to determine where states are failing to comply and giving it the power to issue pilot judgments could be seen as an attempt to de-politicise the process of 'enforcement' by making it the responsibility of the 'judicial arm' of the Council of Europe, rather than that of the Committee of Ministers, a political entity. This may be seen as positive. There is, however, an underlying tension in this, because as a judicial body, the Court is arguably being given a more political role in the pilot judgment procedure. A number of our respondents expressed concern about the Court's role in the light of the development of the pilot judgment procedure. For example, Judge Anatoly Kovler, said that "the task to control the execution of our judgments and to ask ... the states to ensure ... general measures is the task of the Committee of Ministers – it's not the task of the Court".[116] Judge Vladimiro Zagrebelsky suggested that "the Court should not be indicating measures ... which are fairly fluid, in the operative provisions".[117] One commentator has suggested that in focusing more on the question of general measures, the Court's function is becoming blurred with that of a Constitutional Court, and that in prescribing how domestic law should be amended to make it Convention-compliant, the Court is straying into the jurisdiction of sovereign states, and thus over-reaching its powers.[118]

As our case studies in chapters 2-5 demonstrate, to date, the application of the procedure appears to varying degrees dependent on the respondent state's *a priori* acknowledgement that the violation in question is indeed systemic, or the state's anticipated cooperation with the Court in its application of the procedure. A number of respondents in Strasbourg confirmed that in relation to the first pilot judgment, *Broniowski,* the Polish government expressed the requisite political will to find a solution through the pilot judgment procedure and was sympathetic to the aims of the Court. To a certain extent this was also true of the Russian Government vis-à-vis *Burdov (No. 2)* (but this was not the case in respect of *Ivanov*, for example). Therefore, we have sought to explore how this was achieved. In following a 'managerial approach', the nature of cooperation between the domestic authorities and the Court is clearly crucial to successfully negotiating a solution to the problem. Therefore, examples of successful cooperation may help to provide a template for the future practice of the states and the Court.

115 Interview with Erik Fribergh, Court Registry, Strasbourg, 25.3.09.
116 Interview with Judge Anatoly Kovler, Strasbourg, 26.3.09.
117 Interview with Judge Vladimiro Zagrebelsky, Strasbourg, 25.3.09.
118 Valerio Colandrea (2007), 'On the power of the European Court of Human Rights to order specific non-monetary measures: some remarks in light of the Assandize, Broniowski and Sejdović cases' *Human Rights Law Review* 2, pp. 406 and 411.

1.4. THE MECHANICS OF THE PILOT JUDGMENT PROCEDURE

HOW ARE CASES CHOSEN FOR THE APPLICATION OF THE PILOT JUDGMENT PROCEDURE – A QUESTION OF SELECTIVE JUSTICE?

If the only criterion for the application of the pilot judgment procedure were the identification of a systemic violation of the Convention, then there are a large number of repetitive violation cases which have been identified by the European Court (beyond the full pilot judgments issued to date) in which it could have been applied. Commentators have questioned how specific cases are selected for the application of the procedure, as a logical pattern in its application is difficult to discern.[119] Furthermore, it is not clear how the 'lead case' for the pilot judgment is chosen from the wider group of clone cases. It has been acknowledged that there is a risk that individual justice may be prejudiced as the other applicants may not then receive a proper judicial examination of their cases or their cases may be considerably delayed.[120] The 2009 Information Note on the pilot judgment procedure issued by the Court Registrar explains that "it is not every category of repetitive case that will be suitable for a pilot judgment procedure, and not every pilot judgment will lead to an adjournment of cases, especially where the systemic problem touches on the most fundamental rights of the person under the Convention."[121] This inevitably raises the question as to when the procedure is applied and why the Court would apply it selectively, rather than applying it universally to all cases involving systemic violations. For example, Judge Kovler expressed his concern that the process of the selection of cases might appear to be subjective, and subject to political considerations (in the sense of a legislative policy).[122]

The Deputy Registrar of the Court, Michael O'Boyle, told us that the selection depended on a number of factors, some practical, others political. Since applying the pilot judgment procedure is a complex process, section registrars tend to deal first with easier cases, thus delaying the processing of systemic cases.[123] Another

119 Costas Paraskeva (2007), 'Human Rights protection begins at home: the Pilot Judgment Procedure developed by the European Court of Human Rights' *Human Rights Law Commentary* v. 3. https://portal2.nottingham.ac.uk/shared/shared_hrlcpub/Paraskeva.pdf.

120 Renata Degener and Paul Mahoney (2007), 'The prospects for a Test-Case Procedure in the European Court of Human Rights' in *Hanno Hartig Trente ans de droit européen des droits de l'homme – Études à la mémoire de Wolfgang Strasser*, Droit et Justice 74, Emile Bruylant, pp. 173–208.

121 European Court of Human Rights (2009), *The Pilot Judgment Procedure: information note issued by the Registrar* http://www.echr.coe.int/NR/rdonlyres/DF4E8456-77B3-4E67-8944-B908143A7E2C/0/Information_Note_on_the_PJP_for_Website.pdf.

122 Interview with Judge Anatoly Kovler, Strasbourg, 26.3.09.

123 Interview with Michael O'Boyle, Strasbourg, 25.3.09.

factor is that in the application of the procedure, the early practice was for the case to be dealt with by the Grand Chamber (*Broniowski, Hutten-Czapska*). That discouraged section registrars from applying the procedure, as they tend to prefer that cases they are dealing with should remain within their own section.[124] To encourage the procedure's wider application, therefore, section registrars were given the authority to apply the pilot judgment procedure, and to keep the case within their own section.[125] This new policy was apparent in the case of the 'full' pilot judgment of *Burdov (No. 2)*, which did not go before the Grand Chamber, but was processed by the First Section of the Court. Subsequently, *Olaru* and *Suljagić* were handled by the Fourth Section, and *Ivanov* by the Fifth Section.

Broader political considerations might dictate that respondent states may object to being the subject of the pilot judgment procedure.[126] Some of our respondents were firmly of the view that the Court will only proceed with a pilot judgment if it considers it likely that the respondent state will carry out the prescribed measures. As Michael O'Boyle told us:

> "If a procedure was to be hotly contested by a state I think it would damage the efforts that we are making to get this [procedure] on the rails."[127]

A number of respondents in the Court Registry confirmed that the Court had so far been selective in its choice of cases suitable for the pilot judgment procedure; they confirmed that it would be very difficult to issue a pilot judgment if the state were not likely to be cooperative.[128]

A number of interviewees told us that for a pilot judgment to be issued there must be some form of anticipated consent from the government; a respondent state's failure to comply with the measures would damage the authority of the procedure.[129] A Court Registry lawyer suggested that:

> "... if you require something which is not implementable for whatever legal, practical and/or political reasons, the pilot judgment procedure would be compromised."[130]

---

124 *Ibid.*
125 *Ibid.*
126 *Ibid.*
127 *Ibid.*
128 Interview with Santiago Quesada, Strasbourg, 26.3.09; Interview with Michael O'Boyle Strasbourg, 25.3.09.
129 *Ibid.*
130 Interview with Court Registry lawyer, Strasbourg, 27.3.09.

Judge Ineta Ziemele told us that:

> "... if you want the pilot judgment procedure to succeed ... you want to ... have a certain sense whether the state is likely to cooperate ..."[131]

However, it was also emphasised to us by Michael O'Boyle that the state's permission is not in fact a pre-requisite, as such:

> "the pilot judgment procedure is not a consensual exercise – the Court takes its decision in the exercise of its own sovereignty – it doesn't ask a government for consent. We have a sensible procedure where we inform a government that we are considering treating this case as a pilot judgment."[132]

According to our respondents, the mechanics of the process are as follows. The Court Registry lawyers in the relevant section come to an initial view as to whether or not the state will respond cooperatively.[133] At that point, according to one Registry lawyer, the national judge can then over-rule a proposal that the pilot judgment procedure be applied.[134] The Court then asks the parties at the communication stage of the case if they consider that the case is suitable for application of the pilot judgment procedure. If the state agrees then, as, Section Registrar Santiago Quesada told us, this is a 'promising start'.[135] Any case which is symptomatic of a new systemic problem is given high priority by the Court (but other similar cases may be considered 'non-priority' and may therefore be subject to longer delays).[136]

Another Section Registrar confirmed to us that the Committee of Ministers has some influence on the process of selecting a case for the pilot judgment procedure. Should the Committee of Ministers declare the violation in question to be 'structural' or 'systemic' in resolutions concerning earlier judgments of the same nature (as was the case, for example, in *Ivanov*),[137] then this evidently puts

---

131 Interview with Judge Ineta Ziemele, Strasbourg, 26.3.09.

132 Interview with Michael O'Boyle, Strasbourg, 25.3.09. The Grand Chamber has since confirmed this case in the *Demopoulos* case (see chapter five): "...it should go without saying that Contracting States are bound, in any event, to comply with the Court's judgments, whether or not they have been engaged in a dialogue as to their willingness to find general solutions to a widespread problem. The Court's competence to undertake a pilot-judgment procedure in respect of a series of repetitive or clone cases is not conditional on a Government's conduct". See: Demopoulos and others v Turkey, Nos. 46113/99, 3843/02, 13751/02, 13466/03, 10200/04, 14163/04, 19993/04, 21819/04, dec. 1.3.10 (GC), para. 81.

133 *Ibid.*

134 Interview with Lucja Miara, Court Registry, Strasbourg, 26.3.09.

135 Interview with Santiago Quesada, Strasbourg, 26.3.09.

136 Erik Fribergh, *Bringing Rights Home or How to deal with repetitive applications in the future*, Round Table, Bled, Slovenia, 21–22.9.09, paras. 19 & 26.

137 *Yuriy Nikolayevich Ivanov v Ukraine*, No. 40450/04, 15.10.09, para. 87.

greater weight on the respondent state to accept it as such. The Section Registrar suggested that it would be easier for a government to deny that a problem was systemic should the Court alone be claiming it as such.[138]

Our respondents stressed that the Court does not wish to selectively mete out justice via the pilot judgment procedure, but prefers to negotiate a solution consensually with the respondent state. John Darcy, from the Court Registry, emphasised the voluntary nature of the Polish Government's cooperation with the Court in relation to the *Broniowski* case, and its willingness to look at the deeper causes of the problems revealed by that case.[139] The Court Registrar, Erik Fribergh, told us that in the informal discussions with the Russian Federation to try to find a solution to the systemic problem of the non-enforcement of domestic court judgments there were:

> "... internal disputes as to who was responsible for paying the outstanding awards: should it be the region or the federal government, and things like that. Those issues are not for us to be involved in. But you can understand the problems they have and there has been a movement over quite some period to introduce a remedy in the Russian Federation but it has constantly met obstacles, and, in those circumstances, you can say that you have both cooperation and opposition from the government ... you have cooperation from those you deal with – ... the representative – because they want to settle the problems, but then they meet political or administrative obstacles and I think in those circumstances a [pilot] judgment from this court ... could be of great help to them."[140]

Michael O'Boyle confirmed that the Court Registry gauged the political will within the Russian authorities to find a remedy to the problem:

> "We were aware on the Russian side that there were forces in favour of introducing a remedy ... this is a serious problem in Russia and I think a previous attempt to introduce a remedy had failed, so our analysis was that there would not be serious resistance to turning this case into a pilot judgment."[141]

As noted above, the practice of the Court, at the point when the case is communicated to the respondent government, is to ask the parties whether or not they consider that the case is suitable for the application of the pilot judgment procedure. For example, in a number of cases arising from the armed conflict

138 Interview with Section Registrar, Strasbourg 25.3.09. Another example, in which the Committee of Ministers was instrumental in the Court's issuing of an 'Article 46 judgment' is the case of *Kauczor v Poland*, No. 45219/06, 3.2.09 (which we discuss in chapter 2).
139 Interview with John Darcy, Court Registry, Strasbourg, 25.3.09.
140 Interview with Erik Fribergh, Court Registry, Strasbourg, 25.3.09.
141 Interview with Michael O'Boyle, Court Registry, Strasbourg, 25.3.09.

between Russia and Georgia in August 2008, the Court posed the following questions:

> "In view of the nature of the situation which gave rise to the present case and given that more than 3,300 applications having the same situation for their background were lodged with the Court, is the present application suitable for the 'pilot judgment' procedure? The parties are invited to make their comments in the light of the Court's case-law ..."[142]

Another example is the case of *Sinead O'Donoghue v UK*, concerning the restrictions on immigrants' right to marry under the UK's Certificate of Approval Scheme. There, the Court asked the parties the following questions:

> "Do the facts in the present application disclose the existence of a structural problem on account of deficiencies in the impugned national law, which may give rise to numerous similar applications? If so, is the present case suitable for the 'pilot judgment' procedure?" [143]

Therefore, the Court in such cases asks the parties about the 'suitability' of the procedure, thus apparently testing whether or not the respondent state acknowledges the problem to be systemic, and, impliedly, whether it will cooperate with the Court if it lays down general measures in its judgment aimed at the resolution of the structural problem. If the respondent state agrees, then it is likely that a 'full' pilot judgment will be issued. If, however, it does not agree, the Court would then have to consider its options (in the event that the state might not be fully co-operative), but, as we have seen, it would nevertheless not be prevented from issuing a pilot judgment.

What the first three full pilot judgments and some quasi-pilot judgments[144] apparently have in common is an *a priori* recognition by the state's Constitutional Court (or other higher court) that the existing law or practice in question violates the Convention, and that there has been a failure on the part of the executive or the legislature to respond adequately to such findings. In such situations, the higher courts therefore represent the 'forces in favour' which Michael O'Boyle has referred to. The pivotal nature of 'cooperation' between the Constitutional and European Courts in the pilot judgment process has been discussed by Wojciech

142 *Bekoyeva (Elza Alikhanovna) v Georgia*, No. 48347/08 (communicated 26.1.09).

143 *O'Donoghue (Sinead) and others v UK*, No. 34848/07 (communicated 1.12.08).

144 The Albanian *Ramadhi* and *Driza* cases, however, do not appear to fit this model, as in these instances there is no apparent evidence that the Albanian Constitutional Court was acting in consonance with the Strasbourg Court. In the case of *Xenides-Arestis v Turkey* measures had already been taken by the government to increase the rate of compensation for 'TRNC' citizens, which may have been interpreted by the Court as a willingness to comply.

Sadurski in his analysis of the *Broniowski* and *Hutten-Czapska* cases.[145] Through its judgment the European Court is thus requiring the respondent state to comply with the decisions of its own higher national courts.[146] However, as we discuss in Chapter 5, such 'co-operation' by the national courts is certainly not always a feature of the pilot judgment procedure.

An effective response by states in their implementation of the general measures specified by the Court in pilot judgments issued to date is evidently key to the future of the procedure. As we note above, the application of the procedure in a situation where a state then fails to introduce the necessary domestic remedy could discredit it.

---

145 Sadurski, Wojciech (2008), 'Partnering with Strasbourg: Constitutionalization of the European Court of Human Rights, the Accession of Central and East European States to the Council of Europe and the idea of Pilot Judgments', *EUI Working Papers Law* 2008/33.

146 Andrea Gattini sees rather the Court 'conveniently leaning on' the authority of the Constitutional Court. See Andrea Gattini (2007), 'Mass claims at the European Court of Human Rights' in *Stephan Breitenmoser ed. (et al.) Human Rights, Democracy and the Rule of Law: Liber Amicorum Luzius Wildhaber, Nomos*, pp. 271–294, p. 286.

CHAPTER 2

POLAND: THE 'HOMELAND' OF PILOT JUDGMENTS?

2.1. INTRODUCTION

2.1.1. THE STATUS OF THE CONVENTION WITH RESPECT TO DOMESTIC LAW

Poland acceded to the Council of Europe in 1991 and ratified the European Convention on Human Rights in 1993. According to Magda Krzyżanowska-Mierzewska,

> "... the ratification was one of those measures that the newly democratic State regarded as an obvious and necessary thing to take in order to restore democracy and consolidate its return to the family of truly European states."[1]

In 1997 the Polish Constitution was amended, requiring the State to respect international law binding upon it (Articles 9 and 87 of the Constitution).[2] Furthermore, Article 91 of the Constitution provides that a ratified international treaty is part of the domestic legal order and is to be applied directly (unless its application depends on the enactment of a statute). The Constitutional Court has since then consistently clarified in its judgments that the European Convention applies directly in domestic law, and in 2004 stated that domestic law must be harmonised with the Convention.[3]

---

1. Magda Krzyżanowska-Mierzewska (2008), 'The Reception Process in Poland and Slovakia' in Keller, Helen and Alec Stone Sweet (eds.), *A Europe of Rights: the Impact of the ECHR on National Legal Systems*, OUP, p. 536.
2. See further: Andrew Drzemczewski and Marek Nowicki (2001), 'Poland' in Blackburn, Robert and Jurg Polakiewicz (eds.), *Fundamental Rghts in Europe: the European Convention on Human Rights and its member states, 1950–2000*, OUP, pp. 657–79. The Polish Constitution of 1952, and even as amended in 1989 and 1992, was silent as to the relationship between domestic and international law.
3. Magda Krzyżanowska-Mierzewska (2008), 'The Reception Process in Poland and Slovakia' in Keller, Helen and Alec Stone Sweet (eds.), *A Europe of Rights: the Impact of the ECHR on National Legal Systems*, OUP, p. 539. To avoid confusion, 'Tribunal Konstytucjny' will be

There has been a difference of opinion between the Supreme and Constitutional Courts regarding this process of harmonisation, and which court ultimately has the authority to interpret the law in the event of incompatibility.[4] Even before such tensions arose, however, by 1996 the Convention had become a significant point of reference for the Polish courts such that it had *de facto* become a "living instrument in Polish law".

In practice, though, reference to the Convention is more often made in higher court (Constitutional and Supreme Court) judgments than in the lower courts.[5] It has been argued that this is partially the result of judicial culture. Younger judges and prosecutors may be more inclined to invoke the Convention in their judgments, but are discouraged from doing so because their more senior judicial colleagues are less well disposed towards such a practice.[6] Achieving a change in this mentality may be far more of a challenge than amending the law.[7] We heard that there is still little in-depth understanding of how the European Court works, and very few of its judgments or decisions are translated into Polish, which limits the Polish judiciary's access to up-to-date European Court case law.[8] Additionally, although there is now a greater public awareness of the Court, its judgments are not widely reported in the media,[9] and there is rarely systematic or specialist coverage in the press, except in the broadsheet newspaper *Rzeczpospolita*.[10]

---

referred to generically according to its function as 'Constitutional Court' instead of the correct linguistic translation, 'Constitutional Tribunal'.

4 Magda Krzyżanowska-Mierzewska (2008), 'The Reception Process in Poland and Slovakia' in Keller, Helen and Alec Stone Sweet (eds.), *A Europe of Rights: the Impact of the ECHR on National Legal Systems*, OUP, p. 545–6.

5 *Ibid.*, p. 543.

6 *Ibid.*, pp. 544–5.

7 Interview with Adam Bodnar, Secretary of the Board, Helsinki Foundation for Human Rights, 12.05.09. This point is supported by the position of some social scientists who hold that laws may be changed overnight, but the practices of the institutions governed by these laws are much slower to change, see, for example, Douglass North (1990), *Institutions, Institutional Change and Economic Performance*, CUP.

8 Interview with Katarzyna Łakoma and Hanna Machińska, Council of Europe Office, Warsaw, 13.05.09.

9 Interview with Adam Szafrański and Jan Lipiej, Biuro Analyz Sejmowych = the Research Office for the Sejm, Warsaw, 12.5.09; Interview with Igor Dzialuk, Undersecretary of State, Ministry of Justice, 15.5.09.

10 Interview with Adam Bodnar, Secretary of the Board, Helsinki Foundation for Human Rights, Warsaw, 12.5.09; Interview with Adam Szafrański and Jan Lipiej, Biuro Analyz Sejmowych = the Research Office for the Sejm, Warsaw, 12.5.09; Interview with Wojciech Hermeliński, Constitutional Court, Warsaw, 13.5.09; Interview with Marek Nowicki, Helsinki Foundation for Human Rights, Warsaw, 13.5.09. *Rzeczpospolita* has a daily circulation of about 270,000, see: Andrew Drzemczewski and Marek Nowicki (2001), 'Poland' in Blackburn, Robert and Jurg Polakiewicz (eds.), *Fundamental Rghts in Europe: the European Convention on Human Rights and its member states, 1950–2000*, OUP, p. 676.

2.1.2. POLAND'S TRACK RECORD IN RESPONDING TO STRASBOURG

Polish government representatives consistently emphasised to us that they are working hard to respond to Strasbourg and that there is the requisite political will to comply with judgments of the European Court.[11] A 2008 report by the Parliamentary Assembly of the Council of Europe (PACE) stated that data submitted by the Polish Government suggested that there has been progress in respect of the particular problem of the excessive length of judicial proceedings since the *Kudła* judgment of 2000.[12] Evidently the efficiency of the Polish courts has improved, as is shown by a decrease in the number of cases pending for more than five years before domestic courts.[13] The Committee of Ministers, however, stated that they were unable to fully assess this data because "the mechanism for evaluating the average length of proceedings at the national level is not sufficiently clear to make a proper supervision of the evolution of the duration of proceedings possible". Indeed, the way in which the length of proceedings is calculated has given rise to the judgment of *Krawczak v Poland,*[14] as is discussed later in this chapter.

In addition to the problem of the excessive length of proceedings, numerous other Polish applications continue to arrive in Strasbourg. Of those that are found admissible, the principal categories of cases include the excessive length of pre-trial detention and detention on remand (violation of Article 5(3)), interference with prisoners' correspondence (violations of Articles 8 and 34) and cases concerning the unfairness of 'lustration proceedings'.[15] Although the total number of adverse judgments concerning Poland is not inconsiderable, Poland is far from the worst offender.[16] What may also be of concern, however, is that, by 2009, the Court had received the highest number of inadmissible applications

---

11 Interview with Jakub Wołąsiewicz, Government Agent, Warsaw, 14.5.09; Interview with Piotr Styczeń, Undersecretary of State for Infrastructure, 13.5.09; Interview with Igor Dzialuk, Undersecretary of State, Ministry of Justice, 15.5.09.

12 *Kudła v Poland,* No. 30210/96, 26.10.00.

13 Parliamentary Assembly of the Council of Europe. Committee on Legal Affairs and Human Rights (2008) *Implementation of judgments of the European Court of Human Rights: Introductory memorandum,* Rapporteur: Mr Christos Pourgourides, Cyprus, AS/Jur (2008)24, p. 10. http://assembly.coe.int/CommitteeDocs/2008/20080526_ajdoc24_2008.pdf.

14 No. 40387/06, 8.4.08.

15 Directorate General of Human Rights and Legal Affairs (2009), Execution of the Judgments of the European Court of Human Rights. Pending Cases. Current State of Execution, Poland. http://www.coe.int/t/dghl/monitoring/execution/Reports/Current_en.asp. Lustration proceedings are those aimed at exposing persons having worked for or collaborated with the state's security services during the communist period.

16 As at 1.1.09 at least one violation of the Convention had been found in 551 Polish cases. States where the most violations had been found were Turkey (1,676), Italy (1,495), Russia (605). The European Court of Human Rights, Country Fact Sheets 1959–2009, pp. 12–13.

from Poland.[17] Some respondents claimed that a lack of understanding of both the domestic law and the European Court's admissibility requirements explain the high numbers of applications to Strasbourg. According to Katarzyna Łakoma, a lawyer in the Council of Europe Information Office in Warsaw, many applicants from Poland don't understand the need to exhaust domestic remedies before applying to Strasbourg and there is also a tendency for individuals simply to misinterpret the domestic law.[18] This is compounded by the fact that the European Court does not always require applicants from Poland to have exhausted the remedy of an individual constitutional complaint (because of limitations in terms of its scope and the form of redress which it provides).[19] The new remedy of an individual constitutional complaint was introduced in Poland in 1997 (Article 79 of the Constitution) to try to stem the number of cases arriving in Strasbourg. In practice, though, this has not had the desired effect, firstly because of the Court's popularity in Poland, and secondly because a Constitutional Court judgment does not finally resolve an individual complaint. Once an individual has received a Constitutional Court judgment in their favour they must then institute a new set of proceedings to have their case re-opened and reassessed.[20]

How the Polish government responds to Strasbourg judgments evidently continues to be a matter of concern. A former constitutional court judge estimated that to date there had been about 100 Polish cases before the European Court concerning the excessive length of pre-trial detention, but that the requisite domestic remedies had not been fully implemented.[21] This problem is reflected in the increase in Polish cases pending at the Court in 2008.[22] The Committee of Ministers has recently noted that this increase has primarily constituted clone and isolated cases which do not raise new issues related to the adoption of general measures.[23] Nevertheless, a number of interviewees drew our attention to other Polish cases relating to various widespread or systemic violations, including

---

17 By 2009, the Court had declared 30,034 Polish applications inadmissible, see: The European Court of Human Rights, Country Fact Sheets 1959–2009, p. 57.

18 Interview with Katarzyna Łakoma and Hanna Machińska, Council of Europe Office, Warsaw, 13.05.09.

19 See *Szott-Medyńska v Poland*, No. 47414/99, dec. 9.10.03.

20 Magda Krzyżanowska-Mierzewska (2008), 'The Reception Process in Poland and Slovakia' in Keller, Helen and Alec Stone Sweet (eds.), *A Europe of Rights: the Impact of the ECHR on National Legal Systems*, OUP, p. 551–3.

21 Interview with Professor Marek Safjan, University of Warsaw, 13.5.09.

22 Committee of Ministers (2009), *Supervision of the execution of judgments of the European Court of Human Rights, 2nd annual report, 2008*, p. 44.

23 Committee of Ministers (2009), *Supervision of the execution of judgments, 2008, 2nd annual report of the European Court of Human Rights*, p. 44. "Other states, on the contrary, have had a growing number of pending cases (Turkey, Poland, Russian Federation, Romania, Greece, Bulgaria), but the data concerning leading cases … suggest that this growth is mostly related to clone and isolated cases, not raising new issues in respect of the adoption of general measures" Here, 'leading cases' are defined as cases which show evidence of a more systemic problem requiring general measures – see p. 29: 'leading cases include *a fortiori* pilot judgments'.

the excessive length of pre-trial detention (*Kauczor v Poland*),[24] conditions of detention (*Musiał v Poland*),[25] the denial of abortion on therapeutic grounds (*Tysiąc v Poland*)[26] and the protection of gay rights (*Bączkowski v Poland*).[27] The latter judgment condemned Poland for its discrimination against homosexuals in violating their right to freedom of assembly. This occurred three years after the first gay pride Equality Parade in 2004, when the Mayor of Warsaw banned the event.[28] As we discuss below at Section 2.4, the Polish government's failure to respond adequately to Strasbourg judgments, and indeed to its own Constitutional Court, concerning conditions of detention and the excessive length of pre-trial detention resulted in the Court invoking Article 46 in the quasi-pilot judgments of *Kauczor* and *Musiał*.

Why these judgments are not yet fully implemented is not in all cases the result of unwillingness to amend legislation: some decisions will require changes in policy or practice. For example, Adam Bodnar, Secretary of the Board of the Helsinki Foundation for Human Rights (in Poland), suggested to us that changing the law in response to the case of *Tysiąc* will not be the solution – what is needed, in his view, is the provision of adequate clinical facilities in Poland, so that there is sufficient capacity to carry out abortions on therapeutic grounds.[29] A further factor explaining non-implementation may be the extent to which an issue raised in Strasbourg concerns deeply felt moral or social issues – Poland remains of course a predominantly Catholic country. In Poland, for example, issues such as abortion and gay rights concern questions on which the Law and Justice Party, and other parties on the right in Poland, continue to stand at odds with European legislation and the European Convention.[30]

---

24 No. 45219/06, 3.2.09.

25 No. 28300/06, 20.1.09.

26 No. 5410/03, 20.3.07. See para. 85: "... The circumstances of the case revealed the existence of an underlying systemic failure of the Polish legal system when it came to determining whether or not the conditions for lawful abortion obtained in a particular case."

27 No. 1543/06, 3.5.07.

28 Adam Bodnar (2009), 'Shaping the Freedom of Assembly: Counter-Productive Effects of the Polish Road towards Illiberal Democracy' in Sajó, András (ed.), *Free to Protest: Constituent Power and Street Demonstration*, Issues in Constitutional Law v. 5, Eleven International Publishing, pp. 165–187.

29 Interview with Adam Bodnar, Secretary of the Board, Helsinki Foundation for Human Rights (Poland), 12.5.09.

30 However, Bodnar has argued that since the Strasbourg ruling in *Tysiąc* there is a growing awareness among these parties that this type of violation is not acceptable to the international community. See: Adam Bodnar (2009), 'Shaping the Freedom of Assembly: Counter-Productive Effects of the Polish Road towards Illiberal Democracy' in Sajó, András (ed.), *Free to Protest: Constituent Power and Street Demonstration*, Issues in Constitutional Law v. 5, Eleven International Publishing, p. 167.

2.1.2.1. *The problem of ensuring effective parliamentary engagement in the implementation process*

According to academic research published in Poland in 2008, the legislature is heavily influenced by pressure from interest groups and lobbyists and laws consequently reflect the interests of certain groups rather than being geared towards the public interest. This tendency towards meeting short-term goals consequently gives rise to many new amendments to the law.[31] More fundamentally, perhaps, according to a number of our respondents, there is insufficient engagement by parliament in scrutinising draft legislation generally. Igor Dzialuk, Undersecretary of State at the Ministry of Justice, expressed regret that parliament is not more involved in drafting legislation: "I feel it's just very unfortunate that the parliament is not that active in the process of legislation at the initial phase."[32] Complaints about delays in the parliamentary process are also evident. For example, the Marshall's office[33] has been criticised for the time it takes to review draft bills.

Wojciech Hermeliński, formerly the legal representative to Mr Broniowski and now a Constitutional Court judge, recalled that the legislative process can become protracted by parliament's failure to prepare the requisite legislation following a Constitutional Court judgment, particularly in criminal cases.[34] This is apparent from the quasi-pilot judgments of *Kauczor* and *Musiał*, as we discuss below (section 2.4). There is considerable evidence of a particular problem relating to the decisions of the Polish Constitutional Court – that after finding a discrepancy between the Convention and domestic law (prior to, or following, a Strasbourg judgment) there are real difficulties in ensuring that the government and parliament respond appropriately to their judgments. This is compounded by the fact that there is no separate mechanism within the legislative process which scrutinises whether or not draft legislation is Convention-compliant.[35] This problem is considered in the following section.

---

31 Tomasz Stawecki, Wiesław Staśkiewicz, Jan Winczorek (2008), *Między policentrycznością a fragmentaryzacją: wpływ Trybunału Konstytucyjnego na Polski porządek prawny*, Sprawne Państwo, p. 64. = *Between policentrism and fragmentation: the impact of the Constitutional Court on the Polish legal system.*

32 Interview with Igor Dzialuk, Undersecretary of State, Ministry of Justice, 15.5.09.

33 The Marshall has a similar role to the Speaker in the UK Parliament. However, the Marshall's Office has additional powers in that it verifies all draft legislation to make sure that it meets with certain requirements. The Marshall's Office verifies the draft bill itself, and also requires the drafting body to provide supporting documentation, including a justification for the new law and an analysis of the projected consequences in legal, economic and social terms. Additionally there must be a statement concerning compliance with EU law. In the event that the Marshall's Office is not satisfied, the draft bill may be returned to the drafting body for amendment.

34 Interview with Wojciech Hermeliński, Constitutional Court, Warsaw, 13.5.09.

35 Magda Krzyżanowska-Mierzewska (2008), 'The Reception Process in Poland and Slovakia' in Keller, Helen and Alec Stone Sweet (eds.), *A Europe of Rights: the Impact of the ECHR on National Legal Systems*, OUP, p. 584.

2.1.2.2. *The failure of the legislature and the executive to respond to Constitutional Court judgments*

Recent research into the effect of Constitutional Court judgments on Polish legislation suggests that the legislature is not sufficiently responsive to the Court. Evidently the Constitutional Court has limited influence over the legislative process.[36] That there has been a failure to implement Constitutional Court judgments effectively is a view that was expressed by a number of interviewees.[37] One Constitutional Court judge suggested that the failure to implement its decisions is primarily due to inertia on the part of the legislature.[38] Until recently no single institution was responsible for preparing draft bills in response to Constitutional Court judgments. According to one interviewee this has led to delays, as more than one draft of the same bill has then been presented to the Sejm (the lower house of the Parliament).[39] In order to improve implementation, the upper chamber of the Parliament, the Senate, was recently given additional responsibility for the enforcement of Constitutional Court judgments (through changes to its internal procedures in order to ensure prioritisation of legislative initiatives necessary to implement Constitutional Court judgments).[40]

Jakub Wołąsiewicz, of the Ministry of Foreign Affairs, and the current Polish Government agent in Strasbourg, acknowledged that in the past the executive had had a poor disposition towards implementation of Constitutional Court judgments:

> "I have the feeling that the government has a kind of good attitude towards the European Court of Human Rights. Unfortunately, the government in the past has not had such a good attitude towards the Constitutional Court."[41]

A further reason for the relative inertia is that there have been insufficient sanctions that can be applied in the case of non-implementation of a Constitutional Court judgment. To rectify this, measures were relatively recently introduced allowing

36 Tomasz Stawecki, Wiesław Staśkiewicz, Jan Winczorek (2008), *Między policentrycznością a fragmentaryzacją: wpływ Trybunału Konstytucyjnego na Polski porządek prawny*, Sprawne Państwo = *Between policentrism and fragmentation: the impact of the Constitutional Court on the Polish legal system*, pp. 74–5.

37 Interview with Adam Bodnar, Secretary of the Board, Helsinki Foundation for Human Rights (Poland), 12.5.09; Interview with Professor Marek Safjan, University of Warsaw, 13.5.09; Interview with Marek Nowicki, Helsinki Foundation for Human Rights, 13.5.09; Interview with Wojciech Hermeliński, Constitutional Court, Warsaw, 13.5.09; Interview with Jakub Wołąsiewicz, Government Agent, Warsaw, 14.5.09.

38 Interview with Wojciech Hermeliński, Constitutional Court, Warsaw, 13.5.09.

39 Interview with Adam Bodnar, Secretary of the Board, Helsinki Foundation for Human Rights (Poland), 12.5.09.

40 Interview with Judge Wojciech Hermeliński, Constitutional Court, Warsaw, 13.5.09.

41 Interview with Jakub Wołąsiewicz, Government Agent, Warsaw, 14.5.09.

applicants the right to claim compensation in the event that a Constitutional Court judgment which affects them is not implemented. Jakub Wołąsiewicz acknowledged:

> "Maybe, simply, there was no sanction for the government if it fails to implement the judgment of the Constitutional Court. It was only ... 5 or 6 years ago that [there was] a new provision – Article 417 [of the Civil Code] – that in the case of non-implementation of a Constitutional Court judgment, applicants could ask for redress – for compensation."[42]

2.1.2.3. 'Full' Pilot Judgments: Broniowski *and* Hutten-Czapska

In the context of the *Broniowski* and *Hutten-Czapska* judgments, the European Court has proved to be satisfied with the cooperation from the Polish government, the new legislation developed and evidence of implementation of the new domestic measures.[43] Both cases required not only complex legislative changes, but also addressed what citizens in the new Poland could expect in terms of ownership rights in a post-socialist economy. According to the European Court, changes introduced as a result of *Hutten-Czapska*, and the legislative process which ensued, had to strike a 'fair balance' between the interests of landlords and the "general interest of the community".[44] More broadly, therefore, debates over this issue sought to reconcile the state's welfare obligations with its development of market mechanisms.

In both judgments, Strasbourg identified the nature of the violation as being systemic and the Court consequently stipulated that appropriate legislative amendments be made, but did not direct the substance of the settlement, for example, in terms of the amount of compensation due. So, as Judge Vladimiro Zagrebelsky suggested to us, the Court "initiated an important dialogue as far as the government was concerned" – more a dialogue with the Committee of Ministers than with the Court.[45] The Court Registry acted in a mediatory

---

42 Interview with Jakub Wołąsiewicz, Government Agent, Warsaw, 14.5.09. Article 417(1), of the Civil Code states: "The State Treasury, municipality or another legal person wielding public power by virtue of the law shall be liable for damage caused by an unlawful act or omission in the exercise of that power." As cited in *Hutten-Czapska v Poland*, No. 35014/97, 28.4.08, para. 20.

43 Regarding Broniowski, see: Parliamentary Assembly of the Council of Europe. Committee on Legal Affairs and Human Rights (2008) *Implementation of judgments of the European Court of Human Rights: Introductory memorandum* Rapporteur: Mr Christos Pourgourides, Cyprus, AS/Jur (2008)24, p. 4. http://assembly.coe.int/CommitteeDocs/2008/20080526_ajdoc24_2008.pdf. Regarding the Court's satisfaction that measures taken promise to resolve the matter, see *Hutten-Czapska v Poland*, No. 35014/97, 28.4.08, paras. 37–45.

44 *Hutten-Czapska v Poland*, No. 35014/97, 28.4.08, para. 42.

45 Interview with Judge Vladimiro Zagrebelsky, Strasbourg, 25.3.09.

capacity (without applying pressure, as such)[46] but nonetheless played a key role in negotiating the final settlement.[47]

The issue of how much compensation should be paid was politically controversial in the case of *Broniowski*[48] and indeed some of our respondents questioned why the Bug River applicants should be compensated ahead of a large number of unresolved cases, where property was expropriated in the years following the Second World War.[49] However, some interviewees suggested that the Government wished to close a particular chapter in its history by finally dealing with the particularly emotive issue of lost territories of the Kresy region.[50]

2.2. COMPENSATION FOR EXPROPRIATED PROPERTY (*BRONIOWSKI*)

The case of *Broniowski* brought to the fore public consciousness about a number of very sensitive issues relating to the expropriation of property; for some citizens these were perceived to be the result of Poland's occupation by the Soviet Union, an unpopular territorial agreement between the Soviet Union and Nazi Germany, the Polish government's failure to defend its people's rights and the allied forces' failure at the close of the Second World War to maintain Poland's territorial integrity.[51] These issues were apparent in the emotionally charged parliamentary debates of 2003, just before the *Broniowski* law[52] was passed, as the following intervention by a deputy of the Law and Justice Party illustrates:

> "It was very characteristic of the post-war era until 1989 that we were severed from our history, from the history of half of Poland's territory in the East. I very

---

46 Interview with Jakub Wołąsiewicz, Warsaw, 14.5.09.

47 Interview with Katarzyna Łakoma and Hanna Machińska, Council of Europe Information Office, Warsaw 13.5.09; Interview with Wojciech Hermeliński, Constitutional Court, Warsaw, 13.5.09.

48 Interview with Adam Szafrański and Jan Lipiej Biuro Analyz Sejmowych = the Research Office for the Sejm, Warsaw, 12.5.09; Interview with Wojciech Hermeliński, Constitutional Court, Warsaw, 13.5.09.

49 The parliamentary commission which deals with these issues (Sejm Supervisory Commission for monitoring the state project on compensation for property requisitioned by the state, and other property) broadly groups them together as part of the reprivatisation programme.

50 Interview with Katarzyna Łakoma and Hanna Machińska, Council of Europe Information Office, Warsaw 13.05.09; Interview with Wojciech Hermeliński, Constitutional Court, Warsaw, 13.5.09.

51 See, for example, reference to these issues in: Poland. Ministry of Foreign Affairs (2005), *Broniowski v. Poland: Memorandum of the Polish Government*, Warsaw 14 November 2005, pp. 1–6.

52 *Projekt ustawy o realizacji prawa do rekompensaty z tytułu pozostawienia nieruchomości poza obecnymi granicami państwa polskiego* = Bill on the realisation of the right to compensation for property left beyond the present borders of the Polish State, 8.7.05.

> well remember at school in the 1950s and 1960s how Vilnius rather than *Wilno*[53] was used exclusively, and one didn't say '*Lwów*'[54] but '*Lviv*'[55] as it was spelt on all maps and textbooks, which meant that in educational consciousness, in the minds of school teachers, the real Eastern Kresy region was not Polish Eastern Kresy, but some allegedly annexed land. And I think it should be mentioned here that Poland lost the Eastern Kresy territory on the strength of the Ribbentrop-Molotov Pact, whereby Lithuania gained Vilnius, the central section, shall we say, of Kresy went to Belarus and the south-eastern section went to Ukraine. It's also worth mentioning, for those who may not know, that before the war there were basically very few Lithuanians living in *Wilno*. There was a majority of Poles living there, some Jews, a few Germans but Lithuanians formed nothing more than a handful of teachers in a Lithuanian grammar school. That was it. But today nobody questions Poland's boundaries with our Eastern neighbours. There is no viable political force in Poland which questions this [issue], and we fail to remember that the Eastern Kresy lands were Polish territory, similarly in the case of *Lwów*. There were a few more Ukrainians in *Lwów* than there were Lithuanians in *Wilno*, but it formed less than 20% of the population, they were not a numerous group ... But we do not question today's boundaries in Europe, we simply recall them, because there is no reason, just as our greatest opponents – who lost their lands: what is now today's Western region of Poland as the rightful historical judgment in return for their belligerence – remember their right to this land, and want the right to change history and today's laws, but we have to resign ourselves generally to just remembering that [the Eastern Kresy region] was once part of Poland."[56]

A number of the newer Council of Europe states in Central, Southern and Eastern Europe have wrestled with problems arising from reprivatisation generally, and how the state should compensate citizens for property expropriated during the socialist era.[57] However, Poland has been frustrated in developing its laws in this field, as a number of reprivatisation projects which have been presented to parliament as draft bills[58] have been blocked by the President's veto.[59] Some Polish deputies have suggested that in most other comparable states less progress in this area has been made, which has led them to question why Poland in particular was

53 The Polish name of the city.

54 The Polish name.

55 The Ukrainian name.

56 From Marcin Libicki's statement: Poland. Sejm minutes of parliamentary debate of 28.10.2003: *Sprawozdanie Komisji Skarbu Państwa o: ... 2) rządowym projekcie ustawy o zaliczaniu na poczet ceny sprzedaży albo opłat z tytułu użytkowania wieczystego nieruchomości skarbu państwa wartości nieruchomości pozostawionych poza obecnymi granicami państwa polskiego.* 28.10.2003.

57 Andrzej Kozminski (1997), 'Restitution of private property: reprivatization in Central and Eastern Europe' *Communist and Post-Communist Studies* 30:1, pp. 95–106.

58 Interview with Judge Wojciech Hermeliński, Constitutional Court, Warsaw, 13.5.09.

59 Both under Lech Wałęsa and Aleksander Kwaśniewski. Interview with Barbara Grzybowska, Polish Union of Property Owners, 12.5.09.

selected to be the subject of a pilot judgment for failing to compensate 'Bug River' claimants, while certain other countries (such as the Czech Republic, Slovakia and Hungary), subject to comparable systemic violations concerning property ownership, had not been treated in the same way.[60]

In 2007 the MP Artur Górski (Law and Justice Party) suggested in a parliamentary debate that Poland was one of the last of the new EU accession states to resolve the issue of providing claimants compensation for expropriated lands following state boundary changes.[61] Jan Bury, Secretary of State for the Ministry of the Treasury, responded that the scale of the problem had been significantly greater for Poland in terms of the numbers of individuals granted the right to compensation regarding territory now outside the country's boundaries.[62] Moreover, unlike the Czech Republic, Hungary or Slovakia, since the local government reforms of 1990, Poland's 16 provinces (*województwa* – local regions) have been granted legal personality, rights of ownership and other property rights.[63] These reforms have further complicated the process of awarding compensation for expropriated property, as is discussed later in this section.

2.2.1. EVALUATION OF THE EFFECTIVENESS OF THE 'BRONIOWSKI LAW'

Even though further Bug River cases were being lodged with the Court on a monthly basis, the Court decided to close the pilot judgment procedure with respect to the Bug River cases in its admissibility decision in the case of *E.G. v Poland (and 175 other Bug River applications)* in September 2008.[64] This case followed the decisions adopted in December 2007 in *Wolkenberg and Others v.*

60 For example – Elżbieta Streker-Dembińska (Left and Democrats Party): "The change in law came from the European Court of Human Rights and that Poland is the first country to have been subject to this kind of direction. What other countries are contending with this problem?" Andrzej Relidzyński: "This is to do with reprivatisation ... and therefore others in the same position are Czech Republic, Slovakia, Hungary as these are countries where reprivatisation is underway, but not yet completed. Poland is the one country where this law has solved the issue." Elżbieta Streker-Dembińska: "I think Poland has been the most concerned with this problem, but I think it has remained the country for which this is the least problem." Poland. Kancelaria Sejmu, Biuro Komisji Sejmowych (2008), *Biuletyn*, nr.506/VI kad. 9.4.2008, p. 7.

61 Poland. Kancelaria Sejmu, Biuro Komisji Sejmowych (2007), *Biuletyn*, nr. 2224/V kad, 5.7.07, p. 7.

62 Poland. Kancelaria Sejmu, Biuro Komisji Sejmowych (2008), *Biuletyn*, nr. 506/VI kad. 9.4.08, p. 7.

63 Michaela Salamun (2007), 'The laws on the organization of the administration in the Czech Republic, Hungary, Poland and Slovakia: A comparative analysis in the Context of European Integration' *Review of Central & East European Law* 32, pp. 267–301.

64 No. 50425/99, dec. 23.9.08.

Poland[65] and *Witkowska-Toboła v. Poland*.[66] In these cases the applicants claimed that awards amounting to 20% of the value of the property was unsatisfactory compensation,[67] and, additionally, Genowefa Witkowska-Toboła claimed there had been a delay in the processing of her claim. Parliamentary debates just a few months before the decisions in *Wolkenberg* and *Witkowska-Toboła*[68] indicate that MPs were certainly aware of Strasbourg's requirements and the need to expedite the process of awarding compensation. Although some MPs argued that Poland, as a sovereign state, should not be directed by the Strasbourg Court over such matters,[69] the discussion focused mainly on how best to facilitate the necessary administrative changes. One MP expressed his concern that the outcome of the forthcoming Strasbourg decisions would be influenced by evidence of parliament's success in regulating these changes.[70] The Chairman of the Supervisory Commission,[71] Marek Suski, responded that the matter was too complicated to rush through before the decisions were issued, and that the Commission should continue with its work.[72] In its decisions in *Wolkenberg* and *Witkowska-Toboła*, the Court found reasonable the statutory ceiling for compensation set at 20% of the current value of the original property[73] and expressed satisfaction with the implementation of the 2005 'Broniowski law'. The Court cited (from data supplied by the Polish authorities) the number of applications processed (4,000) out of a total which it was estimated had been received (11,000) at the end of 2007.[74] Although the Court noted that the authorities were experiencing difficulties in expediting these applications, as the electronic register of claims was still not fully operational at the time of the judgments,[75] it nonetheless acknowledged that the

---

65 No. 50003/99, dec. 4.12.07.

66 No. 11208/02, dec. 4.12.07.

67 Regarding the rate of compensation, Dr Krystyna Michniewicz-Wanik of the University of Wrocław has argued that 20% is derisory, and that it should be more in the region of 50% or even 100%. See: Krystyna Michniewicz-Wanik (2008), *Mienie Zabużańskie: Prawne podstawy realizacji roszceń, Nortom = Property of the Bug River Region: the legal basis of how claims are dealt with.*

68 Although no mention is made of *Witkowska-Toboła* and *Wolkenberg*, *per se*, in the discussion, reference is made to 'the forthcoming December judgments [*sic*] of the European Court'.

69 Jan Wyrowiński (Civic Platform) Poland. Kancelaria Sejmu, Biuro Komisji Sejmowych (2007), *Biuletyn*, nr. 2224/V kad, 5.7.07, pp. 6–7; Gabriela Masłowska (National People's Movement) (in *ibid.*), pp. 7–8.

70 Artur Górski (Law and Justice Party) Poland. Kancelaria Sejmu, Biuro Komisji Sejmowych (2007), *Biuletyn*, nr.2224/V kad, 5.7.07, p. 7.

71 The Commission's role was to examine the state draft project on the law on property expropriated by the state or other property issues.

72 Marek Suski (Law and Justice Party) Poland. Kancelaria Sejmu, Biuro Komisji Sejmowych (2007), *Biuletyn*, nr. 2224/V kad, 5.7.07, p. 9.

73 *Wolkenberg v Poland*, No. 50003/99, dec. 4.12.07, para. 66; *Witkowska-Toboła v Poland*, No. 11208/02, 04.12.07, para. 66.

74 *Witkowska-Toboła v Poland*, No. 11208/02, dec. 4.12.07, paras. 68–70.

75 *Witkowska-Toboła v Poland*, No. 11208/02, dec. 4.12.07, para. 71.

Government had acted promptly and decisively and that it was not to be censured for any such problems.[76]

During the course of this research we sought to canvas opinions about the effectiveness of the new law introduced in response to the *Broniowski* judgment. Some respondents expressed their satisfaction with the law: that it is effective and has solved the problem, as is evident from the compensation paid to applicants to date.[77] However, Court Registry lawyer Lucja Miara acknowledged that it was problematic for the Court to refer some of the applicants (with *Broniowski*-type claims) back to seek redress within the national system, in view of their advanced ages and the likely length and costs of further domestic proceedings.[78] Furthermore, a number of respondents expressed ongoing concern at the slow rate at which compensation is awarded. The Vice President of the Polish Union of Property Owners, Barbara Grzybowska, suggested that there are problems of implementation and cases of individuals who have still not received compensation.[79] This view was reiterated by the President of the Bug River Region Association who said that the procedure was very slow, that there were no time limits for dealing with applications, nor any sanctions for the failure to compensate applicants.[80] Mr Broniowski's former lawyer, Wojciech Hermeliński, also expressed concern at how the law is being implemented. He identified two causes: firstly, problems with the electronic register of claims which was introduced to register claimants and manage their compensation claims, and, secondly, problems of execution at the provincial level under the supervision of the Governors' offices *(Urząd wojewódzki)*. He explained that if the Governor (*wojewód*) refuses to grant the certificate requested on the basis of the documentation presented by an applicant, then the applicant must apply to a civil court. In turn the procedure of the civil court is complicated by the fact that many people connected with these cases (who would have been witnesses) are now deceased, and in many cases it is simply no

76 *Witkowska-Toboła v Poland*, No. 11208/02, dec. 4.12.07, para. 72.

77 Interview with Adam Bodnar, Secretary of the Board, Helsinki Foundation for Human Rights (Poland), 12.5.09.

78 Interview with Lucja Miara, Strasbourg, 26.3.09.

79 Interview with Barbara Grzybowska of the Polish Union of Property Owners (Polska Unia Właścicieli Nieruchomości), 12.5.09.

80 Telephone interview with Andrzej Korzeniowski, President of the Bug River Region Association (Ogólnopolskie Stowarzyszenie Kresowian Wierzycieli Skarbu Państwa = All-Union Association of the Bug River Region Association of creditors to the State Treasury), 10.2.10. In an email of 11.2.10 (on file with the authors) Mr Korzeniowski stated: "The pilot judgment in the Broniowski case laid down both a fixed term for the execution of the judgment as well as percentages. As is apparent from domestic practice it has not been implemented and that, in turn, is an argument that the pilot judgment is not effective because the Court of Human Rights doesn't supervise its implementation …" He also said that NGOs did not have access to Government data which would enable them to analyse the reasons for the delays in administering payments.

longer possible for applicants to provide the authorities with all the appropriate documentation.[81]

According to the Polish lawyer Magda Krzyżanowska-Mierzewska, the procedure for restitution of property was complicated by the 1990 local government reforms, which devolved responsibility for the administration of compensation payments from central to local authorities. At that time, ownership of real property was transferred from the State Treasury to the local administrative units and the law did not oblige them to compensate the Bug River Region claimants.[82] As we discuss in Chapter one (section 1.2.1.1.) these applicants had a pre-existing right to compensation, but provision for this was not made in the new laws following the local government reforms. This is apparently because the preparatory work before the first local government reforms did not include provision for assessing the claims of these applicants; this failure was most probably the result of an oversight, according to Krzyżanowska-Mierzewska.[83] The problems of implementation experienced at the local level have been discussed in parliament; in 2007 the Parliamentary Commission for the State Treasury, which oversaw the compensation procedure, acknowledged that there had been shortcomings in developing the electronic claims register[84] and at their meeting in 2008 MPs expressed concern that their constituents had still not received due compensation.[85]

In April 2008, Jan Bury, Secretary of State at the Ministry of State Treasury, presented figures to the Parliamentary Commission arguing that the *Broniowski* law had been applied effectively and that there were sufficient funds available for the anticipated future claims for compensation in 2008-2009. Bury did, however, acknowledge that there had been some bottlenecks in implementation at the local level.[86] In response to Bury, MPs complained that their constituents were dissatisfied with the procedure. For example, Jan Kochanowski MP noted that, of 254 appeals to the Ministry of the State Treasury against decisions taken at the provincial level by the Governor (*wojewód*) regarding Bug River applications, only 61 were upheld. From that he concluded that the *wojewód* was clearly not an effective channel of redress for applicants:

81 Interview with Wojciech Hermeliński, Constitutional Court, 13.5.09.

82 There are 308 gmina, that is 'communities' and 16 provinces (województwo).

83 Magda Krzyżanowska-Mierzewska (2008), 'Sprawy mienia zabużańskiego przed ETPCz' *Europejski Przegląd Sądow* 12, pp. 20–25; pp. 20–21= 'Property issues of the Bug River Region inhabitants before the ECtHR' *European Court Review* 12, pp. 20–21.

84 Poland. Kancelaria Sejmu, Biuro Komisji Sejmowych (2007), *Biuletyn*, nr. 2224/V kad, 5.7.07.

85 Poland. Kancelaria Sejmu, Biuro Komisji Sejmowych (2008), *Biuletyn*, nr. 506/VI kad. 9.4.08.

86 Poland. Kancelaria Sejmu, Biuro Komisji Sejmowych (2008), *Biuletyn*, nr. 506/VI kad. 9.4.2008, p. 4.

"... people believe that the state is shirking its responsibility and doesn't want to pay out compensation."[87]

Andrzej Relidziński, the director of the Department of the Registry for Reprivatisation and Compensation at the State Treasury, said that the bottlenecks had resulted from a dispute between the provincial Governors *(wojewóda)* and Ministry of the State Treasury over which was the authority to whom applicants should appeal, as this had not been specified in the 2005 Broniowski law.[88] Delays in implementation had evidently also been caused by technical problems in verifying the authenticity of tens of thousands of documents attesting to claimants' rights to property.[89] According to Wojciech Hermeliński, the proportion of people affected by these administrative difficulties was "not such a small amount, so it is a problem".[90] Jan Bury argued that the work of the local *wojewód* would be streamlined once the new electronic claims register had been introduced enabling speedier processing and verification of claims, and the disbursement of compensation by the national bank.[91]

2.2.2. AMENDMENTS TO THE BRONIOWSKI LAW

The amendments which have been made to the Broniowski law arguably reflect the government's determination to address problems that have arisen in practice since a law was passed in 2003 fixing a ceiling to the compensation at 15% of the original value of the property. There also appears to have been a good deal of active parliamentary engagement in the process of change, as the discussion above has illustrated. In January 2004 a group of MPs applied to the Constitutional Court regarding the constitutionality of, among other things, the 15% statutory ceiling. As a result, in December 2004 the Constitutional Court declared the 15% ceiling to be unconstitutional.[92] The level of compensation was consequently raised to 20% in the amended law which was passed by the lower and upper houses of parliament in July 2005.[93] In 2006 the law was changed to allow, in addition, claims from applicants whose cases concerned an agreement between the Polish state and the Soviet Union in 1951 regarding the exchange

87 Poland. Kancelaria Sejmu, Biuro Komisji Sejmowych (2008), *Biuletyn*, nr. 506/VI kad. 9.4.08, p. 5.

88 Andrzej Relidziński, Kancelaria Sejmu, Biuro Komisji Sejmowych (2008), *Biuletyn*, no. 506/VI kad. 9.4.08, p. 6.

89 *Ibid.*

90 Interview with Judge Wojciech Hermeliński, Constitutional Court, Warsaw, 13.5.09.

91 Jan Bury, Kancelaria Sejmu, Biuro Komisji Sejmowych (2008), *Biuletyn*, nr. 506/VI kad. 9.4.08, p. 6.

92 *Broniowski v Poland*, No. 31443/96, 28.9.05, para. 10.

93 Law on the realisation of the right to compensation for property left beyond the present borders of the Polish State (*Ustawa o realizacji prawa do rekompensaty z tytułu pozostawienia nieruchomości poza obecnymi granicami państwa polskiego*).

of land.[94] Aside from these changes, the other amendments introduced related to the budgetary arrangements for compensation, the ministry responsible for disbursing payments and the timing of the procedure. A further amendment to the law was made in October 2008, after Strasbourg's ruling in *E.G. v Poland*. This provision further clarified that Bug River claimants should apply to the provincial governors (*wojewóda*), and that the *wojewód* is the competent authority to determine whether or not an application is admissible, and whether or not a rejected case could be re-opened.[95]

2.3. STATE RENT-CONTROL AND SUBSIDISATION FOR PROPERTY RENOVATION (*HUTTEN-CZAPSKA*)

In 1997 Maria Hutten-Czapska applied to the European Court concerning a violation of her property rights (invoking Article 1 of Protocol No. 1 to the Convention). Her case exemplified the underlying structural problems of housing legislation which failed to protect landlords' rights by guaranteeing existing tenants from the socialist era the right to remain in subsidised accommodation. Ms Hutten-Czapska had secured the return of her property, expropriated by the state in 1945, but the property was inhabited by tenants whom she was unable to evict under the housing legislation, and the domestic law prevented her from increasing the rent on her property. The case at the European Court became a source of leverage for the Polish Constitutional Court to press for amendments to these housing laws. This was achieved by a complex and lengthy series of Constitutional Court judgments, supported by the Polish Ombudsman and landlords' associations in Poland, and the European Court's three judgments in the case in 2005, 2006 and 2008.[96]

---

94 *Dziennik Ustaw* No. 195, 1437, Ustawa z dnia 8 września 2006 r. "Ustawa z dnia 8 września 2006 r. 'O zmianie ustawy o realizacji prawa do rekompensaty z tytułu pozostawienia nieruchomości poza obecnymi granicami Rzeczpospolitej Polskiej oraz niektórych innych ustaw'" = The law of 8 September 2006 on changes to the "Bill on the realisation of the right to compensation for property left beyond the present borders of the Polish State and other laws." In Article 1, para.1: 1a) "The right to compensation also stretches as far as those whose property concerns an agreement between the Polish state under socialism and the USSR, regarding the exchange of sections of state land from the 15 February 1951."

95 Article 7(3 a) provides as follows: "The rightful organ is the *wojewód* in matters concerning changes or verifying the invalidity or re-opening of procedures in matters of attestation and in making decisions confirming the right to compensation issued according to their individual bylaws ..." See: *Dziennik Ustaw* No. 197, 1223 "Ustawa z dnia 3 października 2008 r. 'O zmianie ustawy o realizacji prawa do rekompensaty z tytułu pozostawienia nieruchomości poza obecnymi granicami Rzeczpospolitej Polskiej'" = Law of 3 October 2008 on changes to the "Bill on the realisation of the right to compensation for property left beyond the present borders of the Polish State."

96 *Hutten-Czapska v Poland*, No. 35014/97, 22.2.05; 19.6.06; 28.4.08.

In 2000 the Constitutional Court declared unconstitutional the 1994 Act on 'Controlled Rent' (*czynsz regulowany*) that prevented landlords raising rent above a specified amount and failed to provide a mechanism to enable landlords to recover expenses incurred as a result of property maintenance.[97] The 1994 Act was consequently repealed and in 2001 the *Law on the protection of tenants, housing provision in the community and on the change to the Civil Code* was introduced.[98] However, the Ombudsman subsequently made an application to the Constitutional Court claiming that the 2001 legislation[99] still failed to provide landlords with sufficient means to recover costs incurred through home improvement. The Constitutional Court subsequently sought supporting data from landlords' associations (such as the Polish Union of Property Owners). These organisations also submitted that the legislation did not sufficiently protect landlords' rights and the Constitutional Court once again found the law unconstitutional.[100] The law was subsequently amended in 2004 – adding provisions to the effect that landlords were not to increase rents by more than 10%. However, the new regulations were still judged unconstitutional by the Constitutional Court. In response to an individual constitutional complaint by J.-M.O in 2004, and an application in January 2005 from the Polish Union of Property Owners, in April 2005 the Constitutional Court upheld its previous ruling, and found that the executive and legislature had failed to amend the law in accordance with the Court's judgments.[101] Also during this period, in January 2005, the Polish government informed the Constitutional Court that the Prime Minister intended to file an application with the Constitutional Court to question the constitutionality of the 2004 amendments which restricted increases in rent to 10%, in that those restrictions constituted an unjustified interference with landlords' property rights.[102]

In May 2006, following an application by the Ombudsman, the Constitutional Court declared unconstitutional a number of provisions of the 2001 law (including the clauses on rent increases). Consequently, Parliament enacted amending legislation in December 2006, which introduced new provisions on rent increases. In September 2006 the Constitutional Court declared unconstitutional further provisions of the 2001 law.[103]

---

97 Poland. Trybunał Konstytucyjny. Judgment of 19 April 2005 K 4/05 Limitation of Rent Increases for living quarters http://www.trybunal.gov.pl/eng/summaries/documents/K_4_05_GB.pdf.

98 Ustawa o ochronie praw lokatorów, mieszkaniowym zasobie gminy i o zmianie Kodeksu cywilnego = Law on the protection of tenants, housing provision in the gmina and on the amendment to the Civil Code.

99 *Ibid.*

100 *Hutten-Czapska v Poland*, No. 35014/97, 22.2.05, para. 108.

101 *Ibid.*, paras. 86, 137 & 108.

102 *Hutten-Czapska v Poland*, No. 35014/97, 22.2.05, para. 138.

103 *Hutten-Czapska v Poland*, No. 35014/97, 28.4.08, paras. 8–18.

It appears that it was not until Strasbourg exerted its influence through the *Hutten-Czapska* judgment that the findings of the Constitutional Court were heeded. In August 2006 Piotr Styczeń, Undersecretary of State for Infrastructure, reported to Parliament about an idea for a proposed law to provide support for renovation and thermo-modernization.[104] However, in June 2006 the Grand Chamber of the European Court had already decided in the *Hutten-Czapska* case that there was a violation of Article 1 of Protocol No. 1 to the European Convention resulting from a systemic problem, arising from the malfunctioning of the domestic legislation.[105] The government apparently then decided that it would be less costly to change the law than pay out compensation to each aggrieved individual.[106] The incremental way in which the law was changed over a period of years, in response to a series of judgments from both the Constitutional and European Courts, indicates to what extent these amendments were contested by different interest groups and the difficulties experienced in finding a satisfactory compromise. The role of the executive in the process was also significant, in the Prosecutor General's application to the Constitutional Court in 2005. However, the pressure for reform (beyond that exerted by the two courts) initially came from an association of property owners, the Helsinki Foundation for Human Rights and academics.[107]

EVALUATION OF THE EFFECTIVENESS OF THE 'RENT MIRROR SCHEME' AND THE LAW ON RENOVATION AND THERMO-MODERNIZATION

In its 2008 *Hutten-Czapska* judgment the European Court assessed the new laws and found that the amendments were "clearly aimed at removing the restrictive aspects of the 2001 Act which were mentioned in the principal judgment".[108] The Court was satisfied that the new provisions introduced by the December 2006 Act clarified the criteria for rent increases, enabling landlords to increase rent to cover costs of maintenance of property and receive a 'decent profit'.[109] Consequently, following a friendly settlement between Ms Hutten-Czapska and the Polish Government, the European Court struck out the case. The Court was satisfied that the Government had shown commitment in taking sufficient measures to resolve the systemic problem, and that the anticipated Law on Renovation and Thermo-Modernization, which had not yet been endorsed by Parliament, promised to be an effective remedy.[110]

---

104 Interview with Piotr Styczeń, Undersecretary of State for Infrastructure, 13.5.09.
105 *Hutten-Czapska v Poland*, No. 35014/97, 19.06.06.
106 Interview with Piotr Styczeń, Undersecretary of State for Infrastructure, 13.5.09.
107 Interview with Judge Wojciech Hermeliński, Constitutional Court, Warsaw, 13.5.09.
108 *Hutten-Czapska v Poland*, No. 35014/97, 28.4.08, para. 39.
109 *Ibid.*, para. 40.
110 *Ibid.*, paras. 41–43.

The most recent amendment (August 2007)[111] to the Land Administration Act of 1997 introduced a 'Rent Mirror'[112] scheme to regulate rents. Under these new provisions, landlords must submit data relating to the age and size of the property and the rent charged. The correlation of this information then enables the average rent in each region to be calculated, thereby facilitating civil courts' adjudication of tenant-landlord disputes arising from rent increases. Furthermore, the Law Supporting Thermo-Modernisation and Renovations,[113] came into force in March 2009. This law makes provision for landlords to claim partial refunds of costs expended on repairs and renovation to property let. Since these amendments have only recently come into force, it is too early to assess levels of satisfaction with the law.

The Vice President of the Polish Union of Property Owners, Barbara Grzybowska, pointed out to us that before claiming state refunds for repairs and renovations, in accordance with the law, property owners must first raise the necessary funds for the work themselves. This, she suggested, inevitably favours those more likely to secure loans from the bank, such as younger people.[114] Furthermore, Ms Grzybowska expressed concern that the 'Rent Mirror' scheme is not functioning as it should do. As a procedure intended to regulate rent by maintaining parity within each region, the mechanism of monitoring is crucial for the regulation process to function effectively. However, according to Ms Grzybowska, this monitoring is not being performed effectively, as the data presented to the authorities is apparently regularly lost.[115]

2.4. 'QUASI-PILOT' JUDGMENTS AND 'THIRD TIER' JUDGMENTS

As we discuss in chapter one, the 'quasi-pilot judgments', or 'Article 46 judgments', issued by the Court in respect of structural or systemic violations, are intended to have the same, or at least a very similar, function to pilot judgments.[116] Like 'full' pilot judgments, these judgments have a very broad application, as they highlight systemic or structural problems, and they impose an obligation on the state to remedy the general problem (as well as providing 'individual measures' in respect of the particular applicant). They (usually) stop short, however, of including any

---

111 *Ustawa o zmianie ustawy o gospodarce nieruchomościami oraz o zmianie niektórych innych ustaw = Bill amending land administration and amending other laws.*

112 *'Lustro Czynszowe'.*

113 Government's Bill on Supporting Thermo-Modernisation and Renovations (*Rządowy projekt ustawy o wspieraniu termomodernizacji i remontów*).

114 Interview with Barbara Grzybowska of the Polish Union of Property Owners (Polska Unia Właścicieli Nieruchomości), 12.5.09.

115 *Ibid.*

116 Interview with Renata Degener, Court Registry, Strasbourg, 26.3.09.

provision in the operative part of the judgment specifying that general measures must be taken by the respondent Government.

In the case of Poland, examples of Article 46 judgments include *Sławomir Musiał*[117] and *Kauczor*.[118] In addition, the Grand Chamber judgment in *Kudła v Poland*[119] is frequently considered to have a significance that is equivalent to the 'Article 46 judgments', because of its status as a precedent: the Court in *Kudła* held for the first time that Article 13 of the Convention guarantees an effective remedy before a national authority for an alleged breach of the requirement under Article 6(1) to hear a case within a reasonable time. Accordingly, we have treated *Kudła* as a 'third tier' judgment (in accordance with the scheme we outline in chapter one). The three decisions are related in that they all concerned criminal proceedings. They raised complaints about the unreasonable length of pre-trial detention and of the excessive length of the criminal proceedings (*Kudła* and *Kauczor*), and of inadequate medical care (*Kudła* and *Sławomir Musiał*) and poor prison conditions (*Sławomir Musiał*). These three judgments are considered in the following sections.

2.4.1. EXCESSIVE LENGTH OF PROCEEDINGS (*KUDŁA*)

The *Kudła* judgment in 2000 pre-dates the pilot judgment procedure but it is widely considered to be equivalent to a pilot judgment. Indeed, Judge Garlicki suggested that it would probably have been issued as a pilot judgment had it arrived at the Court a few years later.[120] Jakub Wołąsiewicz, the Polish Government agent, argued that *Kudła* can be considered as a 'prototype' of the pilot judgment.[121] Igor Dzialuk, Undersecretary of State at the Ministry of Justice, concurred with this view: "... we do consider to a certain extent also *Kudła* as a pilot judgment, because for the first time, the judgment gave [us] an opportunity to think [through] the effective remedy concept".[122] Similarly, Wojciech Hermeliński considered that although it was "not a pilot case, it was founded like a pilot case".[123]

---

117 *Sławomir Musiał v Poland*. No. 28300/06, 20.1.09.

118 *Kauczor v Poland, No.* 45219/06, 3.2.09.

119 No. 30210/96, 26.10.00.

120 Interview with Judge Lech Garlicki, Strasbourg, 25.3.09.

121 Wołąsiewicz, Jakub (2009), 'Pilot judgments from the perspective of the Polish Government Agent and a proposal of provisions related to the existing pilot judgments procedure and so-called simplified pilot judgment procedure' in Wołąsiewicz, Jakub (ed.), *Pilot Judgment Procedure in the European Court of Human Rights and the development of Human Rights standards and procedures : Third informal seminar for government agents and other institutions, Warsaw 14–15 May, 2009*, Kontrast, p. 34.

122 Interview with Igor Dzialuk, Undersecretary of State, Ministry of Justice, Warsaw, 15.5.09.

123 Interview with Judge Wojciech Hermeliński, Constitutional Court, 13.5.09.

The novel element to *Kudła* was the finding that the absence of a remedy before a national authority in respect of cases concerning the undue length of proceedings, violated the right to an effective remedy under Article 13.[124] The Court's judgment in the *Kudła* case established that there was no remedy available in Poland enabling a claimant to enforce the right to a fair hearing within a reasonable time. For that reason it identified a 'systemic' violation of Article 13 of the Convention.

In 1991 Andrzej Kudła was charged with fraud and forgery, and, despite an alleged psychiatric condition, was found fit to be detained in prison. He claimed a violation of Article 3 on the grounds that he had not received adequate psychiatric treatment while in prison. His condition complicated the processing of the criminal proceedings, and resulted in a protracted period of pre-trial detention; others who had been detained with him in relation to the same suspected offence were released significantly earlier. The length of his pre-trial detention amounted to two years, four months and three days.[125] Mr Kudła also complained about the length of the proceedings against him; they had begun in 1991 and in 2000 he was still waiting for the judgment in his appeal to the Supreme Court.[126] The European Court found a violation of Article 5(3) because of the excessive length of his pre-trial detention, but more significantly found that there was no effective domestic remedy (a violation of Article 13) in respect of cases of undue length of proceedings (a violation of Article 6(1)). This novel approach is explained by the escalation in the number of such cases from a growing number of states:

> "If Article 13 is, as the Government argued, to be interpreted as having no application to the right to a hearing within a reasonable time as safeguarded by Article 6§1, individuals will systematically be forced to refer to the Court in Strasbourg complaints that would otherwise, and in the Court's opinion more appropriately, have to be addressed in the first place within the national legal system. In the long term the effective functioning, on both the national and international level, of the scheme of human rights protection set up by the Convention is liable to be weakened".[127]

On this issue, however, there had not been any prior pressure for legislative change from the Constitutional Court.

124 *Kudła v Poland*, No. 30210/96, 26.10.00 para. 146. See also Philip Leach (2005), *Taking a Case to the European Court*, OUP, 2nd ed., pp. 344-5. In previous cases in which the Court found a violation of Article 6(1) it was not considered necessary also to adjudicate on a complaint of Article 13 – usually because Article 6(1) was considered to be the *lex specialis*.

125 *Kudła v Poland*, No. 30210/96, 26.10.00, para.105.

126 *Ibid.*, paras. 119–120.

127 *Ibid.*, para. 155.

Evaluation of the impact of the Kudła judgment on domestic law

In response to *Kudła*, the law which was passed and came into force in September 2004[128] was similar in its design to the Italian *Pinto* Law introduced in the wake of *Bottazzi* and other Italian length of proceedings cases.[129] The 2004 law accordingly made provision for applicants to seek compensation for lengthy domestic proceedings. In 2005 the Supreme Court ruled that applicants could claim retroactively for violations before the 2004 law had come into force.[130] As well as providing compensation, the law also has a remedial function, in that it is possible to request that an order be given for the court before which the case is pending, to take specific procedural measures to speed up the proceedings.[131]

As has been the case with the *Pinto* Law[132] there have been some difficulties with the application of this law, in that claimants have not been granted sufficient redress.[133] During a visit to Poland in early 2009, European Court Registry officials stated that they considered the compensation awarded under the 2004 law to be insufficient and warned that they may take measures to communicate this 'officially' in the near future.[134] According to one respondent, the average award of compensation is only 150 euros.[135] Other problems that have been identified in practice by the Strasbourg Court include the national courts' failure to examine the whole time-frame of the proceedings in question and instead to pass

---

128 *Ustawa o skardze na naruszenie prawa strony do rozpoznania sprawy w postępowaniu sądowym bez nieuzasadnionej zwłoki* = Law on the right to complain of a violation of the right to trial without undue delay.

129 Magda Krzyżanowska-Mierzewska (2008). 'The Reception process in Poland and Slovakia' in Keller, Helen and Alec Stone Sweet (eds), *A Europe of Rights*, OUP, p. 556.

130 *Charzyński v Poland*, No. 15212/03, 1.3.05. paras. 12–23.

131 Magda Krzyżanowska-Mierzewska (2008). 'The Reception process in Poland and Slovakia' in Keller, Helen and Alec Stone Sweet (eds), *A Europe of Rights*, OUP, p. 556.

132 See chapter 4. In March 2009 the Committee of Ministers issued a resolution urging the Italian Government to amend the Pinto Law, undertake measures to better regulate judges' application of the law, and reduce the backlog of cases in domestic courts relating to length of proceedings. See: Committee of Ministers (2009), Interim Resolution CM/ResDH(2009)42 *Execution of the judgments of the European Court of Human Rights concerning the excessive length of judicial proceedings in Italy: Progress achieved and outstanding issues in the context of general measures to ensure compliance with the judgments of the European Court of Human Rights.* https://wcd.coe.int/ViewDoc.jsp?Ref=CM/ResDH(2009)42&Language=lanEnglish&Ver=original&Site=CM&BackColorInternet=9999CC&BackColorIntranet=FFBB55&BackColorLogged=FFAC75. See also Mercedes Candela Soriano (2008), 'The Reception Process in Spain and Italy' in Keller, Helen and Alec Stone Sweet (eds.), *A Europe of Rights: the Impact of the ECHR on National Legal Systems*, OUP, p. 427.

133 Katarzyna Kowalska (2009), 'Effective remedies for excessive length of proceedings' in Wołąsiewicz, Jakub (ed.), *Pilot Judgment Procedure in the European Court of Human Rights and the development of Human Rights standards and procedures : Third informal seminar for government agents and other institutions, Warsaw 14–15 May, 2009*, Kontrast, pp. 166–168.

134 Interview with Judge Wojciech Hermeliński, Constitutional Court, Warsaw, 13.5.09.

135 *Ibid.*

judgment on the basis of only part of the period.[136] For example, in the *Krawczak* case, the Court noted that the practice of the Polish courts when assessing the reasonableness of the length of proceedings was not to include the pre-judicial phase of the proceedings and only to include in their calculation the period of time after 2004, when the new law came into force. The Court reiterated "that a remedy may be accepted as effective only if it is capable of addressing all stages of the impugned proceedings"[137] and consequently found a violation of Articles 6(1) and 13. In the *Tur* case the Court itself decided to consider Article 13 of its own motion, and found a violation as the domestic courts had only examined the period after the entry into force of the 2004 law, and therefore had failed to consider the overall length of the proceedings.[138]

A similar practice in Slovenia has also caused applicants' dissatisfaction with domestic court decisions in length of proceedings cases (see Chapter 3). Unlike the Italian and Slovenian laws, the Polish law only applies to cases where the proceedings are still pending, although damages for cases that are closed may be sought retrospectively in accordance with the Civil Code (and not as a consequence of a violation of the right to trial within a reasonable time).[139]

The government has responded to Strasbourg by amending the law and issuing guidance to streamline administrative procedures. Guidelines were issued in 2008 to improve administrative supervision of the Polish courts in dealing with criminal proceedings.[140] On 20 February 2009 amendments were made to the 2004 law, seeking to make the necessary changes that the European Court had specified.[141] The law was accordingly amended to eliminate the practice of courts inaccurately assessing the length of proceedings by omitting the preparatory stages when the case is under the supervision of the prosecutor during the pre-

136 Katarzyna Kowalska (2009), 'Effective remedies for excessive length of proceedings' in Wołąsiewicz, Jakub (ed.), *Pilot Judgment Procedure in the European Court of Human Rights and the development of Human Rights standards and procedures : Third informal seminar for government agents and other institutions, Warsaw 14–15 May, 2009*, Kontrast, p. 167; Interview with Judge Wojciech Hermeliński, Constitutional Court, Warsaw, 13.5.09.

137 *Krawczak v Poland*, No. 40387/06, 8.4.08, para. 39.

138 *Tur v Poland*, No. 21695/05, 23.10.07, para. 59; similarly a violation of Article 13 in conjunction with Article 6(1) had been found in previous cases after the 2004 law came into force: *Zwoźniak v Poland*, No. 25728/05, 13.11.07.

139 Katarzyna Kowalska (2009), 'Effective remedies for excessive length of proceedings' in Wołąsiewicz, Jakub (ed.), *Pilot Judgment Procedure in the European Court of Human Rights and the development of Human Rights standards and procedures : Third informal seminar for government agents and other institutions, Warsaw 14–15 May, 2009*, Kontrast, p. 165. See for example *Charzyński v Poland*, No. 15212/03, 1.3.05, paras. 12–23.

140 Igor Dzialuk (2009), 'Quasi-Pilot Judgments: comments from the perspective of Poland (cases Musiał and Kauczor)' in Wołąsiewicz, Jakub (ed.), *Pilot Judgment Procedure in the European Court of Human Rights and the development of Human Rights standards and procedures : Third informal seminar for government agents and other institutions, Warsaw 14–15 May, 2009*, Kontrast, pp. 110–111.

141 Interview with Magdalena Brzozowska, Ministry of Justice, 15.5.09.

judicial phase.[142] The 2009 amendments further specified which court would investigate complaints in which instances, and that awards of compensation would be between 2,000 and 20,000 złoties,[143] (approximately 490-4900 euros).[144] This was therefore a significant increase from the average sum of 150 euros awarded under the previous law.

In the *Kudła* judgment, the Court also ruled that Poland had violated Article 5(3) of the Convention because of Mr Kudła's excessive pre-trial detention. There was no suggestion in the judgment that the Court was treating this issue as a 'systemic' one, as such. However, in June 2007, after dozens more Strasbourg judgments against Poland had also found excessive periods of pre-trial detention, the Committee of Ministers of the Council of Europe adopted an Interim Resolution concerning pre-trial detention, identifying it as a structural problem which necessitated changes in legislation or administrative practice.[145] Two years later, the Court considered that there had not been sufficient resolution of this problem, having found a violation of Article 5(3) in a further 32 cases in 2007 and 33 cases in 2008.[146] Consequently in February 2009 the Court applied the 'quasi-pilot judgment' procedure to a further example of this problem, in the case of *Kauczor*, which is discussed below.

2.4.2. EXCESSIVE LENGTH OF PRE-TRIAL DETENTION (*KAUCZOR*)

In February 2000, Adam Kauczor was arrested on suspicion of murder and was detained pending trial for a total period of 7 years, 10 months and 3 days.[147] The grounds for his detention were that he might tamper with evidence relating to his case, but the European Court found that the risk of this happening was not sufficiently justified by the domestic authorities. In its judgment the Court

---

142 Poland. Sejm (2009), *Ustawa z dnia 20 lutego 2009 r. o zmianie ustawy o skardze na naruszenie prawa strony do rozpoznania sprawy w postępowaniu sądowym bez nieuzasadnionej zwłoki* (Dziennik Urząd z dnia 16 kwietnia 2009 r.) = Law of 20 February 2009 amending the law on the right to trial without undue delay (Dziennik Urząd, 16 April 2009). http://www.lex.com.pl/serwis/du/2009/0498.htm (last accessed 9.4.10).

143 Poland. Sejm (2009), Ustawa z dnia 20 lutego 2009 r. o zmianie ustawy o skardze na naruszenie prawa strony do rozpoznania sprawy w postępowaniu sądowym bez nieuzasadnionej zwłoki (Dziennik Urząd z dnia 16 kwietnia 2009 r.) = Law of 20 February 2009 amending the law on the right to trial without undue delay (Dziennik Urząd, 16 April 2009). http://www.lex.com.pl/serwis/du/2009/0498.htm (last accessed 9.4.10).

144 This is according to the exchange rate at 11 February 2010.

145 Committee of Ministers (2007), Interim Resolution CM/ResDH(2007)75 concerning the judgments of the European Court of Human Rights in 44 cases against Poland relating to the excessive length of detention on remand, 6 June 2007. https://wcd.coe.int/ViewDoc.jsp?id=1146407&Site=CM. See also: *Kauczor v Poland*, No.45219/06, 03.02.09, para. 34.

146 *Kauczor v Poland*, No. 45219/06, 3.2.09, para. 56.

147 *Ibid.*, para. 39.

invoked Article 46, and stated that the 2007 Committee of Ministers Resolution taken together with the number of similar cases since then

> "demonstrate that the violation of the applicant's right under Article 5 §3 of the Convention originated in a widespread problem arising from the malfunctioning of the Polish criminal justice system which has affected, and may still affect in the future, an yet unidentified, but potentially considerable number of persons charged in criminal proceedings."[148]

Evaluation of the impact of the Kauczor judgment on domestic law

As the *Kauczor* judgment was only delivered in February 2009, it is too early to fully assess the government's response to the case. However, prior to the Strasbourg judgment, there had been pressure from the Constitutional Court for legislative change, and amendments to the law had been made in 2007. In July 2006 the Constitutional Court judged unconstitutional the provision in the Code of Criminal Procedure[149] which granted courts the right to extend pre-trial detention beyond the existing two year limit. The Constitutional Court reasoned that the conditions under which such an extension could be granted were not sufficiently clearly expressed in the law to protect individuals from arbitrary decisions.[150] As a result of the Constitutional Court judgment, the Code of Criminal Procedure (Article 263(4)) was amended to restrict further the terms under which those on remand could be detained.[151]

The amendment to the Code of Criminal Procedure entered into force in February 2007. Subsequently, following the Committee of Ministers' interim resolution of June 2007, further steps were taken.[152] The new measures were designed to improve the efficiency of the courts' administrative procedures (including scheduling time-limits for hearings well in advance and holding hearings on Saturdays). They

148 *Ibid.*, para. 58.

149 Ustawa o zmianie ustawy Kodeksa postępowaniu karnego oraz niektórych innych ustaw.

150 The provision stated that detention could be extended beyond two years if the pre-trial proceedings could not have been completed because of "important obstacles" which could not have been overcome. See *Kauczor v Poland*, No.45219/06, 3.2.09, para. 26.

151 "The pre-trial detention shall be extended beyond the period specified in paragraphs 2 and 3, only by the court of appeal in whose jurisdiction the proceedings are conducted, upon a motion from the court before which the case is pending, and at the investigation stage, upon a motion from the appellate prosecuting authorities. This can be done if deemed necessary in connection with a suspension of criminal proceedings, in connection with actions aiming at establishing or confirming the identity of the accused, prolonged psychiatric observation of the accused, prolonged preparation of an opinion of an expert, conducting evidentiary action in a particularly intricate case or conducting them abroad, or intentional protraction of proceedings by the accused." See: *Kauczor v Poland*, No.45219/06, 3.2.09, para. 27.

152 *Kauczor v Poland*, No.45219/06, 3.2.09, paras. 32–33.

additionally introduced special training for judges and prosecutors to increase awareness of the European Court's standards in this area.

Following the issue of the *Kauczor* judgment in 2009, however, statements by the Ministry of Justice suggest there is disagreement with Strasbourg's interpretation of the violation as arising from a systemic problem:

> "At [the] present time the problem of the excessive length of pre-trial detention appears in ... isolated cases which are exceptionally complex. However, they should not be treated as revealing the existence in Poland of [a] structural problem connected to the inappropriate application of pre-trial detention."[153]

Igor Dzialuk, Undersecretary of State at the Ministry of Justice, contended that pre-trial detention for periods of more than two years only occurs in complex cases concerning serious crimes and that their number decreased by some 12% between 2007 and 2008.[154] The Institute of Legal Research acknowledges a reduction in these figures, yet maintains that nonetheless these rates still remain too high.[155] The Institute was critical of court practices, and attributed delays to judges' sickness or absence and also to the failure of defendants, or their legal representatives, to appear in court.[156] What was emphasised, was that the full period of detention should be taken into account, starting from the time of the suspect's arrest.[157] Although measures adopted in response to the Committee of Ministers' 2007 Resolution have been welcomed, the Council of Europe has since stated, in August 2009, in its most recent report on the execution of Court judgments, that the problem of excessive length of pre-trial detention remains a structural problem in need of further attention. In this respect the Court recommends additional awareness measures (publication and dissemination of the European Court's judgments) and the monitoring of court practices concerning detention on remand.[158]

---

153 Igor Dzialuk (2009), 'Quasi-Pilot Judgments: comments from the perspective of Poland (cases Musiał and Kauczor)' in Wołąsiewicz, Jakub (ed.), *Pilot Judgment Procedure in the European Court of Human Rights and the development of Human Rights standards and procedures : Third informal seminar for government agents and other institutions, Warsaw 14–15 May, 2009*, Kontrast, p. 111.

154 *Ibid.*

155 Stanisław Momot (2008), Badania aktowe spraw, w których czas trwania tymczasowych aresztowań przekroczył 2 lata, = Research into cases where pre-trial detention has exceeded 2 years, Instytut Wymiaru Sprawiedliwości, p. 5.

156 *Ibid.*, p. 21; p. 38.

157 *Ibid.*, p. 39.

158 Directorate General of Human Rights and Legal Affairs. *Execution of the Judgments of the European Court of Human Rights. Pending Cases. Current State of Execution. Poland*, p. 45, at 26.8.09. http://www.coe.int/t/dghl/monitoring/execution/Reports/Current_en.asp.

Thus the *Kauczor* judgment again displays a commonality of approach by the Polish Constitutional Court and the Strasbourg Court, combining to create added leverage in favour of the executive's compliance with the Convention. In the related case of *Sławomir Musiał*, also concerning pre-trial detention, the applicant pleaded that his conditions of detention were inhuman and degrading. Where Mr Kudła had failed to convince the Court that insufficient provision for prisoners with psychiatric disorders constituted inhuman treatment, Mr Musiał's case was found by the Court to be evidence of a structural problem of overcrowding and inadequate conditions in Polish detention facilities. These issues are considered below.

2.4.3. POOR PRISON CONDITIONS AND INHUMAN TREATMENT (*SŁAWOMIR MUSIAŁ*)

Sławomir Musiał was detained on suspicion of robbery and battery in 2005. Despite a history of serious mental disorders, his period of pre-trial detention of three and a half years was mostly spent in an over-crowded prison, rather than in secure psychiatric care. Mr Musiał therefore pleaded a violation of Article 3 – that he had been subject to inhuman and degrading treatment. Although the Court acknowledged that his lack of care may have been the result of negligence, rather than being intentional, it nonetheless ruled that his treatment was sufficient to find a violation of Article 3. Furthermore, this was considered to be a systemic violation. The Court also found that the over-crowded conditions were sufficient in themselves to violate Article 3, and found this to be an endemic problem.[159] Although psychiatric prisoners constitute a smaller pool of individuals, the issue of over-crowding affects a far larger number of people. As in *Kauczor*, the Court invoked Article 46 of the Convention and stipulated the need for legislative and administrative measures to be adopted in order to improve prison conditions, reduce over-crowding in prisons and guarantee appropriate care for vulnerable detainees.[160]

Evaluation of the impact of the Sławomir Musiał judgment on domestic law

Like *Kauczor*, *Sławomir Musiał* was delivered too recently to allow us to carry out an extensive evaluation of how the general measures highlighted in the judgment have since been addressed. However, similarly to the position in *Kauczor*, there is evidence that the Polish government does not agree that there is an absence of an effective domestic remedy. Igor Dzialuk, Undersecretary of State at the

159 *Musiał (Sławomir) v Poland*, No. 28300/06, 20.1.09, para. 95.
160 *Ibid.*, paras. 106–8.

Ministry of Justice, has argued that there is already provision in Polish law for detainees to complain about their treatment, as they may bring a civil action for this purpose.[161]

The Polish government was already aware that such a judgment was likely to be issued, and so it should not have come as a surprise. The possibility that the Court could issue a pilot or quasi-pilot judgment concerning poor prison conditions had been publicised in the press in 2008. In his *Rzeczpospolita* article of September 2008, Grzegorz Lewocki, of the Institute of Legal Studies of the Polish Academy of Sciences, outlined the problem of overcrowding in Polish prisons, arguing that cells are often packed with so many detainees, that they fail to meet the standards specified in the Polish Criminal Code (Article 110(2) which grants each inmate the right to a minimum of three square metres).[162] In May 2008, the Constitutional Court had issued a judgment finding that Article 248(1) of the Criminal Code, allowing the 'temporary' re-location of detainees, under certain circumstances, into cells of less than three square metres, was incompatible with Article 110(2). As Lewocki noted, a pilot judgment would force the Polish government to heed this Constitutional Court judgment sooner rather than later:

> "If the Strasbourg Court issues the expected pilot judgment, then it will oblige the Polish government, through the recommendation of so called general measures, to eliminate the serious systemic and structural defect that we currently have in operation in the form of the provision and application of Articles 110:2 and 248:1 of the Criminal Code. In the context of the current problem of overcrowding it will thus not be long before appropriate measures are taken in line with recommendations [already made] by the Constitutional Court for future reform."[163]

2.5. EVALUATION OF THE MONITORING OF THE IMPLEMENTATION OF STRASBOURG JUDGMENTS

During the course of this research we asked our interviewees how successfully the implementation of Strasbourg judgments is being monitored within Poland.

---

161 Igor Dzialuk (2009), 'Quasi-Pilot Judgments: comments from the perspective of Poland (cases Musiał and Kauczor)' in Wołąsiewicz, Jakub (ed.), *Pilot Judgment Procedure in the European Court of Human Rights and the development of Human Rights standards and procedures : Third informal seminar for government agents and other institutions, Warsaw 14–15 May, 2009*, Kontrast, p. 108.

162 Grzegorz Lewocki (2008) 'Kauczor et al. Strasburg o przeludnieniu w polskich więzieniach' = 'Kauczor et al.: Strasbourg on the issue of overcrowding in Polish prisons' *Rzeczpospolita* 4.9.08. http://new-arch.rp.pl/artykul/804354.html.

163 *Ibid.*

Although the Polish Government agent in Strasbourg, Jakub Wołąsiewicz, expressed his satisfaction with monitoring,[164] most voiced their concerns. Igor Dzialuk, Undersecretary of State at the Ministry of Justice, explained that, in the justice sector, monitoring of individual cases is performed 'mainly internally', but that there are in any event insufficient resources within the Ministry to monitor all cases that deserve follow up:

> "The individual monitoring [of cases] is definitely internal – this is the communication between the court[s] and the Ministry ... the Ministry itself, although it's a large structure, it wouldn't have enough manpower to monitor all the cases that we believe may require it, while structural monitoring ... – the monitoring of the legislation – it's mostly public – the reports are published on the internet or are published elsewhere."[165]

Additionally, a research institute, the Institute of the Evaluation of Justice (*Instytut wymiaru sprawiedliwości*), financed by the Ministry of Justice, carries out work in this area.[166] The Institute was founded in 1990 and specializes in evaluating whether domestic law is in accordance with European Standards. The former President of the Constitutional Court, Marek Safjan, is the current Director of the Institute. As discussed above (section 2.4.2.1.) a recent report by the Institute investigated cases of pre-trial detention lasting longer than two years and was critical of domestic court practices.[167]

The Committee of Ministers of the Council of Europe expects regular information to be provided on the progress of the execution of relevant judgments.[168] In specific sectors, the relevant ministries in Poland are responsible for collecting this data; for example the Ministry of the State Treasury is responsible for monitoring the *Broniowski* Law. On the Ministry's website there is a general report, updated regularly, which lists the monthly compensation awards made by each of the Governors' Offices and provides a running total for the number of applicants compensated and the total amount of compensation disbursed by the Compensation Fund at the Polish National Bank. The total number of claimants who received compensation for the month of January 2010 was 565 and by that date the total number that had received compensation since the inception of the

---

164 It should be noted that Jakub Wołąsiewicz's approval of the effectiveness of implementation was relative: that in Poland greater heed was paid to the European Court's judgments than to those issued by the Polish Constitutional Court. Interview with Jakub Wołąsiewicz, Warsaw, 14.5.09.

165 Interview with Igor Dzialuk, Undersecretary of State, Ministry of Justice, 15.5.09.

166 *Ibid.*

167 Stanisław Momot (2008), *Badania aktowe spraw, w których czas trwania tymczasowych aresztowań przekroczył 2 lata = Research into cases where pre-trial detention has exceeded 2 years*, Instytut Wymiaru Sprawiedliwości.

168 Interview with Jakub Wołąsiewicz, Government Agent, Warsaw, 14.5.09.

law was 24,681,[169] which is approximately thirty percent of the number of potential applicants, estimated by the Polish Government to be nearly 80,000.[170] However, Jakub Wołąsiewicz has suggested that this figure was an over-estimate, and that the number is more likely to be between 30,000 and 40,000.[171] Wołąsiewicz had a similar view as regards the figures submitted to the Court in the *Hutten-Czapska* case and that 100,000 potential landlords and around 600,000 tenants,[172] were a gross overestimate.[173] As noted above (section 2.2.1), Andrzej Korzeniowski, the President of the Bug River Region Association, told us, however, that the execution of the *Broniowski* judgment is not monitored, and NGOs cannot get access to Government data, which would enable them to analyse the reasons for the slow rate at which applications are dealt with.[174]

In the case of *Hutten-Czapska*, monitoring of follow-up is performed by the Ministry of Infrastructure. There is, however, as yet, no formal monitoring of the 2008 Act on Supporting Thermal Modernization and Renovation, which came into force in March 2009. The Undersecretary of State for Infrastructure, Piotr Styczeń, said that since the law came into force, a provisional voluntary 6 month monitoring procedure had been in operation, whereby those who wanted to make a comment on the new legislation were able to do so. However, there is no active data-collection on the matter, and we were told that at the end of the 6 month period the Ministry may contact some of the organisations representing property owners to solicit their views.[175] The vice president of the Polish Union of Property Owners expressed her dissatisfaction with the monitoring of the 'Rent Mirror' scheme. In her view, although data is collected, it is not used in any way to fine-tune the legislation or the administrative process: "All administrators are required twice a year to provide information – and the information apparently gets lost somewhere."[176]

---

169 Poland. Ministerstwo Skarbu Państwa. Realizacja wypłat rekompensat. Komunikat nr 2/2010 w sprawie wypłat rekompensat z tytułu pozostawienia nieruchomości poza obecnymi granicami Rzeczypospolitej Polskiej, 5.2.10 = Poland. Ministry of the State Treasury. Implementing the disbursement of compensation. Communication nr 2/2010 over the issue of disbursing compensation for those properties left abroad by the Polish government, published 5.2.10. http://msp.gov.pl/portal/pl/118/8820/Komunikat_nr_22010_w_sprawie_wyplat_rekompensat_z_tytulu_pozostawienia_nieruchom.html.

170 European Court of Human Rights (2005), *Press release issued by the Registrar: Recent developments in Broniowski v Poland* 15.6.2005 http://cmiskp.echr.coe.int/tkp197/view.asp?item=1&portal=hbkm&action=html&highlight=recent%20%7C%20developments%20%7C%20in%20%7C%20Broniowski&sessionid=50884070&skin=hudoc-pr-en.

171 Interview with Jakub Wołąsiewicz, Government Agent, Warsaw, 14.5.09.

172 *Hutten-Czapska v Poland*, No. 35014/97, 22.2.05, para. 24.

173 Interview with Jakub Wołąsiewicz, Government Agent, Warsaw, 14.5.09.

174 Telephone interview with Andrzej Korzeniowski, President of the Bug River Region Association (Ogólnopolskie Stowarzyszenie Kresowian Wierzycieli Skarbu Państwa = All-Union Association of the Bug River Region Association of creditors to the State Treasury), 10.2.10 and email of 11.2.10 (on file with the authors).

175 Interview with Piotr Styczeń, Undersecretary of State for Infrastructure, 13.5.09.

176 Interview with Barbara Grzybowska, of the Polish Union of Property Owners, 13.5.09.

Monitoring of the legislation which was developed in response to the *Kudła* case is performed by the Ministry of Justice; data is regularly collected every three months from the regional and appellate courts.[177] As yet, it is too soon to assess the monitoring of legislation and changes in practice developed as a result of the *Kauczor* and *Sławomir Musiał* judgments.

Although there is, therefore, evidence of monitoring of the implementation of European Court judgments, Marek Nowicki, a former member of the European Commission of Human Rights, expressed his doubt that any government issued with a pilot judgment would then adequately monitor implementation. The accumulation of cases which necessitates a pilot judgment, in Nowicki's view, inevitably demonstrates a state's unwillingness to resolve violations at their root, suggesting that the state would be ambivalent to the results of the pilot judgment at the domestic level and would therefore be unlikely to adequately monitor implementation. Accordingly, Nowicki recommends independent domestic mechanisms to ensure execution:

> "For such issues one must have strong NGOs, or ... the ombudsman institution. One should have a certain solid, official partner who could raise the reciprocal question of contesting the governmental practice ... And I think it is a very weak part of the whole concept."[178]

According to Nowicki, once the state has convinced Strasbourg that the issue will be resolved and no longer requires the Court's attention, there is little incentive for the state to deliver:

> "... after one day Strasbourg decides that the government offers appropriate remedies, things look very promising ... and everyone is happy. They are coming here in order to shake hands and to say something in the Foreign Ministry with the Agent of the Government, but what after? What is there the next day? Nothing!"[179]

2.6. CONCLUSION

In this chapter we have noted a greater public awareness in Poland about the European Court of Human Rights, but also that its decisions are not widely reported

[177] Katarzyna Kowalska (2009), 'Effective remedies for excessive length of proceedings' in Wołąsiewicz, Jakub (ed.), *Pilot Judgment Procedure in the European Court of Human Rights and the development of Human Rights standards and procedures : Third informal seminar for government agents and other institutions, Warsaw 14–15 May, 2009*, Kontrast, p. 168. This information is published on the Ministry of Justice's website at: http://www.ms.gov.pl/statystyki/statystyki.php (last accessed 9.4.10).

[178] Interview with Marek Nowicki, Helsinki Foundation for Human Rights, 13.5.09.

[179] *Ibid.*

in the media. There remain significant concerns that the Polish authorities are failing to respond adequately to the decisions of both the Constitutional Court and the Strasbourg Court. There is little evidence of rigorous Parliamentary engagement either in the 'auditing' of draft legislation according to human rights standards, or in the follow up to European Court judgments concerning Poland. Nevertheless, legislation was introduced reasonably rapidly in response to the Court's two 'full' pilot judgments against Poland (although there remain concerns about the effectiveness of their implementation in practice). Other systemic issues, such as the length of legal proceedings, excessive periods of pre-trial detention and poor prison conditions have continued to cause problems. There is no satisfactory system for the monitoring of the effectiveness of measures introduced in response to European Court decisions highlighting structural problems.

2.6.1. WHAT FACTORS HAVE LED THE COURT TO APPLY THE PILOT JUDGMENT PROCEDURE?

Why has Poland been the subject of two 'full' pilot judgments, when only six such judgments have been issued to date? One answer to this might be that the Polish legal system warrants this type of judgment to bring it into line with the Convention. But, since Poland is by no means the only state from which 'clone cases' are appearing at the Court, and as Poland is far from being the worst offender in terms of violations, we must look for other explanations. Our respondents stressed the importance of certain key personnel at the Court in Strasbourg, especially in the Registry, as well as the role played by the Polish government agent.

2.6.1.1. The Role of Individuals

The impact that individuals can have was emphasised by Michael O'Boyle:

> "Individuals count very much in this business ... you need people who have vision, a certain creative spirit and who are willing to challenge traditional thinking".[180]

The senior Court Registry lawyer Renata Degener played an instrumental role in the Court's development of the pilot judgment procedure, as was emphasised to us both in Strasbourg and in Warsaw.[181] Renata Degener herself explained to us that,

[180] Interview with Michael O'Boyle, Strasbourg, 25.3.09.

[181] Interview with Judge Wojciech Hermeliński, Court Registry, Warsaw, 13.5.09; Interview with Judge Lech Garlicki, Strasbourg, 25.3.09.

> "It went beyond my expectations but I must tell you that at some point it became my personal commitment ... to finish the Bug River cases and I think that they came to a very successful end, even though the applicants were not happy. But I think in terms of shaping the pilot judgment procedure and saying that at some point it must be closed, because the issue has been resolved, it was something really important."[182]

The proactive and energetic approach adopted by Jakub Wołąsiewicz, the Polish Government agent, has clearly been important. His approach – of embracing rather than fighting the Court's application of the pilot judgment procedure – has resulted in his becoming one of the procedure's most vocal advocates. Interviewees from NGOs, the European Court Registry and Polish judges confirmed to us that Mr Wołąsiewicz's role had been very considerable.[183] In conjunction with a willingness to cooperate with the Court, Mr Wołąsiewicz apparently enjoys good relations with his government, which significantly facilitates the process of cooperation with the Court.[184] In Strasbourg, a number of interviewees confirmed to us that the decision to apply the procedure to Polish cases (in the first two instances) was to a certain extent 'political' in that there was a degree of expectation that the Polish government would comply with it. Consequently, the procedure can be viewed as a positive and constructive way of working with Strasbourg towards achieving the same goal: the protection of human rights in accordance with the Convention. This collaborative approach is reflected more significantly in the synergy between the Polish Constitutional Court and Strasbourg in the application of the pilot judgment procedure.

2.6.1.2. Collaboration between the Polish Constitutional and European Courts

The process of informal cooperation between the Constitutional and European Courts has been emphasised by a number of interviewees.[185] As Wojciech Sadurski has argued, through the means of a pilot judgment (and the Court's invocation of Article 46), constitutional courts dealing with a recalcitrant legislature and executive may be 'supported' by the European Court in forcing through the

---

182 Interview with Renata Degener, Court Registry, Strasbourg, 26.3.09.

183 Interview with Adam Bodnar, Secretary of the Board, Helsinki Foundation for Human Rights, Warsaw, 12.5.09; Interview with Michael O'Boyle, Strasbourg, 25.3.09; Interview with Renata Degener, Court Registry, Strasbourg, 26.3.09; Interview with Wojciech Hermeliński, Constitutional Court, Warsaw, 13.5.09.

184 We inferred this from an interview with Michael O'Boyle, who told us that Mr Wołąsiewicz had managed to arrange high level discussions with a number of government actors and ministries during the pilot judgment procedure. Interview with Michael O'Boyle, Court Registry, Strasbourg, 25.3.09.

185 Interview with Professor Marek Safjan, University of Warsaw, 13.5.09; Interview with Renata Degener, Strasbourg, 26.3.09.

desired legislative changes.[186] Our current research confirms Sadurski's theory as regards Poland, as well as Slovenia and Italy. In the latter case, the Constitutional Court judge Giuseppe Tesauro told us that although the Italian Constitutional Court was in agreement with the Strasbourg judgments in the cases of *Scordino* and *Sejdović*, there was no active collaboration between the two courts before Strasbourg issued its pilot judgments in relation to Italy.[187] We did find evidence of a certain degree of informal communication between constitutional courts and the European Court, and indeed some movement of personnel between them (for example, the Polish and Slovenian judges at the European Court, Lech Garlicki, and Boštjan Zupančič, were previously Constitutional Court judges).[188]

As this chapter has shown, there is a clear pattern that concerning the cases of *Broniowski, Hutten-Czapska, Kauczor* and *Musiał*, both Courts took a similar line. Prior to the Strasbourg decisions, the Constitutional Court had already issued judgments declaring the relevant legislation (or lack thereof) as being deficient. As the executive and legislature failed to respond adequately to the Constitutional Court's judgments in these instances, the violations continued, as was evident from the further cases found admissible by the European Court. By identifying these violations as 'systemic', and invoking Article 46 to require compliance with the judgment, the European Court has in essence given support to the Constitutional Court in securing the cooperation of the Polish authorities.[189]

---

186 Wojciech Sadurski (2008), 'Partnering with Strasbourg: Constitutionalization of the European Court of Human Rights, the Accession of Central and East European States to the Council of Europe and the idea of Pilot Judgments', *EUI Working Papers Law* 2008/33.

187 Interview with Judge Giuseppe Tesauro, Constitutional Court, Rome, 8.6.09.

188 Interview with Professor Marek Safjan, University of Warsaw, 13.5.09; Interview with Wojciech Hermeliński, Constitutional Court, 13.5.09.

189 A point that was confirmed by a number of respondents: Interview with Wojciech Hermeliński, Constitutional Court, Warsaw, 13.5.09; Interview with Igor Dzialuk, Undersecretary of State, Ministry of Justice, 15.5.09; Interview with Professor Marek Safjan, University of Warsaw, 13.5.09.

CHAPTER 3

THE SLOVENIAN EXPERIENCE OF 'QUASI-PILOT' JUDGMENTS

Has the Court over-reached its powers in length of proceedings cases?

3.1. INTRODUCTION

3.1.1. THE STATUS AND APPLICATION OF THE EUROPEAN CONVENTION IN DOMESTIC LAW

Slovenia ratified the European Convention on Human Rights in 1994, and according to Article 8 of the Slovenian Constitution, international law is binding on domestic law. Therefore, the Convention is in principle implemented directly by Slovenian courts: it has a higher status than ordinary laws, but is subordinate to the Constitution. The Constitutional Court is responsible for ensuring compliance of the domestic law with the Convention.[1]

In practice, however, the judiciary in Slovenia was reported to apply the Convention inconsistently and sporadically. The reason for this, we were told, is insufficient training and awareness of the Convention among judges.[2] Our respondents stated that lower courts are much less likely than higher courts to cite the Convention in their judgments. Evidently, although Constitutional Court judgments make reference to the Convention, judges in other courts only rarely do so. Dean Zagorac, the editor of the legal weekly magazine, *Pravna Praksa*, told us:

---

1 Arne Mavčič (2001), 'Slovenia' in Blackburn, Robert and Jörg Polakiewicz, *Fundamental Rights in Europe: the European Convention on Human Rights and its member states*, OUP, pp. 781–784.

2 Interview with Vita Habjan, Legal Information Centre for NGOs (*Pravno-Informacijski Center nevladnih organizacij*) ("PIC"), Ljubljana, 3.6.09; interview with Dean Zagorac, Editor, *Pravna Praksa*, Ljubljana, 3.6.09.

> "With judges it's even a problem that they very rarely cite the Constitution. They usually only rely on relevant laws, which is OK, but they also have to base their decisions on the Constitution, not only law. So if the Constitution, for them, is something exotic, then you can imagine that the Convention is even more so ..."[3]

Among the general public, however, awareness of the European Court has increased as a result of the *Lukenda* case (concerning the excessive length of legal proceedings – which we discuss below), according to a number of our respondents.[4] Some consider that media coverage of the Court is relatively good, in that daily newspapers such as *Delo* and *Žurnal* report on important European Court cases relating to Slovenia.[5] Others feel the media could do more to contextualise these issues and that the specialist legal weekly magazine, *Pravna Praksa*, is the only publication that reports European Court matters in sufficient detail.[6] According to the Ombudsman's office, there are insufficient resources dedicated to translating European Court judgments into Slovene.[7] Respondents from NGOs considered that people in Slovenia, generally, are insufficiently aware of their rights under the Convention,[8] and to try to rectify this the Legal Information Centre for NGOs (*Pravno-Informacijski Center nevladnih organizacij*) ('PIC'), has recently published a pamphlet providing guidelines on how to take a case to the European Court.[9]

3.1.2. SLOVENIA'S TRACK RECORD IN RESPONDING TO STRASBOURG

3.1.2.1. The Executive

There was a general consensus among our respondents that the government is willing to comply with the Court's *Lukenda* judgment, concerning the particular problem of the excessive length of domestic legal proceedings. However, aside from that issue, NGO respondents expressed their concern that there are a number of other human rights issues (on which the European Court has issued judgments) that have not been addressed by the Slovenian Government. These

3 Interview with Dean Zagorac, Editor, *Pravna Praksa*, Ljubljana, 3.6.09.
4 Interview with Neža Kogovšek, Peace Institute, Ljubljana 1.6.09; Interview with Dean Zagorac, Editor, *Pravna Praksa*, Ljubljana, 3.6.09.
5 Interview with Ivan Šelih and Jernej Rovšek, Ombudsman's Office, Ljubljana, 2.6.09.
6 Interview with Neža Kogovšek, Peace Institute, Ljubljana 1.6.09, Interview with Dean Zagorac, Editor, *Pravna Praksa*, Ljubljana, 3.6.09.
7 Interview with Ivan Šelih and Jernej Rovšek, Ombudsman's Office, Ljubljana, 2.6.09.
8 Interview with Neža Kogovšek, Peace Institute, Ljubljana 1.6.09; Interview with Vita Habjan, PIC, Ljubljana, 3.6.09.
9 Interview with Vita Habjan, PIC, Ljubljana, 3.6.09.

have also been described as systemic problems. Two concern discrimination: the state's failure to protect Roma rights,[10] or to grant redress to the 'Erased.'[11] The 'Erased' are a group of more than 18,000 former Yugoslav citizens who became officially stateless after the authorities deleted their names from the Slovenian State Register in 1992. The authorities also destroyed documents attesting to these individuals' residency status in Slovenia and they subsequently became known as 'erased persons'. Many of the 'erased' were Croats or Serbs, which is why this act was perceived as motivated by the ethnic tensions between the constituent republics of the Former Yugoslavia.[12] In its partial admissibility decision in *Makuc and others v Slovenia*, concerning the issue of the 'Erased', the Court gave notice to the Slovenian Government of the applicants' complaints relating to the failure to ensure the retrospective recognition of permanent residence (Article 8), the lack of an effective legal remedy (Article 13), the allegedly discriminatory treatment (Article 14) and the denial of pension benefits (Article 1 of Protocol No. 1).[13] Given also the large numbers of people affected by this systemic issue (more than 18,000), it is suggested that this is the sort of case for which the Court might issue a pilot or quasi-pilot judgment.

Other notable issues which have arisen in recent judgments concerning Slovenia include the authorities' failure to investigate allegations of police brutality or negligence by the medical profession, as will be discussed later in relation to the cases of *Matko* and *Šilih*.

3.1.2.2. The Legislature

According to our respondents, the legislature also bears some degree of responsibility for the failure to address systemic violations. Parliament fails to implement Constitutional Court judgments adequately, and the delays which occur before laws which have been declared unconstitutional are subsequently amended frequently leave judges in confusion as to which version of the law they should apply. Simple amendments can evidently be processed fairly quickly, but when laws concern systemic issues, delays can be considerable, lasting a year or even longer.[14] Although in theory parliamentarians can propose draft laws, the Government and its competent ministries perform this duty in the main.[15] According to one of our respondents, they do not, however, draft workable laws

---

10 Interview with Aldo Mihlonić, Peace Institute, Ljubljana, 3.6.09; Interview with Vita Habjan, PIC, Ljubljana, 3.6.09.

11 Interview with Neža Kogovšek, Peace Institute, Ljubljana, 1.6.09.

12 For an account of the plight of the 'erased' see: Brad Blitz (2006) 'Statelessness and the Social (De)Construction of Citizenship: Political Restructuring and Ethnic Discrimination in Slovenia' *Journal of Human Rights*, pp. 453–479.

13 *Makuc (Milan) and others v Slovenia*, No. 26828/06, dec. 31.5.07, para. 216.

14 Interview with Judge Marija Krisper Kramberger, Constitutional Court, Ljubljana, 3.6.09.

15 Interview with Neža Kogovšek, Peace Institute, Ljubljana, 1.6.09; e-mail 7.11.09.

which respect human rights principles. Neža Kogovšek, of the Peace Institute, suggested that "the lack of knowledge among the members of the parliament about human rights is definitely a problem".[16] Furthermore it was suggested to us that this problem is accentuated by the fact that there are very few parliamentarians in Slovenia who are lawyers by profession, that generally MPs are simply not aware of human rights issues[17] and so have insufficient expertise to amend bills.[18] Consequently, debate in parliament about draft legislation tends to be rather ineffectual, and in Slovenia is manifested in consensus among opposition and ruling parties over these issues.[19]

The unanimous approval by the Parliament's lower house, the National Assembly,[20] of the recent 2009 amendments to the 2006 *Act on the protection of the Right to*

---

16 E-mail from Neža Kogovšek, Peace Institute, Ljubljana, 7.11.09.

17 Interview with Darja Lavtižar Bebler, National Assembly, Ljubljana, 2.6.09.

18 Interview with Neža Kogovšek, Peace Institute, 1.6.09; e-mail 7.11.09.

19 Interview with Darja Lavtižar Bebler, National Assembly, Ljubljana, 2.6.09. However there may also be other reasons for this commonality of approach over such policies; some commentators have noted that issues generally regarding Europe have often become 'valence' issues, where there is consensus among all parties, as European issues tend to cut across traditional party cleavages, making it risky for parties to adopt a strong stance on Europe for fear of alienating some of their supporters (Philippe Schmitter (2009), 'The changing politics of organised interests' in Goetz, Klaus H., Peter Mair and Gordon Smith (eds.), *European Politics: Pasts, presents, futures*, Routledge, pp. 199–203). Although before accession to the EU (especially around the accession referendums of 2003) some political parties in CEE did shape their platforms around euroscepticism or in favour of accession, after 2004 this factor has waned considerably (see, for example: Paul Lewis and Zdenka Mansfeldová (2006), *The European Union and Party Politics in Central and Eastern Europe*, Palgrave). One could argue by analogy, that since judicial reform and compliance with European human rights standards was emphasised in the Copenhagen criteria of 1993, on the basis of which Slovenia and Poland (among others) ratified the European Convention, it is possible that ECHR issues may already have become 'valence issues' in the new member states. For a discussion on 'valence' versus 'positional' issues, see Herbert Kitschelt, Zdenka Mansfeldová, Radoslaw Markowski, Gábor Tóka (1999), *Post-Communist Party Systems: competition, representation, and inter-party cooperation*, CUP. In the context of the new member states of CEE, the accession process itself tended to create a strong executive at the expense of the legislature and judiciary. This 'executive bias' has in particular been identified in the mechanism which developed during the accession process whereby the legislature was obliged to hastily endorse laws submitted by the executive in order to meet the conditions for EU accession, resulting in the parliament's 'rubber-stamping' of legislation. See, e.g.: Heather Grabbe (2006), *The EU's Transformative Power: Europeanization through conditionality in Central and Eastern Europe*, Palgrave, pp. 207–208. In some states, however, as we note for example in the cases of *Olaru* and *Manole v Moldova* in Chapter 5, there has since developed a tendency for opposition parties to use Strasbourg judgments to support their own platforms, or even to help institutionalise their own power. What is interesting is that whereas the EU developed an 'executive bias', in contrast the dynamic of the European Court may act to some extent in the opposite way, enabling opposition parties and domestic higher courts more effectively to challenge the executive when it either introduces a dysfunctional law, or otherwise fails to execute European Court judgments.

20 The bicameral structure of parliament in Slovenia is based on the French model, where the upper house, the National Council, is elected by local officials and representatives of interest groups to represent regional and commercial interests rather than political interest groups or

a trial without undue delay – the 'Lukenda Law'[21] – could be interpreted as a reflection of this consensus position, or alternatively of Parliament's exasperation at the ongoing saga of the unresolved problem of overly long domestic proceedings. This legislation was amended just one week before the Court issued another judgment relating to the excessive length of domestic proceedings – the *Robert Lesjak* case (see section 3.4).[22]

3.2. THE CAUSES OF THE EXCESSIVE LENGTH OF LEGAL PROCEEDINGS IN SLOVENIA

According to a number of our respondents, court procedures became very protracted after the reorganisation of the court system in Slovenia in the 1990s. This reorganisation involved the creation of a second type of first instance court in 1994 based on the Austrian model. During the period that followed a lot of court staff were transferred, causing considerable disruption to judicial proceedings.[23] Boštjan and Mateja Verstovšek, the applicants' legal representatives in the cases of *Lukenda* and *Robert Lesjak*, told us:

> "... the reorganisation took about a year, and nobody worked during that time ... and more cases were filed to the courts ... We explained to every client that he would have to wait three years to the first hearing from filing the lawsuit. And for courts this was the normal state."[24]

The 1997 EU Accession Report on Slovenia estimated that it took as long as five years for civil cases to be brought to court. The report attributed key causes for delays to the fact that judges were poorly paid and there were too few judges as a result of the minimum age requirement of 30.[25] The problems caused by reorganisation have been compounded by the fact that litigation is very commonplace in Slovenia, according to our respondents, who consider that the large volume of cases that come to court is a significant cause of the delays in processing and the subsequent deferment of proceedings in Slovenian courts. The resultant backlog has in turn led to a mass of applications to the European

---

parties. Deputies to the lower house, the National Assembly, are elected according to party in national elections.

21 *Zakon o varstvu pravice do sojenja brez nepotrebnega odlašanja (ZVPSBNO)* 12.5.06 = *Act on the Protection of the Right to a trial without undue delay* [this will be referred to hereafter as the 2006 Law].

22 *Lesjak (Robert) v Slovenia*, No. 33946/03, 21.7.09.

23 Peter Pavlin, Slovenian Government Agent, written response to questions, 28.11.09.

24 Interview with Boštjan and Mateja Verstovšek, legal represenatives for *Lukenda* and *Robert Lesjak*, 17.6.09.

25 European Commission (1997), *Agenda 2000 – Commission Opinion on Slovenia's Application for Membership of the European Union*, http://ec.europa.eu/enlargement/archives/pdf/dwn/opinions/slovenia/sn-op_en.pdf.

Court alleging a violation of the right to trial within a reasonable time. By the end of 2009 there had been 209 adverse judgments against Slovenia concerning this violation of the European Convention.[26]

Other aspects of the prevailing legal culture have exacerbated these delays. According to the Constitutional Court Judge Marija Krisper Kramberger, parties to legal proceedings generally do not trust lower courts to have sufficient legitimacy and therefore they tend to utilise all the available ordinary and extraordinary legal appeals, and, after that, they lodge a constitutional complaint with the Constitutional Court. They consider the latter to be an appellate court, rather than a court which has the competence to decide constitutional complaints against decisions violating human rights. Judge Marija Krisper Kramberger told us that the practice of lodging constitutional complaints in 'minor cases' has even resulted in backlogs at the Constitutional Court. The Act amending the Constitutional Court Act (adopted in 2007) was aimed at limiting the number of constitutional complaints. The Constitutional Court is thus no longer competent to decide 'minor cases' (save in exceptional cases – when a decision concerns an important constitutional question which exceeds the importance of the concrete case), and will accordingly reject such complaints. Nevertheless, the influx of such cases still burdens the Constitutional Court:

> "... I think that our judicial culture is still not mature enough to allow us to really make people understand that we are not – in simple words – a rubbish bin."[27]

It was even suggested to us – by both the Ombudsman's Office and the Ministry of Justice – that a culture of lengthy trials has become institutionalised, in that judges are reluctant to take decisions or process cases quickly as they perceive an expectation among litigants that unless proceedings have taken a certain length of time, then they cannot have been investigated properly.[28] In some instances where cases have been speedily processed, individuals have complained to the Ombudsman claiming that the length of the trial was insufficient to allow a thorough investigation of the case.[29] However, we were also told that this argument could simply be an excuse, on the part of an unsuccessful applicant, in support of their case being re-opened, or according to one respondent, self-justification on the part of the judge responsible for a delay.[30]

---

26 European Court of Human Rights (2010), *The European Court of Human Rights: Some facts and figures*, p. 17, http://www.echr.coe.int/NR/rdonlyres/ACD46A0F-615A-48B9-89D6-8480AFCC29FD/0/FactsAndFigures_EN.pdf.

27 Interview with Judge Marija Krisper Kramberger, Constitutional Court, Ljubljana, 3.6.09.

28 Interview with Ivan Šelih and Jernej Rovšek, Ombudsman's Office, Ljubljana, 2.6.09; Interview with Peter Pavlin, Ministry of Justice, Ljubljana, 1.6.09.

29 Interview with Ivan Šelih and Jernej Rovšek, Ombudsman's Office, Ljubljana, 2.6.09.

30 Interview with Neža Kogovšek, Peace Institute, Ljubljana, 1.6.09.

Respondents also attested that there is a widespread lack of respect for the courts in Slovenia. For example, it was said that when the courts summon individuals, they often fail to turn up. As a result, the courts waste resources by re-sending summons, which slows down the procedure considerably.[31] Additionally, delays are caused by problems in delivering official documents to the parties.[32] When summoned either as a witness or even as a defendant,[33] individuals fail to appear in court and there are insufficient sanctions to discourage this practice.[34] One NGO lawyer described to us how this has led in some instances to 'inertia' on the part of judges:

> "There was ... one criminal proceeding where the ... suspect hadn't shown up 5 or 6 times and the judge didn't want to bring him before the Court to put him in custody ... she tried to avoid that – I really don't understand why ... The [victim] was actually handicapped after the car accident and she didn't take any actions – I was a bit surprised and shocked about it."[35]

It is possible that such leniency could perhaps be explained by the judge's low expectations of the efficacy of the sanctions that could be applied, or that there are insufficient sanctions available. According to the Verstovšek lawyers, who have represented many such cases, the majority of cases relating to length of proceedings are compensation claims filed against insurance companies, who are said to be particularly prone to drawing out the procedures and the courts have no way to take sanctions to prevent such delays. For example in 2006, the number of Slovenian cases dealt with by the European Court that originated from cases against insurance firms was approximately 60% of all length of proceedings cases.[36] 86 of these cases[37] in 2006 had originally been filed against one particular insurance firm, 'Z.T.'[38] According to one NGO lawyer, insurance companies often only pay a certain amount of the damages owing and then postpone paying the

31 Interview with Ivan Šelih and Jernej Rovšek, Ombudsman's Office, Ljubljana, 2.6.09; Interview with Neža Kogovšek, Peace Institute, Ljubljana, 1.6.09; Interview with Vita Habjan, PIC, Ljubljana, 03.06.09.

32 Interview with Ivan Šelih and Jernej Rovšek, Ombudsman's Office, Ljubljana, 2.6.09.

33 Interview with Vita Habjan, PIC, Ljubljana, 3.6.09.

34 Interview with Ivan Šelih and Jernej Rovšek, Ombudsman's Office, Ljubljana, 2.6.09; Interview with Neža Kogovšek, Peace Institute, Ljubljana, 1.6.09.

35 Interview with Vita Habjan, PIC, Ljubljana, 3.6.09.

36 There were some 203 Slovenian length of proceedings cases, of which 118 constituted cases which originated against insurance firms. These figures were compiled through research using HUDOC. http://cmiskp.echr.coe.int/tkp197/search.asp?sessionid=44332630&skin=hudoc-en.

37 That is about 70% of all cases originally filed against insurance companies that were judged by the European Court in 2006 (against Slovenia). These figures were compiled through research using HUDOC. http://cmiskp.echr.coe.int/tkp197/search.asp?sessionid=44332630&skin=hudoc-en.

38 Zavarovalnica Triglav = Triglav Insurance. This is the largest insurance firm in Slovenia, and has branches in Croatia and Bosnia and Herzegovina: Peter Pavlin, Slovenian Government Agent, written response to questions, 28.11.09.

remainder. In these cases, claimants often lack the means to start proceedings against the insurance companies and, in urgent need of the compensation, agree to settle for less to guarantee receipt of their claim in the short term. In this way insurance companies pay less in compensation; or if claimants do file for more damages then the proceedings are further drawn out.[39] The lawyers Boštjan and Mateja Verstovšek told us:

> "... 90 per cent of lawsuits were for personal injuries ... – people hurt in accidents and so on ... and ... no interest on [damages] ... was granted ... from filing the lawsuit to the first court decision. There was no sanction for the insurance companies for that delay. They could argue in court for years and there was no [monetary] sanction ..."[40]

According to members of the judiciary with whom we spoke, there are various problems; a number of these are cultural or institutional and others are the result of legislation. One judge told us that there is administrative malpractice,[41] which some respondents explained as being the result of an incentive system that fails to reward efficiency and fails to sanction malpractice.[42] Laws are evidently not always clear,[43] and are sometimes conflicting,[44] which can lead to difficulties for judges in interpreting legislation. Moreover, legislation is constantly changing, which inevitably slows down the legal process as judges need time to familiarise themselves with new laws and amendments.[45] According to one respondent, since the emphasis is on written documentation, rather than the oral testimony of witnesses, judges are required to perform more administrative work than they do in other legal systems, and their attempts to obtain information or data to support their judgments can meet with no response:

> "... judges are doing a lot of administrative work, writing to different institutions ... and, of course, before you write a letter it takes a week, before you get an answer it takes a month, before you ask for additional information it takes a few weeks ..."[46]

According to Peter Pavlin, Undersecretary of the Directorate for Legislation on the Justice system in the Ministry of Justice, two-thirds of lengthy trials have

39 Correspondence with Vita Habjan, Legal Information Centre (Pravno-Informacijski Center, Ljubljana, 2.11.09.

40 Interview with Boštjan and Mateja Verstovšek, 17.6.09.

41 Interview with Zinka Strašek, President of the Higher Court, Celje, 1.6.09.

42 Interview with Vita Habjan PIC, Ljubljana, 3.6.09. Interview with Neža Kogovšek, Peace Institute, Ljubljana, 1.6.09; Interview with Zinka Strašek, President of the Supreme Court Celje, 1.6.09.

43 Interview with Ivan Šelih and Jernej Rovšek, Ombudsman's Office, Ljubljana, 2.6.09.

44 Interview with Zinka Strašek, President of the Higher Court, Celje, 1.6.09.

45 Interview with Neža Kogovšek, Peace Institute, Ljubljana, 1.6.09.

46 Interview with Neža Kogovšek, Peace Institute, Ljubljana, 1.6.09.

been the result of systemic problems and the appeal process. Furthermore, delays resulting from cases being referred back and forth between courts of first and second instance (a process he described as 'ping-pong justice'), have been particularly problematic.[47]

Other respondents argued that personnel and staffing issues contribute to inefficiency and delays. The common perception that judges are not very well paid was also considered to be significant,[48] and according to some interviewees, individuals are often promoted to judicial positions with insufficient 'life-experience' and training for the post.[49] It was also claimed by some respondents that as the majority of Slovenian judges are women, and are relatively young, judges' maternity leave and other staff turnover have caused disruption to legal proceedings.[50] A number of interviewees considered that an increase in staff providing technical support, such as court assistants, could expedite proceedings considerably.[51]

In the next section we provide a brief case-study of the local courts in Celje which have been the cause of a particularly large number of applications to the European Court (including *Lukenda*).

THE PARTICULAR PROBLEM IN CELJE

Undue length of proceedings is apparently particularly problematic for the courts in the area of Celje, the third largest town in Slovenia, situated in the Savinjsko Region. Although some relevant data was forthcoming, our research did not allow a thorough investigation of this matter and we were therefore unable to draw firm conclusions as to why this is so. According to one respondent the Celje courts have been less efficient than other courts mainly because of particular practices by judges in these courts and bad management.[52] The current President of the Higher Court of Celje, Zinka Strašek, confirmed that in the past bad practice and management was a significant causal factor in delays to proceedings.[53] The scale of this problem is apparent from the fact that the vast majority of cases

---

47 Interview with Peter Pavlin, Ministry of Justice, Ljubljana, 1.6.09.

48 Interview with Boštjan and Mateja Verstovšek, legal represenatives for *Lukenda* and *Robert Lesjak*, 17.6.09.

49 Interview with Ivan Šelih and Jernej Rovšek, Ombudsman's Office, Ljubljana, 2.6.09; Interview with Neža Kogovšek, Peace Institute, Ljubljana, 1.6.09; Interview with Zinka Strašek, President of the Supreme Court Celje, 1.6.09.

50 Interview with Ivan Šelih and Jernej Rovšek, Ombudsman's Office, Ljubljana, 2.6.09; Interview with Neža Kogovšek, Peace Institute, Ljubljana, 1.6.09.

51 Interview with Zinka Strašek, President of the Higher Court, Celje, 1.6.09; Interview with Vita Habjan, PIC, Ljubljana, 3.6.09.

52 Interview with Boštjan and Mateja Verstovšek, 17.6.09.

53 Interview with Zinka Strašek, President of the Higher Court, Celje, 1.6.09.

concerning length of proceedings complaints that have been submitted to Strasbourg were originally filed at the Celje courts. This may in part be due to the efforts of one law firm, Verstovšek, which has been particularly active in this field, and the catchment area of its clients. As noted in a number of European Court judgments this firm represented some hundreds of applicants to the Court in length of proceedings cases. According to the Verstovšek lawyers, the number of applicants the firm represented in total at the time of the *Lukenda* judgment, in 2005, was around 800, including the applicants in both the *Lukenda* and *Robert Lesjak* cases. When asked why these cases were particularly prevalent in the Celje courts, the Verstovšek lawyers replied:

> "Because the court in Celje ... is blocked. Every case in Celje ... from filing the lawsuit to the first hearing of the court took approximately two to three years – and then the procedure took on average two to three years for the decision."[54]

Precisely why this is the case in Celje, however, is difficult to determine. Some respondents suggested it is because the courts tend not to investigate these cases.[55] In spite of the fact that there appears to be a disproportionate problem with delays in proceedings from Celje, the 2006 Law stipulated that all civil proceedings for damages that would normally fall within the jurisdiction of the District Court of Maribor are to be dealt with by the District Court in Celje.[56] We can infer from this that the number of cases coming to Celje would accordingly have increased. The rationale for re-directing Maribor cases to Celje was, according, to Government Agent Peter Pavlin, because there was a concern that the Maribor court, the second largest in Slovenia, would develop backlogs dealing with these cases. Provision for this extra anticipated workload was made to compensate the courts in the form of funding for the appointment of more judges and court clerks.[57] However, as we touch on later, in section 3.3.1.4., problems with these provisions in Celje were identified by the European Court in 2007. Nonetheless the 2009 amendments to the law clarify that the jurisdiction should 'exclusively' lie with the Celje District Court.[58] It is possible that as a result of this clarification, it is likely that the court will receive even more cases. Indeed when asked whether the proposed 2009 amendments to the law would improve the situation in the

---

54 Interview with Boštjan and Mateja Verstovšek 17.6.09.

55 Interview with Judge Klakočar of the Supreme Court, Ljubljana, 1.6.09.

56 Similarly, according to this clause, all such cases normally falling within the jurisdiction of Ljubljana would be dealt with by the District Court in Kranj. *Zakon o varstvu pravice do sojenja brez nepotrebnega odlašanja (ZVPSBNO) 49/2006 2091 12.05.06, 20(4) = Law on the Right to trial without undue delay (ZVPSBNO)* 12.5.06, Article 20(4) http://www.uradni-list.si/1/content?id=73309&part=&highlight=ZVPSBNO (last accessed 9.4.10).

57 Peter Pavlin, Slovenian Government Agent, written response to questions, 28.11.09.

58 *Zakon o spremembah in dopolnitvah Zakona o varstvu pravice do sojenja brez nepotrebnega odlašanja (ZVPSBNO-A), 58/2009, 2867 27.07.09, 20(4) = Law amending the implementation of the law on the right to trial within reasonable time*, 27.7.09, Article 20(4) http://www.uradni-list.si/1/content?id=93400&part=&highlight=ZVPSBNO-A (last accessed 9.4.10).

Celje Higher Court, the President of the Court said that it would make it worse, as there were an increasing number of similar applications filed.[59]

3.3. EXCESSIVE LENGTH OF PROCEEDINGS: THE CASES OF *BELINGER & LUKENDA*

The problem of unreasonably long legal proceedings, and the lack of an effective domestic remedy in Slovenia to provide redress, was first raised at the European Court in the case of *Belinger* which was declared admissible in 2001. In its decision the Court found the existing remedies, in particular the 1977 and 1997 Administrative Disputes Acts, to be ineffective on the basis of the evidence of the backlogs in the Slovenian courts, as noted by the EU Commission during Slovenia's accession negotiations. The Court therefore ruled that the applicant was not obliged to have availed himself of these remedies before applying to Strasbourg.[60]

The parties in the *Belinger* case subsequently agreed to a friendly settlement (with the Slovenian Government simply paying compensation of €3,700), and the case was struck out in 2002.[61] The systemic problem in the domestic courts was accordingly not considered by the European Court, and it certainly wasn't resolved. Had the *Belinger* case been decided on the merits, the Court could at that stage have indicated the systemic nature of the problem in Slovenia. Instead, however, the Court struck out the case as having been settled, invoking Article 39 of the Convention. It also found that the settlement was "based on respect for human rights", in accordance with Article 37. Of course, the Convention always provides the parties with the option of settlement, which arguably reflects the notion of subsidiarity, but, in a case of this nature, to allow the parties to come to an individual agreement, without resolving a structural problem, could be considered to be ill-judged. It means that the systemic problem remains unresolved, that others will accordingly become victims of it too, and that more 'clone' applications will appear at the European Court. The better course in such situations, in spite of any agreement between the parties, is arguably for the Court to continue the examination of the case, as it may do under Article 37, if "respect for human rights … requires" – a decision dealing with the substantive issue being 'required' in order to try to resolve the core structural problem. By the time of the *Lukenda* judgment in 2005, hundreds of similar applications from

59 Interview with Zinka Strašek, President of the Higher Court of Celje, 1.6.09.
60 *Belinger v Slovenia*, No. 42320/98, dec. 2.10.01, pp. 9–10.
61 *Belinger v Slovenia*, No. 42320/98, 13.6.02, para. 11.

Slovenia had been declared admissible by the Court,[62] and the Court found this to be evidence of the Slovenian Government's failure to expedite court cases and amend the Administrative Disputes Act to provide an effective complaints procedure, in response to the *Belinger* case.[63] Indeed the Slovenian Government has confirmed that the *Lukenda* judgment came as no surprise.[64]

3.3.1. THE 'QUASI-PILOT' JUDGMENT OF *LUKENDA V SLOVENIA*

Franjo Lukenda was injured at work, in a lignite mine, in 1994 and consequently received disability benefits through his employer's insurance company (his disability was assessed at 13%). In 1998, he requested from the insurance company a 7% increase to his benefits, on the basis of an expert medical opinion, which was rejected. He began civil proceedings at the Celje Local Court, and in 2002 the court upheld his claim in part. Mr Lukenda appealed to the Celje Higher Court and in 2004 the court decided to increase his disability benefits and awarded him costs and expenses. Mr Lukenda's subsequent complaint to the European Court, that the proceedings (lasting more then 5 years and three months) were unreasonably long, was upheld in October 2005. Both Article 6(1) and Article 13 of the European Convention were found to have been violated. The Court noted that there had been no substantive changes to the Administrative Disputes Act since its decision in *Belinger*, and in view of the continuing backlog of cases in the Slovenian courts, it found that there was no effective domestic remedy. Citing the Committee of Ministers' 2004 Resolution,[65] applying Article 46, and relying on a variety of sources, the Court signalled that the problem necessitated legislative and administrative change:

> "In view of the persistent backlog in the Slovenian courts in general, as reported in the latest statistics published by the Ministry of Justice of the respondent State, it is clear that the length of judicial proceedings remains a major problem in Slovenia. In addition, the Government, with the aid of the Supreme Court, produced a document in 2002 in which it conceded that there were delays in judicial proceedings. The European Commission reached similar conclusions in its last report on the readiness of Slovenia to accede to the European Union published in November 2003. Furthermore, the Slovenian Human Rights Ombudsman

---

62 *Lukenda v Slovenia,* No. 23032/02, 6.10.05, para 40. The judgment states that the Verstovšek lawyers were representing other applicants in nearly 400 other length of proceedings cases at the European Court.

63 *Lukenda v Slovenia*, No. 23032/02, 6.10.05, paras. 51–53.

64 Interview with Peter Pavlin Ministry of Justice, Ljubljana, 1.6.09.

65 Committee of Ministers (2004), *Resolution Res(2004)3 of the Committee of Ministers on judgments revealing an underlying systemic problem (adopted by the Committee of Ministers on 12 May 2004, at its 114th Session).* https://wcd.coe.int/ViewDoc.jsp?id=743257&Lang=fr.

observed in his report for the year 2004 that the most serious problem facing the Slovenian legal system was the length of court proceedings ..."

"It is intrinsic to the Court's findings that the violation of the applicant's right to a trial within a reasonable time is not an isolated incident, but rather a systemic problem that has resulted from inadequate legislation and inefficiency in the administration of justice. The problem continues to present a danger affecting every person seeking judicial protection of their rights."[66]

The obligation placed on the Slovenian Government to "secure the right to a trial within a reasonable time" was included in the operative provisions of the Court's judgment.[67]

At the time, there were about 500 length of proceedings cases against Slovenia pending at the Court.

3.3.1.1. The impact of Lukenda *on domestic law*

A month before the *Lukenda* decision was published, the Constitutional Court issued a judgment, in September 2005, in response to a complaint filed by a Ljubljana lawyer, Marta Dominika Jelačin, in February 2005, concerning the alleged unconstitutionality of the Administrative Disputes Act.[68] The Constitutional Court judgment declared the Act incompatible with Article 15(4) of the Constitution, and Article 6(1) of the European Convention, and required that the Government remedy the matter within a year of publication of the judgment. The judgment stated that the right to compensation for a delay in proceedings should only apply to proceedings which had been concluded and that compensation should be awarded, not as damages according to the criteria of civil liability, but rather "due to the omission of the positive duty of the state to ensure a system or organization of proceedings such that would enable the individual to obtain a decision of the court within a reasonable time."[69]

As a consequence of both the *Lukenda* European Court judgment and the *Jelačin* Constitutional Court judgment, the Slovenian Government undertook an investigation and launched an initiative, known as the 'Lukenda Project', with the goal of eliminating domestic court backlogs by the end of 2010.[70] The project

---

66 *Lukenda v Slovenia*, No. 23032/02, 6.10.05, paras. 91–93.

67 As we discuss in chapter one (see section 1.2.2), this is not usual for a 'quasi-pilot' or 'Article 46' judgment. However, as the Court did not expressly state that it was applying the pilot judgment procedure, we have not characterised the case as a 'full' pilot judgment (see section 1.2.1.7).

68 *Zakon o upravnem sporu* 50/97, 65/97, amended 70/2000.

69 U-I-65/05 22.9.05.

70 *Joint state project 'the elimination of court backlogs: the Lukenda project, operational plan* Ljubljana, 12.12.05, p. 1.

sought to introduce a package of reforms in the wake of *Lukenda* to address the Court's recommendations. In particular, the 2006 *Law on the Protection of the Right to Trial Without Undue Delay,* (ZVPSBNO)[71] was introduced in January 2007. The legislation was based on the Italian *Pinto* Act, and on the Polish and Czech laws of 2004.[72] It stipulated maximum time limits for case processing in courts and issued standards for the length of procedures, including the preparatory stages of legal proceedings, prior to trials. It gave applicants the right to lodge a 'supervisory appeal', in which case the president of the court must determine whether or not the complaint is justified. If the president dismisses the complaint because there is no 'indication of circumstances or other particulars concerning the case, which demonstrate that the court is unduly protracting the decision-making', then applicants have no right of appeal against the president's decision. In the event that the complaint is not dismissed, then the relevant judge is required to explain the reasons for the duration of the proceedings, and complete them within four months of receipt of the supervisory appeal. If the president considers that the judge is protracting the decision-making, then deadlines may be set for completion of certain aspects of the proceedings. Deadlines set by the president can range from fifteen days to six months. Should an applicant's appeal be dismissed at that stage, then a motion for a deadline may be lodged. If the motion is considered justified, the president can then set deadlines ranging from fifteen days to four months. Should the president consider that the judge in question is overburdened with work, or that the delay is the result of extended absence, the president may reassign the case to another judge. Applicants may claim compensation after lodging a supervisory appeal or motion for deadline but are not allowed to file further appeals until existing deadlines have been exceeded.[73] This law applies to civil, administrative and criminal proceedings.[74]

Furthermore, a new appeal procedure was set up to handle complaints and 140 new judges, 650 new technical personnel and 175 administrative staff were appointed to help expedite proceedings.[75] The legislative amendments introduced as part of the *Lukenda* Project were considerable, as we discuss below.

---

71 *Zakon o varstvu pravice do sojenja brez nepotrebnega odlašanja (ZVPSBNO)* 12.5.06 = *Act on the Protection of the Right to a trial without undue delay.*

72 Peter Pavlin (2006), *Overview of the contents of the protection of the right to a trial without undue delay act of the Republic of Slovenia of 2006*, Ministry of Justice, p. 7.

73 See, *e.g.*, *Žunič (Branko) v Slovenia*, No. 24342/04, dec. 18.10.07, paras 20–22.

74 Sections 1 and 2 of the 2006 Law.

75 Interview with Peter Pavlin, Ministry of Justice, Ljubljana, 1.6.09.

3.3.1.2. *Changes in the law to make administrative procedures in courts more efficient*

As we have discussed above (see section 3.2), our respondents referred to various administrative problems that cause delays in legal proceedings. The Government has sought to address some of these problems by adopting legislative changes. For example, the Civil Procedure Act ('*Zakon o pravdnem postopku*') was amended in 2008 to introduce tougher sanctions for failing to respond to court summons.[76] As a way to discourage the parties from re-scheduling hearings, which was causing delays, a new Court Fee Act introduced a fine for cancelling hearings. Additionally, the law stipulated that higher courts could not return cases to lower courts, in order to eliminate delays caused by 'ping pong justice'.

3.3.1.3. *Alternative means of dispute resolution*

According to our respondents, one of the main reasons for the unreasonable length of legal proceedings in Slovenia is the large volume of cases taken to court (and appealed) each year (especially civil proceedings). Clearly one strategy for improving the length of proceedings would be to reduce the number of cases coming to court each year. For this purpose, the government is trying to encourage individuals to make use of alternative forms of dispute resolution, such as mediation.[77] In 2008 amendments to the Civil Procedure Act made greater provision for the use and encouragement of mediation.[78] This is considered an important step towards reducing the number of cases flooding the courts in Slovenia each year, as Constitutional Court Judge Marija Krisper Kramberger suggested to us.[79]

THE ATTORNEY'S LAW (ZAKON O ODVETNIŠTVU)

However, we also heard concerns that measures taken to reduce the number of cases coming to court had been at the expense of the independence of the legal profession and public access to justice. The argument runs as follows: by increasing court fees and consistently awarding just a small percentage of the legal costs to successful applicants, this is acting as a disincentive for applicants to file cases. Additionally where previously the Bar Association had determined rates for legal fees which were then approved by the Ministry of Justice, following *Lukenda*, in 2009 the Attorney's Law was passed, making Parliament responsible for determining lawyers' fees.[80] One lawyer told us:

---

76 The law came into force on 1 October 2008.

77 Interview with Vita Habjan, PIC, Ljubljana, 3.6.09.

78 Interview with Zinka Strašek, President of the Higher Court, Celje, 1.6.09; Interview with Vita Habjan, PIC, Ljubljana, 3.6.09.

79 Interview with Judge Marija Krisper Kramberger, Constitutional Court, Ljubljana, 3.6.09.

80 Zakon o odvetništvu, 27.3.09.

> "In this way, the Parliament is able to undermine the independence of the profession, in the sense that it regulates the obedience of lawyers through inadequate fees which do not suffice for normal work."[81]

However, this section of the law was held to be unconstitutional in April 2009, following an application to the Constitutional Court by one third of the parliament demanding a referendum on the issue. Although the Constitutional Court rejected holding a referendum, it held this aspect of the law to be unconstitutional on the basis that it would not ensure the effective implementation of legal aid.[82] It reasoned that if Parliament were to set attorneys' fees, this would reduce the wage below attorneys' expectations, and would make them reluctant to agree to represent clients on a legal aid basis. So, once again, the Bar Association has regained its right to set fee levels.[83]

3.3.1.4. *How effective was the application of the pilot judgment procedure in the case of* Lukenda?

When asked whether the situation had improved following the 2006 Law, respondents agreed that it had.[84] Statistics from the Ministry of Justice indicated some improvement and the Ombudsman's Office told us their impressionistic view confirmed this.[85] We were informed that there was a 4% reduction in the number of cases pending in 2008, compared with the previous year.[86] However, the legislation may have given rise to other procedural problems, such as those experienced at the Supreme Court. According to Judge Klakočar, from the Supreme Court, there was some confusion as to how the law should be applied, and whether or not it should be applied in accordance with administrative or civil procedure. Additionally, there was no provision in the law for appeal to the Supreme Court. Under these difficult circumstances the Supreme Court was

---

81 E-mail response to questionnaire from Zlatko Lipej, lawyer, Medvode, 15.7.09.

82 Slovenia. Ustavno Sodišče. *Odločba o ugotoviti, da bi odložitvijo uveljavite oziroma z zavrnitvijo zakona o spremembah in dopolnitvah zakona o odvetništvu lahko nastale protiustavne posledice = The decision to determine whether the proposed postponement with respect to the rejection of the amendments to the Attorney's law will have unconstitutional consequences*, Uradni list RS, št. 35/2009, 08.05.09, http://www.uradni-list.si/1/content?id=92090 (last accessed 9.4.10).

83 Government Communication Office. News. 09.05.09. 'Amended Attorney's Act Takes Effect' See: *http://www.ukom.gov.si/en/news/newsletter_slovenia_news/news/article/393/147/f210e94b84/?tx_ttnews%5Bnewsletter%5D=7*; *http://www.uradni-list.si/1/objava.jsp?urlid=200935&stevilka=1644*.

84 Interview with Ivan Šelih and Jernej Rovšek, Ombudsman's Office, Ljubljana, 2.6.09; Interview with Neža Kogovšek, Peace Institute, Ljubljana, 1.6.09; Interview with Peter Pavlin, Ministry of Justice, Ljubljana, 1.6.09.

85 Interview with Ivan Šelih and Jernej Rovšek, Ombudsman's Office, Ljubljana, 2.6.09.

86 As of 31 December 2007 there were 287,175 cases pending and at 31 December 2008 this had reduced to 276,332; Interview with Peter Pavlin and Zoran Skubic, Ministry of Justice, Ljubljana, 1.6.09.

bombarded with applications for supervisory review.[87] Thus we may well question whether the application of the pilot judgment procedure in the case of *Lukenda* has had the desired effect.

A number of respondents expressed their concern that the 2006 Law has not in fact helped to solve the endemic problem of lengthy legal proceedings and that the European Court judgment had simply 'repatriated' cases, requiring applicants to exhaust another domestic remedy before being eligible to apply to Strasbourg.[88] Neža Kogovšek, of the Peace Institute, suggested that:

> "... the 2006 Law actually ... doesn't remove the systemic problems that are causing lengthy [proceedings]. I will use a very basic example. In Slovenia, before the trial starts there are a few months and if the trial is not finished in the first phase it is postponed for several months, depending on how busy the judge dealing with the case is, or the court in general. So the trial is postponed ... and then the witness doesn't show up and the trial is postponed, and then the defendant doesn't show up and it's again postponed ... every time it's postponed for a couple of months, even for half a year if ... the judge ... can't do it earlier ... and ... cases are being transferred from one judge to another ..."[89]

This view is redolent of Judge Josep Casadevall's partly dissenting opinion in *Kudła*, in which he objected to the Court's requirement that Poland provide a new domestic remedy on the grounds that it would further lengthen the procedure for applicants: "ultimately only the litigant would suffer the consequences of this situation".[90] Similarly, Judge Vladimiro Zagrebelsky's partly dissenting opinion in *Lukenda* did not dispute that there had been a systemic violation of Article 6, but rather questioned whether the Court had over-reached its powers in specifying in the operative provisions of the judgment that Slovenia must introduce "appropriate legal measures and administrative practices [to] secure the right to a trial within a reasonable time". Judge Zagrebelsky suggested that such directives should instead be issued by the Committee of Ministers:

> "In my view, such an indication to the Government falls outside the scope of a judgment of this Court (and probably of any court). It appears to me to be too general. It implies the need to identify the requested measures and, in so doing, to examine whether the laws concerning procedures must be changed (and if so how), to evaluate whether the number of judges and administrative personnel and their level of qualification are commensurate with the task, to increase and modernise the resources made available to the judiciary, to adjust the national

[87] Interview with Judge Klakočar of the Supreme Court, Ljubljana, 1.6.09.
[88] Interview with Ivan Šelih and Jernej Rovšek, Ombudsman's Office, Ljubljana, 2.6.09.
[89] Interview with Neža Kogovšek, Peace Institute, Ljubljana, 1.6.09.
[90] *Kudła v Poland*, No. 30210/96, 26.10.00, Partly Dissenting Opinion of Judge Casadevall, para. 5.

> yearly budget accordingly, and to tackle the issue of the number of lawyers, their level of qualification and their role in dealing with civil disputes. When there is a 'systemic problem' underlying the incapacity of a State to provide trials within a reasonable time, all these questions must be taken into consideration. In addition a particular system might labour under other specific difficulties … the Court is requesting the Government to change the national system in law and in practice. Nothing more, nothing less.
>
> I do not think that this can be regarded as a judgment of a court. It is not an order that can be executed as judicial orders usually are. The timing and monitoring of the quality and suitability of the 'execution' measures that the Government should introduce can only be guessed at. In my view it is up to the Committee of Ministers to identify, request, suggest, secure and monitor the measures which appear to be necessary."[91]

Since the *Lukenda* judgment, and the ensuing package of reforms, the Court continued communicating cases to Slovenia concerning excessive length of proceedings, which indicated that this problem remained unresolved. By May 2007, there were almost 1,700 such cases pending at the Court against Slovenia.[92] In that month, however, in the cases of *Grzinčič* and *Korenjak* the Court found that, in principle, the remedies available under the 2006 Law provided a means of preventing the continuation of the violation of the right to a hearing without undue delay and provided adequate redress for a violation that had occurred. The Court found that there was no reason to doubt the effectiveness of the new Law at that time, although the decisions acknowledged the difficulties inherent in making such an assessment:

> "It is true that no long-term practice of domestic authorities applying the 2006 Act can be established at this time. However, it is clear that the Act was specifically designed to address the issue of the excessive length of proceedings before domestic courts and there is no reason to doubt its effectiveness at this stage. However, the Court's position may be subject to review in the future and the burden of proof as to the effectiveness of the remedies in practice remains on the Slovenian Government."[93]

The decision in the case of *Žunič v Slovenia,*[94] however, was different. Unlike the *Grzinčič* and *Korenjak* cases, where the applicants had not made use of the Lukenda Law, Branko Žunič had appealed in accordance with the 2006 Law. However, his request to have his case expedited was dismissed by the Celje District

---

91 *Lukenda v Slovenia*, No. 23032/02, 6.10.05, Partly Dissenting Opinion of Judge Zagrebelsky.

92 *Korenjak v Slovenia*, No. 463/03, 15.5.07, para. 69.

93 *Grzinčič v Slovenia*, No. 26867/02, 3.5.07, para. 108; *Korenjak v Slovenia*, No. 463/03, dec. 15.5.07, para. 73.

94 *Žunič (Branko) v Slovenia*, No. 24342/04, dec. 18.10.07.

Court, apparently because the judge concerned was overburdened. The European Court noted that:

> "... the President of the Celje District Court ... relied on the fact that the applicant's case had not been granted priority; that the judge C.K ... had to deal with 264 other cases, some of them much older than the applicant's; that the order of precedence had to be respected; and that the delays in the present case had resulted from systemic problems and were not the fault of the judge. The President of the Celje District Court therefore deemed it impossible to order any of the measures stipulated in the 2006 Act ... [noting] that since other judges were likewise overburdened, it would not be sensible to assign the case to another judge. Moreover, seven new judicial posts had been created at the court as a result of the Lukenda Project ... three of which had been filled, and the rest of which were in the process of being filled. According to him, this would, reduce delays in the future."[95]

Although the Court found the situation in Celje 'regrettable', it nevertheless acknowledged that the judicial system required time to resolve the issues underlying the problem, including the inefficiency of the court system:

> "... the Court is aware of the fact that the reasons underlying the systemic problem of excessive length of judicial proceedings, such as inefficiency in the administration of justice, cannot be eliminated immediately ... Article 13 ... offers an alternative: a remedy is 'effective' if it can be used either to expedite the proceedings or to provide adequate redress, such as just satisfaction, for delays that have already occurred ..."[96]

Not without some hesitation, the Court acknowledged the reasons why Mr Žunič's application for accelerative remedies was rejected and dismissed the case on the understanding that Žunič would still be able to claim compensation under the 2006 Law. Since the President of the Celje Higher Court has expressed concern that the amendments to the 2006 Law are likely to impose a greater burden on judges, it is possible that workload problems may continue to impact upon the speed of processing overall in Celje.[97]

The Court in *Žunič* went out of its way to emphasise the need for the Slovenian government to show evidence that proceedings were being expedited as a result of the *Lukenda Project*:

---

95 *Ibid.*, para. 13.
96 *Ibid.*, para. 45.
97 Interview with Zinka Strašek, President of the Higher Court of Celje, 1.6.09.

> "... the national authorities should take particular care to ensure that the 2006 Act is applied in conformity with the Convention and the Court's case-law. In particular, the national authorities should ensure that the aggrieved party has a prompt access to the compensatory remedy once he or she has made use of the accelerative remedies ... in order to comply with Article 13 of the Convention the possibility to seek compensation should be open to the applicant no later than within the coming year, provided that he acts with due diligence in the remaining part of the proceedings and that no special difficulties, which would justify their prolongation, arise."[98]

3.4. THE SEQUEL TO *LUKENDA*: THE *ROBERT LESJAK* JUDGMENT

Since *Lukenda*, the European Court has found the new remedies introduced by the 2006 Law to be effective in expediting cases before first and second instance courts (as in the *Korenjak* decision)[99] but has also found that there is no effective complaints procedure in respect of delays occurring in the course of the appeal process to higher courts. This was an issue which the Ombudsman's office also drew to our attention.[100]

After sustaining injuries in a car accident in 1999, Robert Lesjak instituted civil proceedings against the other driver and the driver's insurance company. In 2006 the Celje District Court issued an interim judgment in favour of Mr Lesjak, awarding him damages and finding the other driver entirely responsible for the accident. The other driver appealed to the Celje High Court, and in May 2007 the Court ruled that the driver and his insurance company should be responsible for 70% of the damages. The insurance company appealed against this judgment to the Supreme Court, and the case was still pending at the time of the European Court's judgment in July 2009.[101] Mr Lesjak petitioned the European Court on account of the excessive length of the proceedings, and the absence of an appropriate domestic remedy for delays incurred during the appeal to the Supreme Court. The Court found a violation of Articles 6(1) and 13 of the Convention, in that the 2006 Law failed to provide an effective remedy in respect of delays in Supreme Court proceedings: the new remedies were found in those circumstances to be too complicated and uncertain.[102]

---

98 *Žunič (Branko) v Slovenia*, No. 24342/04, dec. 18.10.07, para. 54.
99 *Korenjak (Matej) v Slovenia*, No. 463/03, dec. 15.5.07, para. 78.
100 Interview with Ivan Šelih and Jernej Rovšek, Ombudsman's Office, Ljubljana, 2.6.09.
101 *Lesjak (Robert) v Slovenia*, No. 33946/03, 21.7.09, paras. 6–15.
102 *Ibid.*, paras. 54–55.

THE 2009 AMENDMENTS TO THE 2006 LAW

The 2006 Law was amended in July 2009,[103] in fact a week before the *Robert Lesjak* judgment was delivered.[104] Article 19 of the 2006 Law provided that a party could file a motion within 9 months of the final resolution of the case. The amended law of 2009 extended this provision to the further stages of appeal to the Supreme Court, thus providing a mechanism for complaint to be made about the length of proceedings at the Supreme Court.[105] At the session of the National Assembly when the 2009 amendments to the law were discussed and approved, Boštjan Škrlec, Secretary of State at the Ministry of Justice, suggested that the 2006 Law had

> "until now stood the test well at the ... Court of Human Rights in Strasbourg as an effective and appropriate system to protect the right to trial without undue delay in accordance with the European Convention on Human Rights. The proposed amendments merely enhance[e] its effect and complement existing legal solutions in accordance with the standards achieved in this area."[106]

Other amendments to the 2006 Law included provisions to prevent the problems experienced in Poland with the legislation adopted after *Kudła*, whereby the duration of proceedings has been calculated by the courts in a way that fails to reflect their full length. The amended law places greater burden on first instance courts to try to discourage the practice of their referring cases to higher courts (which lengthens the procedure) and court presidents have a more significant role in proceedings, so as to increase their accountability. However, this increased accountability may itself lengthen procedures, as, according to President Strašek

---

103 *Zakon o spremembah in dopolnitvah Zakona o varstvu pravice do sojenja brez nepotrebnega odlašanja (ZVPSBNO-A)* 15.7.09 = *Supplementary Amendments to the Act on the Protection of the Right to a trial without undue delay.*

104 Peter Pavlin has stated that the Government had been made aware of this particular lacuna, as a result of the Court's judgment of *Tomažić v Slovenia*. No. 38350/02, 13.12.07 and that the legislative response coinciding with the Court's judgment in Lesjak, 18 months later, was coincidental. Written response to questions, 13.11.09.

105 "The party may file such a motion concerning their case under Article 2 within 9 months from the day the final decision of the court was served, or from the day the decision of the Supreme Court of the Republic of Slovenia that ends the proceedings was served when, in their case under Article 2, an extraordinary legal remedy to be decided by the Supreme Court of the Republic of Slovenia was filed." See, *Zakon o spremembah in dopolnitvah zakona o varstvu pravice do sojenja brez nepotrebnega odlašanja (ZVPSBNO-A) Uradni List*, 58, 27.7.09, p. 8138, Slovenian Ministry of Justice translation.

106 Boštjan Škrlec, Republika Slovenija Državni Zbor Nadaljevanje 8. seje (15. julij 2009) = Republic of Slovenia. National Assembly, continuation of Session 8, 15.7.09. http://www.dzrs.si/index.php?id=97&cs=1&st=s&vt=15&fts=julija&unid=SZA|AAE1930FB30A1C00C1257632003892FE&showdoc=1. No reference was made to the forthcoming judgment of *Robert Lesjak* at this parliamentary session.

of the Celje High Court, it will require a greater emphasis on the need to justify decisions made at each level, which will increase the bureaucracy for the courts.[107]

Although the National Assembly adopted the law unanimously, there was some disagreement from the Slovenian Democratic Party (SDS) over the nature of the amendments. Eva Irgl said that legal experts in her party had scrutinised the bill and considered the changes were cosmetic, and made little substantive difference to the law. Instead, the SDS proposed that to expedite cases the courts should simplify and standardise their procedures. Since then, there has been some discussion in the National Assembly as to the nature and cause of the continuing backlog of cases. Irma Pavlinič Krebs of the Liberal Democratic Party argued that increasing judges' wages will help expedite cases. Boštjan Škrlec of the Ministry of Justice argued that increasing the number of judges will not improve the situation and that backlogs are the result of inefficiencies in the judicial system which requires overhaul.[108] Alenka Jeraj of the Slovenian Democratic Party argued that an important way to reduce backlogs would be to spend more on introducing e-procedures to expedite proceedings.[109]

In October 2009 the Constitutional Court held that provision must be made for applicants who have exhausted the 2006 Law to allow them to appeal to the Constitutional Court and file a complaint.[110]

3.5. 'THIRD TIER' JUDGMENTS – THE CASES OF *MATKO* AND *ŠILIH*

In addition to the excessive length of domestic proceedings, other cases concerning the way in which injuries or fatalities are investigated by the authorities have also

---

107 Interview with Zinka Strašek, President of the Higher Court, Celje, 1.6.09.

108 Magnetogram 12. izredne seje Državnega sveta Republike Slovenije, 29.9.09 = minutes of the 12th extraordinary session of the National Council RS, 29.9.09. *http://www.ds-rs.si/?q=dejavnost/seje&CategoryID=95.*

109 Slovenia. Državni Zbor. *Odbor Državnega zbora Republike Slovenije za notranjo politiko, javno upravo in pravosodje. 1. nadaljevanje 6. seja 1.07.09 = [Minutes of the] Committee on domestic politics, public management of justice, National Assembly of the Republic of Slovenia*, 1.7.09 = http://www.dz-rs.si/index.php?id=97&cs=7&vt=15&fts=zvpsbno&unid=PMT|665FD5521ECE60C7C12575E700207487&showdoc=1.

110 Slovenia. Ustavno Sodišče. Judgment No. U-I-93/07, 22.10.09 http://odlocitve.us-rs.si/usrs/us-odl.nsf/o/3BA096F20C0B1BACC1257662004E4EA2 "2. When an aggrieved person opines that the Court does not operate in such manner [decides a case without undue delay], it is then available to her to request adequate judicial protection due to violation of the right to a trial without undue delay as is provided by the Act on the Protection of the Right to a Trial without Undue Delay (Official Gazette No. 49/06 and following – ZVPSBNO). After its exhaustion [of its acceleratory legal remedies] it can file the constitutional complaint in accordance with provisions of Articles 50–53 of the Constitutional Court Act (Official Gazette No. 64/07)" [Translation provided by Peter Pavlin].

been treated in Slovenia as being systemic violations. The cases of *Matko* and *Šilih* both concern a failure by the authorities to instigate an independent and/or effective investigation.

3.5.1. INVESTIGATION INTO CLAIMS OF POLICE BRUTALITY: *MATKO*

The case of *Matko v Slovenia*, in 2006, concerned alleged police brutality involving the same body (the Slovenj Gradec Police – a special unit operating under the control of the Ministry of Internal Affairs) that had been the subject of criticism in the 2000 judgment in *Rehbock v Slovenia*,[111] and led to a finding by the Court of a violation of Article 3 because of the failure to carry out a thorough and effective investigation. In *Butolen* there was also an alleged violation of Article 3 for the same reasons; at the time of writing the Court's judgment in this case was still pending.[112]

Aleksander Matko was arrested by the police in 1995 for speeding and was released some hours later. However, during his arrest he was subject to alleged police brutality and sustained significant bruising and other injuries, as was confirmed by a medical examination. He consequently filed a criminal complaint against the police,[113] which was dismissed in 1997 by the Public Prosecutor.[114] In his application to the Strasbourg Court Mr Matko complained of a violation of Article 3 as a result of his ill-treatment and the failure to investigate his complaint, both of which the Court upheld, finding (amongst other things) that there was a lack of institutional independence in the investigation of the case.[115] Although there was no explicit statement by the Court that the problem was systemic, it noted that a similar investigation had been criticised by the Court in *Rehbock*,[116] and it cited with approval a recent Slovenian Constitutional Court judgment which had found that an independent investigation had not been carried out in relation to the death of a person who had died during a police operation (relying on both Article 15 of the Constitution and Article 13 of the European Convention).[117]

Interestingly, the Slovenian government agent, Peter Pavlin, has suggested that the judgment was systemic in nature:

---

111 *Rehbock v Slovenia*, No. 29462/95, 28.11.00 Ernst Rehbock had been assaulted by police while being arrested in 1995 on suspicion of drug smuggling.
112 *Butolen (Boris) v Slovenia*, No. 41356/08, dec. 9.6.09.
113 *Matko v Slovenia*, No. 43393/98, 2.11.06, paras. 10–29.
114 *Ibid.*, para. 34.
115 *Ibid.*, paras. 89–91.
116 *Ibid.*, para. 94.
117 *Ibid.*, para. 66.

"It was not a pilot case *per se* ... It shows that the police are not ... totally capable of investigating crimes or alleged crimes of its own officers or members."[118]

The effect of the Matko *judgment on domestic law*

A direct result of the *Matko* case was the amendment of the State Prosecutor's Act in February 2007, which established a new department within the Prosecutor's Office to investigate any alleged malpractice by the police or other home affairs officials.[119] The State Prosecutor's Office was made responsible for directing the investigation and supervising the transfer of relevant staff to ensure impartiality.[120]

3.5.2. INVESTIGATION OF MEDICAL MALPRACTICE: *ŠILIH V SLOVENIA*

The 2009 Grand Chamber judgment in *Šilih* concerned the failure by the authorities to investigate the death of the applicants' son, which they alleged was the result of medical negligence.[121] Franja and Ivan Šilih's twenty-year old son Gregor died in 1993 after he was admitted to hospital for allergy treatment and suffered anaphylactic shock as a result of the drugs administered. The Šilihs subsequently made a criminal complaint against the duty doctor responsible but this was dismissed in 1994 because of insufficient evidence.[122] After a series of unsuccessful attempts to have the matter investigated, through both criminal and civil proceedings, in 2006 the Maribor District Court dismissed the case.[123]

---

118 Peter Pavlin (2009), *Discussion* in Jakub Wołąsiewicz (ed.) (2009), *Pilot judgment procedure in the European Court of Human Rights and the future development of Human Rights' standards and procedures: Third Informal Seminar for Government Agents and other institutions, Warsaw 14–15 May 2009*, Kontrast, Warsaw, p. 127.

119 *Zakon o spremembah in dopolnitvah zakona o državnem tožilstvu (ZDT-D)* 14/2007 602, 16.2.07 = *Law amending the implementation of the State Prosecutor's Act*, 16.2.07. See: Peter Pavlin (2009), *Discussion* in Jakub Wołąsiewicz (ed.) (2009), *Pilot judgment procedure in the European Court of Human Rights and the future development of Human Rights' standards and procedures: Third Informal Seminar for Government Agents and other institutions, Warsaw 14–15 May 2009*, Kontrast, Warsaw, p. 127.

120 This law has been amended a number of times since, making minor changes to the terms and conditions of officials' employment in the special department, and the transfer of police officers, or other officials, during the investigation. This provision was also incorporated into the Criminal Procedure Act. See: *Zakon o spremembi in dopolnitvi Zakona o kazenskem postopku* (ZKP-H) 14/2007 601, 16.2.07 = *Law amending the implementation of the Criminal Procedure Act*, 16.2.07; *Zakon o spremembah in dopolnitvah Zakona o državnem tožilstvu* (ZDT-E) 40/2007 2171, 7.5.07 = *Law amending the implementation of the State Prosecutor's Act*, 7.5.07; *Zakon o spremembah in dopolnitvah Zakona o državnem tožilstvu* (ZDT-G) 87/2009 3840, 2.11.09 = *Law amending the implementation of the State Prosecutor's Act*, 2.11.09.

121 *Šilih v Slovenia*, No. 71463/01, 9.4.09.

122 *Ibid.*, paras. 10–18.

123 *Ibid.*, para. 73.

An appeal to the Constitutional Court, concerning the alleged violation of their right to equality before the law, the inviolability of human life, the right to equal protection, the right to judicial protection and the right to legal remedies, was still pending at the time the European Court published its judgment in April 2009.[124]

The Court held that there had been a procedural violation of the right to life (Article 2), as in practice neither the civil nor criminal proceedings had proved to be effective, primarily because of inefficiencies and serious delays.[125] Although Article 46 was not applied, as in the case of *Matko*, the Slovenian Ministry of Justice has also indicated that it considers the judgment identified a systemic violation, and for that reason we have treated it as a 'third tier' judgment. Peter Pavlin has said:

> "... *Šilih* [is] ... not a pilot case, but it is also a case, which shows some systemic problems. It concerns a person, who died in hospital in 1993 and his parents are totally convinced this is as a result of [the] physicians' mistake or negligence ... it seems ... that some parliamentary decisions shall be required and there is some concern [that] the investigations of these physicians' mistakes [is] left completely within the ... chamber of physicians. Maybe [it is necessary to form] some independent body or more independent body or impartial body within the chamber of physicians."[126]

The effect of the Šilih *judgment on domestic law*

In July 2009 the MP Eva Irgl of the Slovenian Democratic Party raised the *Šilih* case in the National Assembly:

> "... the European Court of Human Rights ... decided that in Slovenia there no are effective legal procedures to investigate medical malpractice. This is an important issue that also relates to the protection of human rights."[127]

---

[124] *Ibid.*, para. 78.

[125] *Ibid.*, paras. 197–211. The Slovenian Ombudsman had also been critical of judicial conduct of the case (see paras. 81–85).

[126] Peter Pavlin, 'Discussion' in Wołąsiewicz, Jakub (ed.) (2009), *Pilot judgment procedure in the European Court of Human Rights and the future development of Human Rights' standards and procedures: Third Informal Seminar for Government Agents and other institutions, Warsaw 14–15 May 2009*, Kontrast, Warsaw, p. 127. On the question of disciplinary proceedings (which were not in fact instituted in this case), the European Court had simply found that the Government had not shown that proceedings before the Medical Tribunal would have provided an effective remedy: *Šilih v Slovenia*, No. 71463/01, 9.4.09, para. 199.

[127] Eva Irgl, Republika Slovenija Državni Zbor Nadaljevanje 8. seje (15. julij 2009) = Republic of Slovenia. National Assembly, continuation of Session 8, 15.7.09. http://www.dz rs.si/index.php ?id=97&cs=1&st=s&vt=15&fts=julija&unid=SZA|AAE1930FB30A1C00C1257632003892FE& showdoc=1.

The Constitutional Court issued a judgment on 7 October 2009 which explicitly upheld the Strasbourg decision in finding a procedural violation of Article 2, in the failure to investigate the death. The Constitutional Court overturned the Maribor District Court's judgment, and stated that that court's restriction on the applicants' right to present evidence was a breach of their constitutional rights. The Constitutional Court held that blocking an applicant's right to present evidence (in accordance with Article 286 of the Civil Procedure Act) was a breach of Article 22 of the Slovenian Constitution. Although the Constitutional Court judgment noted that the European Court had not required the Slovenian Government to amend the procedure for investigating malpractice by the medical profession, the Constitutional Court did question the District Court's use of discretionary powers to prevent the admissibility of certain evidence (under the Civil Procedure Code).[128] The Committee of Ministers stated in its October 2009 report on monitoring execution of judgments that it was waiting for further information on measures taken or envisaged to prevent similar violations concerning medical malpractice.[129]

3.6. EVALUATING HOW THE IMPLEMENTATION OF STRASBOURG JUDGMENTS IS MONITORED

In Slovenia the Ministry of Justice is responsible for monitoring laws that have been amended or introduced as a result of the *Lukenda Project*. Official statistics tend to group length of proceedings cases together with court and police procedures generally, so that it is difficult to establish the precise number of cases that concern complaints over length of proceedings. This was apparent from data presented to us at the Ministry of Justice and the Ombudsman's Office. For example, the Ombudsman's office stated that 456 cases were referred to them in 2007 which concerned court and police procedures generally, and in 2008 this figure rose to 492. However, the Ombudsman's Office said they believed, anecdotally, that there had been a reduction in the number of length of proceedings cases, and an increase in those relating to criminal cases.[130]

---

128 Slovenia. Ustavno Sodišče. Judgment, Up-2443/08-22, 7.10.09, para. 19, see: http://odlocitve.us-rs.si/usrs/us-odl.nsf/o/C11D8876A72E2582C12576560043BF48 Article 22 of the Constitution provides "Everyone shall be guaranteed equal protection of rights in any proceeding before a court and before other state authorities, local community authorities, and bearers of public authority that decide on his rights, duties, or legal interests." See: Constitution of the Republic of Slovenia, http://www.dz-rs.si/index.php?id=351&docid=25&showdoc=1.

129 Directorate General of Human Rights and Legal Affairs (2009), *Execution of the Judgments of the European Court of Human Rights. Pending Cases. Current State of Execution, Slovenia*, p. 1. *http://www.coe.int/t/dghl/monitoring/execution/Reports/Current_en.asp* (As at: 7.10.09).

130 Interview with Ivan Šelih and Jernej Rovšek, Ombudsman's Office, Ljubljana 2.6.09.

Representatives of the Ombudsman's Office told us that they do not consider their role should be extended to monitoring compliance with Strasbourg judgments, and urging the Slovenian Government to take the necessary remedial measures. They also indicated that they do not consider it appropriate that they should act as an 'agent of pressure' on behalf of the Council of Europe Commissioner for Human Rights. This point stems from recommendations made by the Group of Wise Persons in their 2006 Report[131] and a series of roundtables organised by the Commissioner for Human Rights, Thomas Hammarberg, to develop cooperation between the Commissioner's Office and local national human rights structures, in particular national ombudsmen. The initiative was aimed at creating an active network so as to disseminate appropriate information on human rights to the public and, as far as the Ombudsmen's competence permits, take action on alleged violations and abuses. Among other things, the Commissioner's Office requested that ombudsmen monitor the implementation of European Court judgments, and alert the Commissioner to possible repetitive cases that were indicative of a systemic violation.[132] The Ombudsman's Office felt its role as impartial arbiter could be questioned if it were in effect forced to act 'on behalf of', or 'in support of' the Court or Commissioner's Office.[133] Additionally, it was said that the Ombudsman's Office does not have sufficient resources for such monitoring and for the lobbying of parliament and government.

3.7. CONCLUSIONS

3.7.1. WHAT FACTORS LED THE COURT TO ISSUE 'QUASI-PILOT' AND 'THIRD TIER' JUDGMENTS AGAINST SLOVENIA?

Evidently the sheer number of cases submitted against Slovenia concerning violations of the right to a trial within a reasonable time was the main reason why the Court issued a quasi-pilot judgment in the case of *Lukenda*. The Slovenian Government agent informed us that the Government had acknowledged the problem as being systemic, and he suggested that its acceptance of the problem

---

131 Committee of Ministers (2006), CM(2006)203. *Report of the Group of Wise Persons to the Committee of Ministers*, 15 November 2006, 979bis Meeting https://wcd.coe.int/ViewDoc.jsp?id=1063779&BackColorInternet=9999CC&BackColorIntranet=FFBB55&BackColorLogged=FFAC75.

132 The Commissioner for Human Rights, Thomas Hammarberg, made a statement at a press conference in Ljubljana which touched on the importance of cooperation with the national ombudsman. See: *Statement by Thomas Hammarberg, Commissioner for Human Rights at Press Conference in Ljubljana*. http://www.dosta.org/en/node/159.

133 Interview with Ivan Šelih and Jernej Rovšek, Ombudsman's Office, Ljubljana, 2.6.09.

was evident in the fact that they did not seek the referral of the case to the Grand Chamber (as they did, for example, in the *Šilih* case).[134]

The problem of the excessive length of legal proceedings has plagued Slovenia for a number of years. As we have seen, problems remained even with the 2006 Law which was introduced in the wake of *Lukenda*. The amendments made to the 2006 Law in accordance with the European Court's decisions arguably demonstrate a degree of willingness on the part of the Slovenian Government to comply with Strasbourg over this issue. Whether or not the Court might in any event have been inclined to issue a second pilot judgment in the case of *Robert Lesjak*, or a similar case, is highly questionable. This would arguably have been counterproductive for the Court, in that it would have shown the procedure to have failed in its application to *Lukenda*. Indeed, since the pilot judgment procedure is relatively new, it has never been applied in its full form twice in respect of the same type of violation (to the same respondent state); however length of proceedings cases appear to be the exception to the rule, necessitating, for example in the case of Slovenia (cases such as *Belinger*, *Lukenda* and *Robert Lesjak*) and Italy (cases such as *Bottazzi* and *Scordino*) a number of judgments to be issued, even after the systemic problem has been very clearly flagged up. Similarly, as we discuss in Chapter Two, the 2009 amendments to the *Kudła* law in Poland (relating to length of proceedings) resulted from the follow-up judgment in the case of *Krawczak*.[135]

Cooperation between the Slovenian Constitutional Court and the European Court

Respondents agreed that there are good relations between the Constitutional Court and the European Court, which one interviewee partly explained as being the result of a 'career path' from Constitutional Court to Strasbourg.[136] At the very least, according to Dean Zagorac, Editor of *Pravna Praksa,* there is general agreement between the two courts:

> "I could not imagine our Constitutional Court working against the judgments of the European Court - no way."[137]

Saša Zagorc, Assistant Professor of Constitutional Law, at the University of Ljubljana has argued that the two courts have 'co-operated' with each other.[138]

---

134 Interview with Peter Pavlin, Ministry of Justice, Ljubljana, 1.6.09.
135 *Krawczak v Poland*, No. 40387/06, 8.4.08.
136 Interview with Dean Zagorac, Editor, *Pravna Praksa*, Ljubljana, 3.6.09.
137 *Ibid.*
138 Saša Zagorc (2005), "Dvojna Predramitev za slovensko oblast: odprava kršitev pravice do sojenja v razumnem roku - kako naprej? = Double wake-up call for Slovenian authorities effective legal remedies for the violation of the right to trial within a reasonable time - now what?" *Revus* 5, p. 46.

The Constitutional Court Judge, Marija Krisper Kramberger explained that the proceedings in the case of *Lukenda* before the European Court of Human Rights and the proceedings in the case of *Jelačin* before the Constitutional Court were run simultaneously:

> "... the Constitutional Court ... found on its own that in Slovenia, there is no effective legal remedy for violations of the right to a trial within a reasonable time. Besides, the Constitutional Court respects the jurisprudence of the European Court of Human Rights. In most decisions of the Constitutional Court we directly refer to the decisions of the European Court of Human Rights, irrespective of the respondent state, and we use the same standards of protection that are used by the latter court when interpreting the Convention."
>
> "The importance of the case-law of the European Court of Human Rights is also shown in the work of the legislature. If the Constitutional Court follows a ... judgment of the European Court of Human Rights, again irrespective of the respondent state, the Slovene legislature responds [swiftly] to our decisions as well. In this way, for example, the legislative procedure following the decisions in [the] cases of *Jelačin* and *Lukenda* started only two months after they were published and the law was passed in the spring [of] 2006."[139]

In spite of this cooperation between the courts, and something of a flurry of activity within the executive, legislature and judiciary, the Lukenda project, and further amendments resulting from the *Robert Lesjak* case, are still work in progress. This leads us to question whether the issuing of a 'quasi-pilot' judgment was in fact effective from the point of view of the respondent state or the Court.

3.7.2. THE EFFICACY OF THE 'QUASI-PILOT' JUDGMENT IN *LUKENDA*

Although in its judgment in *Lukenda*, the European Court exerted pressure on the executive and legislature, in effect, to comply with the Constitutional Court, there is evidence that the application of this procedure in the case of endemic dysfunction, such as the excessive length of proceedings, is problematic as it results in another process of 'ping pong justice' – the movement back and forth of cases between the national courts and Strasbourg, and long-term haggling over the effectiveness of domestic remedies.

---

139 Interview with Judge Marija Krisper Kramberger, Constitutional Court, Ljubljana, 3.6.09.

3.7.3. THE *ERGA OMNES* IMPLICATIONS OF *LUKENDA*

As was noted in Chapter One, judgments concerning endemic problems such as length of proceedings violations from international courts can be considered problematic in some quarters, especially when a prescriptive approach is adopted by the international court. Misgivings over the application of the pilot judgment procedure to such endemic malfunctioning were expressed in the dissenting opinions of Judges Casadevall and Zagrebelsky in the *Kudła* and *Lukenda* judgments. The Slovenian Government Agent, Peter Pavlin, also suggested to us that the Court's specification of measures in the operative part of the *Lukenda* judgment was inappropriate, and *ultra vires*.[140] Nonetheless in the *Kudła* judgment, the resolution of this problem was clearly identified as being something expected of all states.[141] Furthermore, in the wake of *Lukenda*, judgments of a similar nature (some of which are 'quasi-pilot' judgments) continue to be issued to various states, including Bulgaria, France, Germany, Moldova, Serbia and Slovakia.[142] This clearly shows the pressing need for a greater understanding and *application* of the '*erga omnes*' principle as regards Strasbourg judgments – state authorities must act swiftly in response to European Court judgments against other states which lay down standards in relation to systemic issues which are also relevant to their situation.

140 Interview with Peter Pavlin, Ministry of Justice, Ljubljana, 1.6.09.

141 *Kudła v Poland*, No. 30210/96, 26.10.00, paras 147–148.

142 See, for example, *Donnadieu v France (No. 2)*, No. 19249/02, 7.2.06; *Kounov v Bulgaria*, No. 24379/02, 23.5.06; *Sürmeli v Germany*, No. 75529/01, 8.6.06; *Ilić v Serbia*, No. 30132/04, 9.10.07; *Karamitrov and others v Bulgaria*, No. 53321/99, 10.1.08; *Boboc v Moldova*, No. 27581/04, 4.11.08; *Berková v Slovakia*, No. 67149/01, 24.3.09.

CHAPTER 4

ITALY: PINTO, AZZOLINI AND THE ELEVATION OF THE STATUS OF THE EUROPEAN CONVENTION IN DOMESTIC LAW

4.1. INTRODUCTION

4.1.1. THE STATUS OF THE CONVENTION WITH RESPECT TO NATIONAL LAW

Until recently, the European Convention on Human Rights had the same status as ordinary law in Italy, and the Italian Constitution contained no specific provision concerning the position of the Convention with respect to domestic law.[1] Following constitutional reform in 2001, Article 117 of the Constitution now provides that the legislative authorities of the State and the regions must exercise their powers in compliance with international treaties (such as the Convention).[2] In 2007, by interpreting Article 117, two Constitutional Court judgments (348 and 349) had the effect of raising the status of the Convention above that of ordinary law – to sub-constitutional status[3] (which we discuss further below). These judgments followed directly from the European Court's 'quasi-pilot' judgment in *Scordino*

---

1 Mercedes Candela Soriano (2008), 'The Reception Process in Spain and Italy' in Keller, Helen and Alec Stone Sweet (eds.), *A Europe of Rights*, p. 405. As Oreste Pollicino has explained, therefore the European Convention could be abrogated by any successive statutory law that conflicted with it. See Oreste Pollicino (2008), 'Italy – Constitutional Court at the crossroads between constitutional parochialism and co-operative constitutionalism. Judgments No. 348 and 349 of 22 and 24 October 2007' *European Constitutional Law Review* 4, p. 369.

2 Article 117(1) of the Italian Constitution provides: 'Legislative power belongs to the state and the regions in accordance with the Constitution and within the limits set by European Union law and international obligations.' See: Italy. Constitution (1948), http://www.servat.unibe.ch/icl/it00000_.html.

3 Italy. Corte Costituzionale. Judgment 348 of 22 October 2007 http://www.cortecostituzionale.it/versioni_in_lingua/eng/attivitacorte/pronunceemassime/recent_judgments_2007.asp, para. 4.5. See also: Directorate General of Human Rights and Legal Affairs. *Execution of the Judgments of the European Court of Human Rights. Pending Cases. Current State of Execution, Italy* p. 12, at 7.10.09. http://www.coe.int/t/dghl/monitoring/execution/Reports/Current_en.asp.

v Italy.[4] Although our respondents perceived this rise in status as a positive step towards the direct application of the Convention in domestic law, the nature of this change and what it means in practice is still rather open to interpretation,[5] as we discuss in Section 4.3 below. However, only judges, regions and states may petition the Constitutional Court directly to contest the constitutionality of a law in Italy; unlike in Poland and Slovenia, individuals have no right of direct complaint.[6] The European Court is the only judicial body where individuals may make a direct claim of a violation of their fundamental rights.[7]

Commentators have voiced concern that in practice the courts in Italy may experience difficulties in applying the Convention, as lawyers and judges are insufficiently trained with respect to the Convention and the judiciary needs to be reformed.[8] The view that Italian lower court judges are insufficiently aware of the Convention was expressed by a number of our interviewees.[9] We were also told that the higher courts rather than the lower courts tend to invoke the Convention in their judgments.[10] According to our interviewees a significant hurdle for the Italian judiciary is language, as there is insufficient translation of European Court judgments from English or French.[11] We were told that the older generation of judges and lawyers do not have sufficient fluency in English or French to read judgments issued by the Court.[12]

To improve access to European Court case-law, an Italian NGO, *Unione Forense per la Tutela dei Diritti dell'Uomo* (comprising lawyers, judges and academics) was granted funds to translate the most important European Court judgments and all judgments in cases against Italy – the 'ECHR Observatory' (Osservatorio

---

4 *Scordino v Italy (No. 1)*, No. 36813/97, 29.7.04; 29.3.06 (GC); *Scordino v Italy (No. 2)*, No. 36815/97, 15.7.04; *Scordino v Italy (No. 3)*, No. 43662/98, 6.3.07.

5 See Giacinto della Cananea (2008), 'The Italian Constitutional Court and the European Court of Justice: From Separation to Interaction?' *European Public Law* 14:4, p. 528.

6 Marcello Flores [2009], *Supranational rights litigation, implementation and the domestic impact of Strasbourg Court jurisprudence: A case study of Italy, Juristras: final case study report*, p. 3. http://www.juristras.eliamep.gr/?cat=8.

7 *Ibid.*, p. 4.

8 Antonio Bultrini (2008), 'Le sentenze 348 e 349/2007 della Corte costituzionale: l'inizio di una svolta?' = The Constitutional Court judgments 348 and 349: the beginning of a turning point?' *Diritto Pubblico Comparato ed Europeo* = Comparative public rights and Europe; Giacinto della Cananea (2008), 'The Italian Constitutional Court and the European Court of Justice: From Separation to Interaction?' *European Public Law* 14:4, p. 528.

9 Interview with Giuseppe Tesauro, Constitutional Court, Rome, 8.6.09; Interview with Professor Barbara Randazzo and Professor Valerio Onida, University of Milan, 10.6.09.

10 Interview with Vitaliano Taccioli and Patriarca Pier Ludovico, Ombudsman's Office, Rome, 8.6.09.

11 Interview with Professor Barbara Randazzo and Professor Valerio Onida, University of Milan, 10.6.09.

12 Interview with Professor Barbara Randazzo, University of Milan, 10.6.09; Interview with Marco Cerase, Camera, Rome, 10.6.09.

CEDU).[13] However, in 2008, the funding for this public resource was discontinued, and it has been superseded by a website created for Italian judges, which is no longer free as access to this website is limited to paid subscribers only.[14]

4.1.2. ITALY'S TRACK RECORD IN RESPONDING TO STRASBOURG

By the beginning of 2010 the European Court had delivered 1,095 judgments against Italy finding a violation of the right to trial within a reasonable time. This constituted 27% of all violations concerning excessive length of proceedings from the establishment of the Court in 1959 to 2009.[15] The vast number of such 'clone' cases on this issue indicate the extent of the problems within the Italian legal system, and the authorities' failure to remedy its causes. In its March 2009 Interim Resolution, the Committee of Ministers noted that statistics for 2006-2007 still showed an increase in the length of cases pending before certain jurisdictions, and recorded the significant backlogs of both civil and criminal cases (approximately 5.5 million civil cases and 3.2 million criminal cases pending before domestic courts).[16] Nevertheless, according to the Ministry of Justice, the Government is now more responsive to the Court's judgments, as, we were told, was demonstrated by the measures taken in the wake of the *Sejdović* and *Scordino* judgments.[17] A number of our respondents expressed their concern, however, at how the Government responds to the Court's judgments.[18]

---

13 Interview with Mario Lana and Professor Andrea Saccucci, Rome, 9.6.09. See also the website of the Prime Minister's Office, www.osservatoriocedu.it (last accessed 9.4.10) – and the Parliament's website, http://www.camera.it/europ_rap_int/14489/20512/documentotesto.asp (last accessed 9.4.10).

14 See: http://www.italgiure.giustizia.it/. (last accessed 9.4.10) Interview with Professor Andrea Saccucci, *Unione Forense per la Tutela dei Diritti dell'Uomo*, Rome, 9.6.09.

15 The total number of violations concerning length of proceedings was 4008; 1095 of these (27%) were judgments against Italy. The European Court of Human Rights: some facts and figures, pp. 15–16. http://www.echr.coe.int/NR/rdonlyres/ACD46A0F-615A-48B9-89D6-8480AFCC29FD/0/FactsAndFigures_EN.pdf.

16 Committee of Ministers (2009), Interim Resolution CM/ResDH(2009)42, *Execution of the judgments of the European Court of Human Rights concerning the excessive length of judicial proceedings in Italy: Progress achieved and outstanding issues in the context of general measures to ensure compliance with the judgments of the European Court of Human Rights*. https://wcd.coe.int/ViewDoc.jsp?Ref=CM/ResDH(2009)42&Language=lanEnglish&Ver=original&Site=CM&BackColorInternet=9999CC&BackColorIntranet=FFBB55&BackColorLogged=FFAC75.

17 Interview with Emilia de Bellis, Ministry of Justice, Rome, 9.6.09.

18 Interview with Mario Lana and Andrea Saccucci, Rome, 9.6.09; Interview with civil servant, Rome, 9.6.09.

The majority of Italian cases submitted to the European Court are still those concerning excessive length of proceedings.[19] Other widespread violations relate to the expropriation of property and the administration of justice.[20] It has been argued that this is because there are gaps in the legislative system in respect of these areas, and that the rights violated are not adequately protected by the Constitution.[21] Additionally, there are ongoing concerns about police brutality, mass expulsions of legal and illegal immigrants and 'rendition' of individuals suspected of terrorism, directed in particular against minority groups.[22] In the case of renditions, the Court has issued a number of judgments finding violations of Article 3, as we discuss in Sections 4.1.2.2 and 4.4.1.2. Other cases raising repetitive violations that are currently under the supervision of the Committee of Ministers include judgments relating to Article 8 (concerning the monitoring of prisoners' correspondence), and Article 1 of Protocol No. 1 (expropriation and bankruptcy laws).[23] The Strasbourg Court has issued a significant number of judgments concerning violations of prisoners' privacy rights because of the authorities' interception of their correspondence.[24] Although the Committee of Ministers stopped monitoring this issue in 2005, following the introduction of new legislation on 'Restrictions and control of correspondence',[25] it decided to resume its supervision of the problem in 2009.[26]

---

19 Italy. Presidenza del Consiglio dei Ministri (2008), *L'esecuzione delle pronunce della Corte europea dei diritti dell'uomo nei confronti dello stato italiano Legge 9 gennaio 2006, n. 12 : Relazione al Parlamento Anno 2008=The execution of the decisions of the European Court of Human Rights with respect to the Italian State, law of 9 June 2006, no. 12 : Report to the Parliament, 2008.*

20 Marcello Flores [2009], *Supranational rights litigation, implementation and the domestic impact of Strasbourg Court jurisprudence: A case study of Italy, Juristras: final case study report,* p. 7. http://www.juristras.eliamep.gr/?cat=8.

21 *Ibid.*

22 *Ibid.*, p. 8.

23 Directorate General of Human Rights and Legal Affairs. *Execution of the Judgments of the European Court of Human Rights. Pending Cases. Current State of Execution, Italy,* at 26/08/2009. http://www.coe.int/t/dghl/monitoring/execution/Reports/Current_en.asp.

24 Directorate General of Human Rights and Legal Affairs. *Execution of the Judgments of the European Court of Human Rights. Pending Cases. Current State of Execution, Italy,* p. 14, at 07/10/2009. http://www.coe.int/t/dghl/monitoring/execution/Reports/Current_en.asp.

25 Committee of Ministers (2005), ResDH(2005)55. *Resolution concerning the judgments of the European Court of Human Rights relating to the monitoring of prisoners' correspondence and the right to an effective remedy (case of Calogero Diana against Italy and 6 other cases) Adopted by the Committee of Ministers on 5 July 2005 at the 933rd meeting of the Ministers' deputies.* https://wcd.coe.int/ViewDoc.jsp?Ref=ResDH(2005)55&Language=lanEnglish&Site=CM&BackColorInternet=DBDCF2&BackColorIntranet=FDC864&BackColorLogged=FDC864.

26 Directorate General of Human Rights and Legal Affairs. *Execution of the Judgments of the European Court of Human Rights. Pending Cases. Current State of Execution, Italy,* p. 14 at 16.11.09. http://www.coe.int/t/dghl/monitoring/execution/Reports/Current_en.asp.

4.1.2.1. *Implementation of Constitutional Court judgments*

Once the Constitutional Court has held a law to be unconstitutional it may no longer be applied by the courts, and the preceding law automatically comes into force from the day after the judgment is published.[27] However, as Judge Tesauro pointed out to us, this may be highly problematic in particular where in some situations a Constitutional Court ruling of this kind may give rise to a series of quashed laws, as has been the case with expropriation legislation (see Section 4.2.2).

Regarding the response to Strasbourg judgments, since the executive and legislature appear to engage ineffectually with human rights issues, as the next section discusses, legislative change in response to Strasbourg judgments tends to follow a slow and tortuous path.

4.1.2.2. *The implementation of Strasbourg judgments – the roles of the executive and legislature*

According to Professor Andrea Saccucci, the executive and legislature are, generally, insufficiently aware of Strasbourg judgments and the need to apply the Convention in Italian legislation.[28] We were also told that the Parliament is not 'tuned in' to human rights issues,[29] and tends to focus on domestic questions rather than those that emanate from Strasbourg.[30] According to one Constitutional Court Judge, Parliament engages in debating legislation in response to Strasbourg judgments but it is not sufficiently aware of the issues concerned.[31] For example, human rights lawyers Professor Andrea Saccucci and Anton Lana consider that the six month detention-period of asylum seekers and illegal immigrants constitutes a violation of the European Convention which Parliament has failed to address.[32] Judge Giuseppe Tesauro, of the Constitutional Court, suggested that in Italy Parliament often perceives Constitutional Court judgments regarding human rights as favourable towards criminals:

> "A law could be an advantage for a mafia man or a terrorist or so on, so it's psychologically easy. In the parliament they say always [to the Constitutional Court] – you defend mafia and criminals ... It's very easy to speak on television ... It's not so easy to make a law, and to make a judgment: to let these people free."[33]

---

27 *Scordino v Italy (No. 1)*, No. 36813/97, 29.3.06 (GC), para. 51.
28 Interview with Professor Andrea Saccucci, *Unione Forense per la Tutela dei Diritti dell'Uomo*, Rome, 9.6.09.
29 *Ibid.*
30 Interview with Professor Barbara Randazzo and Professor Valerio Onida, University of Milan, 10.6.09.
31 Interview with Giuseppe Tesauro, Constitutional Court, Rome, 8.6.09.
32 Interview with Professor Andrea Saccucci and Anton Lana, Rome, 9.6.09.
33 Interview with Giuseppe Tesauro, Constitutional Court, Rome, 8.6.09.

Judge Tesauro expressed the view that pilot judgments could encourage the lower and upper houses of Parliament, the Camera and the Senate, to work much harder than they currently do in resolving these violations – in such areas pressure from Strasbourg for legislative change through the pilot judgment procedure would be welcome.[34]

According to the lawyer Alessandra Mari, since Prime Minister Berlusconi's time in office, Parliament has actively legislated in violation of human rights and the Convention.[35] However, Senator Pietro Marcenaro claimed that some members of Parliament are aware of Strasbourg judgments and debate such issues. He cited the example of the Italian Government's decision to deport a number of Tunisian citizens from Italy, which the Strasbourg Court had held to be in violation of Article 3.[36] Although in some instances the Tunisians have been deported, Senator Marcenaro and other colleagues in the Senate questioned why the Italian Government refused to follow the Court's ruling.[37] The applicant in the case of *Ben Khemais v Italy* had already been deported by the time his case was considered by the European Court, in spite of the Court's 'interim measures' ruling that he should be allowed to remain in Italy.[38] The Italian Government claimed in its defence that it had secured diplomatic assurances from the Tunisian Government that the applicant would not be mistreated, and argued that this was sufficient guarantee of Mr Ben Khemais's safety.[39] The Court, however, did not subscribe to the Government's viewpoint.[40] Although Article 46 was not applied in this case, another similar case, the Grand Chamber judgment in *Saadi v Italy*, was described in the 2008 Azzolini Report as a 'true pilot judgment'. We discuss this further in Section 4.4.1.2 below.

Many of our interviewees considered the pilot judgment procedure to be a positive way to bring about legislative change,[41] and the former President of the Constitutional Court, Professor Onida, views the procedure as an effective mechanism in situations where there is no system or procedure to execute the

---

34 *Ibid.*

35 Interview with Alessandra Mari, legal representative for Scordino and Guiso-Gallisay, Rome, 9.6.09; Interview with civil servant, Rome, 9.6.09.

36 See, for example, *Saadi v Italy*, No. 37201/06, 28.2.08, para. 193; *O. v Italy*, No. 37257/06, 24.3.09, para. 59; *Sellem v Italy*, No. 12584/08, 5.5.09, para. 61.

37 Interview with Pietro Marcenaro, the Senate, Rome, 9.6.09.

38 *Ben Khemais v Italy*, No. 246/07, 24.2.09 Directorate General of Human Rights and Legal Affairs. Execution of the Judgments of the European Court of Human Rights. Pending Cases. Current State of Execution, Italy, at 7.10.09, pp. 19–20. http://www.coe.int/t/dghl/monitoring/execution/Reports/Current_en.asp.

39 *Ben Khemais v Italy*, No.246/07, 24.2.09, paras. 26–27.

40 *Ibid.*, para. 61.

41 Interview with Judge Tesauro, Constitutional Court, 8.6.09; Interview with Pietro Marcenaro, the Senate, Rome, 9.6.09; Interview with Professors Barbara Randazzo and Valerio Onida, University of Milan, 10.6.09.

European Court's judgments.[42] The following two sections evaluate a number of key Italian 'quasi-pilot' judgments.

4.2. 'QUASI-PILOT' JUDGMENTS IN ITALIAN CASES

In the case of Italy the Court has, as yet, delivered no 'full' pilot judgments. Nevertheless, a number of 'quasi-pilot' judgments have been issued in relation to Italy, concerning, notably, the right to a fair trial (Articles 6(1), 6(2) and 6(3)), and the right to compensation for expropriated property (Article 1 of Protocol No. 1 to the Convention). Some examples are discussed below.

4.2.1. THE RIGHT TO A FAIR TRIAL (ARTICLE 6)

Two quasi-pilot judgments have been issued in relation to violations of the right to a fair trial, with respect to the practice of holding trials *in absentia* (*Sejdović v Italy* in 2004 and 2006;[43] and *R.R. v Italy* in 2005).[44] By the time *Sejdović* was considered by the Grand Chamber in 2006, the Court found there was no need for general measures since the Italian Government had amended the Code of Criminal Procedure in 2005 with respect to trial in absentia.[45] As has been discussed by Mercedes Candela Soriano, the first Italian case in which the Court found such a violation of the right to a fair hearing was *Colozza v Italy*[46] in 1985.[47] Consequently changes were made to the Code of Criminal Procedure in 1989, but these were deemed insufficient in the later judgments of *Somogyi* and *Sejdović*.[48] The Code of Criminal Procedure still provided that the defendant had to prove that his failure to appear in court was not caused by negligence on his part.[49] Secondly, the legislation provided insufficient opportunity for the defendant to have a case re-opened following a trial *in absentia*.[50] Following *Somogyi* and the first judgment of *Sejdović* in 2004, the Code of Criminal Procedure was amended in 2005, so that the defendant was no longer required to prove that the court had failed to contact him by a summons. Instead the prosecutor must prove that

---

42 Interview with Professor Valerio Onida, University of Milan, 10.6.09.

43 No. 56581/00, 10.11.04; 1.3.06 (GC).

44 No. 42191/02, 9.6.05.

45 No. 56581/00, 10.11.04; 1.3.06 (GC), paras. 122–4.

46 No. 9024/80, 12.2.85.

47 Mercedes Candela Soriano (2008), 'The Reception Process in Italy and Spain' in Keller, Helen and Alec Stone Sweet (eds.), *A Europe of Rights*, p. 415.

48 Directorate General of Human Rights and Legal Affairs. *Execution of the Judgments of the European Court of Human Rights. Pending Cases. Current State of Execution, Italy*, p. 6, at 07/10/2009. http://www.coe.int/t/dghl/monitoring/execution/Reports/Current_en.asp.

49 Article 175(2) & (3) of the Code of Criminal Procedure.

50 *Somogyi v Italy*, No. 67972/01, 18.5.04, para. 36.

the defendant had been made aware of a hearing, but had subsequently failed to attend court.[51] We would also note that the Court of Cassation's interpretation of the Code of Criminal Procedure was somewhat different to the authorities' application of it in the case of *Sejdović*. Instead of 'negligence' or lack of interest on the defendant's part, the Court of Cassation stipulated that there must have been "intentional conduct designed to avoid taking cognisance of the procedural steps."[52] We discuss the particular circumstances of both the cases of *Sejdović* and *R.R.* below.

4.2.1.1. Sejdović v Italy

Ismet Sejdović (a national of the former Federal Republic of Yugoslavia) applied to the European Court in 2000, alleging a violation of the right to a fair trial (Article 6) on the grounds that he had been convicted *in absentia* without having had the opportunity to present his defence before the Italian courts. In 1992, there had been a shooting incident, and witnesses claimed Mr Sejdović had been responsible for the fatality.[53] A few weeks later the investigating judge ordered Mr Sejdović's detention pending trial, but the authorities evidently could not find him. Assuming he was evading arrest, counsel was appointed on his behalf and the trial proceeded in his absence. In 1996 he was found guilty and sentenced to 21 years' imprisonment.[54] Mr Sejdović claimed that he knew nothing of the judgment, or the trial, until he was arrested in Hamburg in 1999; he also denied that he had been evading arrest. Although the Italian authorities requested the extradition of Mr Sejdović, the German authorities refused.[55] Therefore he was unable to avail himself of the relevant (Italian) domestic remedy, which would have allowed him to contest his trial *in absentia* (within the stipulated timeframe) and have the case reopened. Mr Sejdović was detained for two months before his release. In its 2004 chamber judgment, the European Court found that there had been a violation of Article 6 of the Convention, and that Italian law did not provide sufficiently for a defendant's case to be reopened following a trial *in absentia*. The Court invoked Article 46, requiring the Italian Government to amend the relevant legislation:

> "The facts of the case disclose the existence, within the Italian legal order, of a shortcoming as a consequence of which anyone convicted *in absentia* who has not been effectively informed of the proceedings against him may be denied a retrial. It also finds that the deficiencies in national law and practice identified

---

51 *Sejdović v Italy*, No. 56581/00, 1.3.06 (GC), para. 122.
52 *Ibid.*, para. 23.
53 No. 56581/00, 10.11.04, paras. 8–9.
54 *Ibid.*, paras. 10–12.
55 *Ibid.*, paras. 13–16.

in the applicant's particular case may subsequently give rise to numerous well-founded applications."[56]

The Italian Government contested the application of Article 46 (before the Grand Chamber), and argued that the Court's new practice of prescribing general measures:

> "ran the risk of nullifying the principle that States were free to choose the means of executing judgments. It also ran counter to the spirit of the Convention and lacked a clear legal basis."[57]

Moreover the Italian Government suggested that the Court's judgments should remain 'declaratory' in nature, and that there was no legal basis for the Court to prescribe measures, and that by so doing the Court was encroaching on the role of the Committee of Ministers. The Government also argued that, should this new practice continue, then it must be clarified in the Rules of the Court, and upon communication of a case, the parties should be asked whether or not they consider the violation in question to be systemic.[58]

4.2.1.2. R.R. v Italy

Following the first *Sejdović* judgment (but before the second), the Court issued an Article 46 judgment relating to a trial held *in absentia* in the case of *R.R. v Italy* in 2005.[59] The applicant, a French citizen, complained of a violation of the right to defend himself before the Italian courts, during separation proceedings in 1995, instituted by his wife. The court decided in his absence that he should pay the monthly sum of 1,000,000 lira (approximately €500) in alimony. In 1992, the applicant had left the conjugal home on account of his wife's alleged infidelity and relocated to France. In 1993, his wife filed proceedings against him for failing to pay alimony, which is a criminal offence under the Italian criminal code. Between the hearing in 1995 and four subsequent hearings between 1998 and 2000 the court was unable to contact the applicant, because they did not have his correct contact details. A lawyer was appointed to represent him at the hearings and although he was not present, he was not officially noted as 'absent.'[60] In 2000 he was sentenced to 6 months' imprisonment for failing to pay alimony, having left his wife and children without justification. In January 2002 there was a further hearing, at which the applicant was officially declared 'absent'. The court added a fine of €30,987 to the 6 month sentence. The applicant claimed that he only found

56 *Sejdović v Italy*, No. 56581/00, 10.11.04, para. 44.
57 *Sejdović v Italy*, No, 56581/00, 1.3.06 (GC), para. 115.
58 *Ibid.*, paras. 116–118.
59 *R.R. v Italy*, No. 42191/02, 9.6.05.
60 *Ibid.*, paras. 10–16.

out about this judgment in November 2002 after his sister faxed him a copy of it.[61] In its judgment the European Court found a violation of Article 6(1) of the Convention on the same basis as *Sejdović* – resulting from the lack of a procedure to enable a defendant to re-open a case after a trial *in absentia*. Although the Italian Government had already amended the relevant legislation (Article 175 of the Code of Criminal Procedure) by the time of the judgment in 2005, the Court invoked Article 46 highlighting the deficiency that there clearly had been in the domestic legal system. The Court determined that it was too soon to assess the efficacity of the new law in practice,[62] and for that reason did not specify general measures.

In April 2005, Parliament passed the Law no. 60/2005 which amended Article 175 of the Code of Criminal Procedure to allow defendants who had been tried *in absentia*, and were not aware of the proceedings against them, the right to appeal against the judgment (with the exception of defendants who have deliberately chosen not to attend the hearing). Applications must be made within thirty days of the date when a defendant became aware of the judgment.[63] As in the judgment of *R.R. v Italy*, the Grand Chamber in *Sejdović* in 2006 decided that it was too soon to evaluate the compatibility of the new law with the Convention. Since the Government had taken steps to redress the problem, the Court decided there was no need to prescribe general measures.[64]

Emilia de Bellis of the Ministry of Justice told us that the Ministry considered *Sejdović* to be a pilot judgment in that the Court had found that the violation was a systemic problem. According to Emilia de Bellis, in response to the various Strasbourg judgments, the Ministry of Justice had examined the domestic law on trial *in absentia*, in order to remedy the problem which had arisen.[65]

Since the *Sejdović* Grand Chamber judgment in 2006, the Committee of Ministers has expressed itself to be satisfied with the amendments to the Code of Criminal Procedure and the implementation of the Court's judgment. Furthermore, in its report on the case, the Committee of Ministers positively appraised the intervention of the Court of Cassation in a subsequent case in requiring a local appellate court to apply the European Court case law in respect of such a violation:

> "the Court of Cassation reaffirmed the direct effect of the Convention and of the case-law of the European Court in Italian law, not least in respect of judgments having the status of *res judicata*. It thus affirmed the retroactive application of

61 *Ibid.*, paras. 17–27.
62 *Ibid.*, paras. 66–68.
63 *Sejdović v Italy*, No. 56581/00, 1.3.06 (GC), paras. 25–27.
64 *Sejdović v Italy*, No. 56581/00, 1.3.06 (GC), paras. 122–124.
65 Interview with Emilia de Bellis, Ministry of Justice, Rome, 9.6.09.

> Article 175 of the CCP. The case-law of the Court of Cassation has been applied by the Verona Tribunal ... thereby indicating that it seems possible to rely directly on the direct effect of the Convention to resolve these cases."[66]

In the case of expropriation laws, there have been a number of Constitutional Court judgments holding the relevant legislation to be unconstitutional, as we discuss in the next section.

4.2.2. COMPENSATION FOR EXPROPRIATED PROPERTY (ARTICLE 1 OF PROTOCOL NO. 1)

The issue of reconciling Italian expropriation laws with the Convention poses a significant challenge to the Italian Government, and also to the European Court as to how prescriptive its judgments should be in assessing appropriate rates of compensation. To some extent this problem arose in the Polish cases of *Broniowski* and *Hutten-Czapska*, as discussed in Chapter Two. In those situations, though, the Court did not prescribe rates of compensation, but rather left the matter for the state to resolve, and reserved the right to assess the solution proposed by the state.

In 1971 a law was passed in Italy providing regional authorities with the right to expropriate land for development in the public interest, referred to as 'indirect expropriation'.[67] The new criteria in the 1971 Law (amended in 1974 and 1977) prescribed a flat, basic rate of compensation for all types of land expropriated, but the Constitutional Court subsequently held this provision to be unconstitutional in 1980.[68] As discussed above (at Section 4.1.2.1), once a law is found to be unconstitutional the previous law automatically comes back into force with immediate effect. Between 1980 and 1999 the Constitutional Court issued a number of judgments declaring expropriation laws unconstitutional. This situation has therefore given rise to considerable confusion in the allocation of compensation.

Aside from questioning the amount of compensation, applicants to Strasbourg have complained of delays following the authorities' issue of notices of expropriation, and the time taken for a plan of development to be finally determined by the

66 Directorate General of Human Rights and Legal Affairs. *Execution of the Judgments of the European Court of Human Rights. Pending Cases. Current State of Execution, Italy*, p. 4, at 7.10.09. http://www.coe.int/t/dghl/monitoring/execution/Reports/Current_en.asp. See also *Cat Berro v Italy*, No. 34192/07, dec. 25.11.08.

67 "Law no. 865/1971 (supplemented by section 4 of Legislative Decree no. 115/1974, which subsequently became Law no. 247/1974, and by section 14 of Law no. 10/1977)" *Scordino v Italy, no. 1 (36813/97)*, 29.3.06, para. 49.

68 *Scordino v Italy (No. 1)*, No. 36813/97, 29.3.06 (GC), paras. 49–50.

regional authorities and the expropriation executed. Once the authorities have issued a notice of expropriation, the owners of the land in question are then prohibited from developing the land.[69] Applicants have therefore also sought additional compensation at the European Court for the time during which they have been, in effect, denied the use of their land.

This section examines the quasi-pilot judgments of *Scordino* (No. 1) and *Scordino* (No. 3), in which Article 46 of the Convention was applied regarding violations of the applicants' property rights with respect to the adequacy of compensation for expropriated property. Although in the related case of *Scordino* (No. 2) the Court did not apply Article 46, nor did it do so in the similar cases of *Elia SRL*, *Terazzi*, or *Rossitto*, these cases are examined in this section, as is the case of *Guiso-Gallisay* which is, in effect, the 'sequel' to *Scordino* (No. 1) and (No. 3). These judgments explore how the Government has responded to this issue since the *Scordino* 'quasi-pilot' judgments and reflect the persistence of systemic violations with respect to Article 1 of Protocol No. 1 of the Convention. The *Guiso-Gallisay* case raises the thorny issue of how the Court deals with systemic violations of Article 1 of Protocol No. 1, and how much discretion should be left to respondent states in determining compensation.

4.2.2.1. Scordino v Italy (No. 1)

In its first *Scordino* judgment of 2004, the Court found a violation of the applicants' right to peaceful enjoyment of possessions (Article 1 of Protocol No. 1) and the right to a fair hearing within a reasonable time (Article 6(1)).[70] The Italian Government contested the judgment and requested that the case be referred to the Grand Chamber which subsequently confirmed the chamber judgment, and went on also to invoke Article 46.[71]

Giovanni, Elena, Maria and Giuliana Scordino originally filed their case in 1993 to contest the amount of compensation which the family had received for land expropriated from their father, and the unreasonable length of the court proceedings in resolving their case. In 1982 the Reggio di Calabria District Council had decided to re-develop some land owned by Mr. Scordino.[72] The amount offered for the land was in accordance with Law no. 865/1971 and was offered on the basis that the final amount would be determined once a law had been enacted laying down new compensation criteria for building land.[73] Mr. Scordino refused the particular offer of compensation, and the Regional Council

[69] *Elia S.r.l. v Italy*, No. 37710/97, 2.8.01, para. 29.
[70] *Scordino v Italy (No.1)*, No. 36813/97, 29.7.04.
[71] *Scordino v Italy (No.1)*, No. 36813/97, 29.3.06 (GC).
[72] *Ibid.*, paras. 1–3.
[73] *Ibid.*, para. 15.

offered a slightly higher amount, which he again refused.[74] The Constitutional Court found the terms relating to compensation to be unconstitutional, as they were subject to the enactment of a future law. Consequently the previous law, 2359/1865, came back into force which offered compensation at a rate equivalent to the market value of the land at the time of expropriation. The Regional Council awarded Mr. Scordino a sum which it claimed was commensurate with the market value of the land.[75]

In 1990 Mr. Scordino brought proceedings against the District Council and the Cooperative in the Reggio di Calabria Court of Appeal to contest the amount of compensation. During the course of the proceedings, a new law came into force: Law No. 359 of 8 August 1992 ('Urgent measures aimed at stabilising public finances'). Section 5 *bis*[76] of the 1992 law specified new criteria for calculating compensation for the expropriation of building land. The law also applied to pending proceedings, such as Mr. Scordino's case.[77] After Mr. Scordino died in 1992, his family continued the proceedings, in 1993, disputing the terms of compensation.[78] Compensation was awarded according to section 5 *bis* of the 1992 law, in 1997.[79]

In its 2004 judgment the Court found a violation of the right to a fair hearing for two reasons. Firstly, there was a breach of the reasonable time requirement – the domestic proceedings had lasted about eight and a half years. Secondly, Article 6 was violated because the enactment of a new law regulating the award of compensation, which applied to *pending* proceedings, amounted to an interference, by the legislature, with the judicial process. As to the right to peaceful enjoyment of possessions, the Court held that the price paid to the applicants was

74 *Ibid.*, paras. 16–18.
75 *Ibid.*, paras. 19–21.
76 "Section 5 *bis* of Law no. 359 of 8 August 1992 introduced a "temporary, exceptional and urgent" measure aimed at stabilising public finances, to remain valid until structural measures were adopted. That provision applied to any expropriation under way and to any pending proceedings related thereto. Section 5 *bis* of Law no. 359/1992, which was published in the Official Gazette on 13 August 1992, came into force on 14 August 1992. Section 5 *bis* provides that the compensation payable for the expropriation of building land is to be calculated using the following formula: market value of the land plus the total of annual ground rent multiplied by the last ten years, divided by two, minus a 40% deduction. In such cases, the compensation corresponds to 30% of the market value. That amount is subject to tax, deducted at source at a rate of 20% (in accordance with section 11 of Law no. 413/1991). The 40% deduction can be avoided if the basis for the expropriation is not an expropriation order but a "voluntary agreement" for the transfer of the land or, as in the instant case, if the expropriation took place before section 5 *bis* came into force (see the Constitutional Court's judgment no. 283 of 16 June 1993). In such cases, the resulting compensation corresponds to 50% of the market value. Again, that amount is subject to tax at a rate of 20%", see: *Scordino v Italy (No.1),* No. 36813/97, 29.3.06 (GC), paras. 56–58.
77 *Scordino v Italy (No.1),* No. 36813/97, 29.3.06 (GC), paras. 22–29.
78 *Ibid.*, para. 30.
79 *Ibid.*, paras. 36–39.

not reasonably related to the value of the expropriated property. The decision was then referred up to the Grand Chamber which, in its 2006 judgment, in essence followed the line taken by the chamber judgment, but in addition laid particular emphasis on the systemic issue which had arisen:

> "... the violation ... originated in a widespread problem arising out of a malfunctioning of the Italian legislation which has affected, and may still affect in the future, a large number of people. The unjustified hindrance in obtaining compensation for expropriation 'reasonably related to the value of the property' was not caused by an isolated incident; neither is it attributable to the particular turn taken by events in the case of the applicants. It arises from the application of a law to a specific category of citizens, namely, persons affected by the expropriation of land."[80]

The Court also noted frankly, that, aside from certain indications made by the Constitutional Court, "the existence and systemic nature of this problem have not been acknowledged by the Italian judicial authorities".[81] As a consequence, the Court stipulated that the Italian authorities should:

> "... above all, remove every obstacle to the award of compensation bearing a reasonable relation to the value of the expropriated property, and thus ensure, by appropriate statutory, administrative and budgetary measures, that the right in question is guaranteed effectively and rapidly in respect of other claimants affected by the expropriation of property ...".[82]

4.2.2.2. *Scordino v Italy (No. 3)*

A year later, there was still apparently no domestic remedy in place, so that in the third *Scordino* judgment, the Court identified a violation in the Italian legal system (the illegal expropriation of land) whereby a whole class of people were clearly deprived arbitrarily of their property rights, which, the Court noted, could give rise in the future to numerous well-founded applications.[83] The Court also found that the large numbers of individuals concerned indicated that this was a systemic dysfunction. As in *Scordino* (No.1), the Court held that compensation should be commensurate with the value of the property expropriated and that damages for loss of use of the property should, ideally, also be awarded.[84]

---

80 *Ibid.*, para. 229.
81 *Ibid.*, para. 230.
82 *Ibid.*, para. 237.
83 *Scordino v Italy (No. 3)*, No. 43662/98, 17.5.05; 6.3.07, para. 11.
84 *Ibid.*, paras. 15–16.

The Committee of Ministers reiterated these views in its 2007 Resolution concerning the practice of 'indirect expropriation' and expressed its dissatisfaction with the emergency expropriation of land by local authorities (without any formal procedure), the lack of clear and predictable rules concerning the transfer of property and compensation, and the absence of mechanisms to afford redress, including the inadequacy of compensation awarded.[85] More recently, the Court has re-assessed this situation in the case of *Guiso-Gallisay.*

4.2.2.3. Guiso-Gallisay

As a sequel to the *Scordino* cases, *Guiso-Gallisay* signalled a change to the application of the Convention as regards the calculation of compensation for the expropriation of land. In the Court's 2008 judgment in this case[86] the Second Section departed from the usual method of calculating compensation under Article 41. The new method was based on the market value of the property on the date when the right of ownership to the property had been lost, rather than the market value of the land increased by the value of the buildings erected on it by the local authority. The Court's intention was to iron out potential disparities in value, which might depend on the nature of the works carried out on the land.[87] The case was subsequently referred to the Grand Chamber which upheld the chamber judgment and, noting that the domestic courts had taken account of the European Court case law, found that the new method by which compensation had been calculated in the case should be applied to all similar pending and future cases before the Italian courts.[88] This, in effect, overturned the means of calculating compensation which had been extensively applied, notably in Italian cases, including *Scordino* (No. 1).[89]

Reporting on the 2008 Section judgment in the *Guiso-Gallisay* case, the Prime Minister's Office characterised the case as a 'pilot judgment' and suggested that

---

85 Committee of Ministers (2007), Interim Resolution CM/ResDH(2007)3, *Systemic violations of the right to the peaceful enjoyment of possessions through 'indirect expropriation' by Italy (adopted by the Committee of Ministers on 14 February 2007 at the 987th meeting of the Ministers' Deputies).* https://wcd.coe.int/ViewDoc.jsp?id=1095781&Site=CM&BackColorInternet=9999CC&BackColorIntranet=FFBB55&BackColorLogged=FFAC75.

86 *Guiso-Gallisay v Italy,* No. 58858/00, 21.10.08.

87 But on this question, and the application of the principle of *restitutio in integrum,* see the dissenting opinion of Judge Tulkens to the chamber judgment, and the dissenting opinion of Judge Spielmann to the Grand Chamber judgment.

88 *Guiso-Gallisay v Italy,* No. 58858/00, 22.12.09 (GC). It resulted in a pecuniary damages award of €2,145,000.

89 As applied, for example, in *Papamichalopoulos v Greece,* No. 14556/89, 31.10.95; *Belvedere Alberghiera S.r.l. v Italy,* No. 31524/96, 30.5.00; *Carbonara and Ventura v Italy,* No. 24638/94, 30.5.00; *Scordino v Italy* (No. 1), No. 36813/97, 29.3.06; *Scordino v Italy (No.3),* No. 43662/98, 6.3.07; *Pasculli v Italy,* No. 36818/97, 4.12.07.

the European Court had heeded the Italian Government's objections to previous rulings which had imposed:

> "... particularly punitive, as well as illogical, contradictory and unfair, terms for the state involved in the proceedings. With the ... change in direction ... the European Court has come much closer to the Italian Government's thinking – harmonising the compensation criteria with that used also by the national judge in the domestic system ..."[90]

The Court did not apply the pilot judgment procedure in *Guiso-Gallisay* (nor invoke Article 46 in the manner of a 'quasi-pilot' judgment). The Prime Minister's Office Report does not offer any explanation as to its characterisation of *Guiso-Gallisay* as a pilot judgment. We might conclude that the Prime Minister's Office would be glad to categorise it as such since it lends the judgment greater weight as a precedent for future awards of compensation, in a way which is more favourable to the Italian authorities.

4.2.2.4. Prohibition of building on land for expropriation

The Scordino family filed a further application with the European Court concerning the terms under which the expropriation had proceeded. Their complaint was that in 1975 Mr. Scordino had been informed of the authorities' decision to expropriate the land, as part of the General Urbanisation Plan, and that such notification expressly prohibited owners from developing the land in the interim. It was only five years later, however, in 1980, that the Council formulated any concrete plans as to how they would develop the land.[91] In its 2004 judgment the Court held that the Italian Government should pay compensation for this delay.[92] This had been preceded by a Constitutional Court judgment in 1999 which found the lack of statutory provision for compensation in such cases to be unconstitutional.[93] A series of similar cases have been taken to the European Court, such as *Elia SRL v Italy*,[94] *Terazzi v Italy*[95] and more recently *Rossitto v Italy*.[96]

---

[90] Italy. Presidenza del Consiglio dei Ministri (2008), *L'esecuzione delle pronunce della Corte europea dei diritti dell'uomo nei confronti dello stato italiano Legge 9 gennaio 2006, n. 12 : Relazione al Parlamento Anno 2008=The execution of the decisions of the European Court of Human Rights with respect to the Italian State, law of 9 June 2006, no. 12: Report to the Parliament, 2008*, pp. 26–27 [translation by Federica Arisco].

[91] *Scordino v Italy (No. 2)*, No. 36815/97, 15.7.04, paras 12–14.

[92] *Ibid.*, para. 132.

[93] Judgment No. 179 of 12–20.5.99. See: *Elia S.r.l. v Italy*, No. 37710/97, 2.8.01, para. 47; *Scordino v Italy (No. 2)*, No. 36815/97, 15.7.04, para 44.

[94] No. 37710/97, 2.8.01.

[95] No. 27265/95, 17.10.02.

[96] No. 7977/03, 26.5.09.

In its January 2010 report on the execution of Court judgments, the Committee of Ministers noted that the Italian Government had failed to introduce an effective remedy in relation to the State's inaction in such situations, or to provide a mechanism for the compensation of landowners when restrictions on building were maintained after the expiry of the deadlines set by the law. The Italian Government had informed the Committee of Ministers secretariat, following the *Terazzi* judgment, that such a remedy would come into force in 2003 but, according to the Committee of Ministers, no progress had been made.[97] These issues were not addressed in the 2008 Report from the Prime Minister's Office, which, however, discussed in some detail the issue of length of proceedings and the implementation of the Pinto Act (which we discuss in the next section).

4.2.3. RIGHT TO TRIAL WITHIN A REASONABLE TIME (ARTICLE 6(1))

In response to the perennial problem of excessively long proceedings before the Italian courts, the Pinto Law of 2001[98] sought to provide redress by enabling the courts to make awards of just satisfaction. The Pinto Law was introduced in the wake of the *Bottazzi v Italy* judgment, in 1999,[99] in which the Grand Chamber first identified a systemic violation of the right to trial within a reasonable time in the Italian legal system. Although the Court did not invoke Article 46 in its judgment, nor was there a violation of Article 13, the Court expressly identified a systemic violation, amounting to a 'practice' that breached the Convention, and which required the Italian authorities to take general measures to rectify the situation:

> "The frequency with which violations are found shows that there is an accumulation of identical breaches which are sufficiently numerous to amount not merely to isolated incidents. Such breaches reflect a continuing situation that has not yet been remedied and in respect of which litigants have no domestic remedy. This accumulation of breaches accordingly constitutes a practice that is incompatible with the Convention."[100]

---

97 Directorate General of Human Rights and Legal Affairs. *Execution of the Judgments of the European Court of Human Rights. Pending Cases. Current State of Execution, Italy*, pp. 19–20 at 7.10.09. http://www.coe.int/t/dghl/monitoring/execution/Reports/Current_en.asp.

98 Law no. 89 of 24 March 2001 on the right to trial within a reasonable time (Legge Pinto: durata ragionevole del processo ed equa riparazione-nuovo 375 cpc, Legge 24.3.01 n° 89, G.U. 03.04.2001). It is more commonly known as the 'Pinto Law', named after Senator Michele Pinto who presented the bill to Parliament.

99 No. 34884/97, 28.7.99.

100 No. 34884/97, 28.7.99, para. 22.

Therefore, we would categorise *Bottazzi* as a 'third tier' judgment, akin to cases like the Polish length of proceedings judgment in *Kudła*, as discussed in Chapter Two. Interestingly, in his dissenting opinion in *Bottazzi*, Judge Türmen was critical of the majority's finding of an 'administrative practice', arguing that there was no evidence of official state tolerance of the problem. Given the dialogue that was at the time ongoing between the Committee of Ministers and the Italian authorities, Judge Türmen could see no basis for this finding.

However, the Court was soon to find deficiencies in the Pinto Law, as hundreds of new applications were submitted to the Court complaining about its application. The Court responded by issuing the *Scordino* judgment in 2006,[101] as we discuss in the next section.

Scordino v Italy (No.1) *and the ineffectiveness of the Pinto Law*

The domestic proceedings in the *Scordino* case had been adjourned by the local courts on a number of occasions, such that in 2002 the Scordino family appealed to the Reggio di Calabria Court of Appeal, invoking the Pinto Law, and seeking compensation for the unreasonable length of the proceedings. Later in 2002 the Court of Appeal judged that the length of proceedings should only be calculated from 1993, when the Scordino family had continued the proceedings following the death of Mr. Scordino, and therefore it amounted to three and a half years. The Court of Appeal found that this was therefore only six months in excess of the European Court 'standard' (three years at first instance and two years at second instance courts).[102] The Court of Appeal accordingly awarded a nominal amount for non-pecuniary damages.[103] The Grand Chamber in *Scordino* (No. 1) in 2006 found this award to be about 10% of awards made by the European Court in similar Italian cases. Contrary to the decision of the Court of Appeal, the Grand Chamber held that the entire length of the proceedings should have been taken into account: eight and a half years.

In November 2003, the Court of Cassation had issued a number of judgments on appeal from decisions delivered by the courts of appeal in Pinto proceedings, in which it emphasised that it was imperative that the domestic courts should apply

101 *Scordino v Italy (No. 1)*, No. 36813/97, 29.3.06 (GC). A further eight Article 46 judgments were issued by the Grand Chamber in respect of the right to trial within a reasonable time, on the same day: *Cocchiarella v Italy*, No. 64886/01, 29.3.06 (GC), *Zullo (Ernestino) v Italy*, No. 64897/01, 29.03.06 (GC), *Apicella v Italy*, No. 64890/01, 29.3.06 (GC), *Mostacciuolo (Giuseppe) v Italy (No. 1)*, No. 64705/01, 29.3.06 (GC), *Mostacciuolo (Giuseppe) v Italy (No. 2)*, No. 65102/01, 29.3.06 (GC), *Musci v Italy*, No. 64699/01, 29.3.06 (GC), *Pizzati (Riccardi) v Italy*, No. 62361/00, 29.3.06 (GC) and *Procaccini (Giuseppina and Orestina) v Italy*, No. 65075/01, 29.3.06 (GC).

102 *Scordino v Italy (No. 1)*, No. 36813/97, 29.3.06 (GC), para. 43.

103 *Ibid.*, paras. 42–46.

the Pinto Law in accordance with the European Court's rulings.[104] Nevertheless, in spite of this important affirmation by the Court of Cassation, the Pinto Law had not solved the problem of excessively lengthy proceedings in Italian courts; it simply offered a compensatory mechanism. The Grand Chamber in *Scordino* found that Pinto had "admittedly saved the Court the trouble of finding these violations, but the task has simply been transferred to the courts of appeal, which were already overburdened themselves".[105] Instead, the Pinto Law had given rise to a new new variety of clone case appearing in Strasbourg: the failure to execute judgments issued in accordance with the new law:

> "Hundreds of cases are currently pending before the Court in respect of awards made by the courts of appeal in 'Pinto' proceedings ... The Court ... regrets to observe that where a deficiency that has given rise to a violation has been put right, another one related to the first one appears: in the present case the delay in executing decisions. It cannot over-emphasise the fact that States must equip themselves with the means necessary and adequate to ensure that all the conditions for providing effective justice are guaranteed."[106]

In 2009, in *Simaldone v Italy*,[107] the European Court again found a violation of Article 6(1) on the basis of excessive length of domestic proceedings and delays in proceedings under the Pinto Law itself. The Court also drew attention to the systemic failings of the Pinto Law, noting that since March 2006 it had delivered more than 50 similar judgments arising from delays in the payment of compensation under the Pinto Law. The Court concluded from the high number of applications lodged since September 2007 that there were problems with the way the Law was operating. Nevertheless, the Court found no violation of Article 13, and could not conclude that the Law was structurally ineffective (taking note of the 16,000 decisions made by the courts of appeal under the Pinto Law between 2005 and 2007).[108]

In March 2009, a Committee of Ministers' Resolution strongly urged the Italian authorities:

> "... to consider amending Act No. 89/2001 (the Pinto Law) with a view to setting up a financial system resolving the problems of delay in the payment of compensation

---

104 *Ibid.*, para. 64.

105 *Ibid.*, para. 223.

106 *Ibid.*, para. 238. See also: Third annual report on the excessive length of judicial proceedings in Italy for 2003 (administrative, civil and criminal justice), CM/Inf/DH(2004)23, 24 September 2004; Interim Resolution ResDH(2005)114 concerning the judgments of the European Court of Human Rights and decisions by the Committee of Ministers in 2183 cases against Italy relating to the excessive length of judicial proceedings, 30 November 2005.

107 No. 22644/03, 31.3.09.

108 *Ibid.*, paras. 82–85. See also *Cocchiarella v Italy*, No. 64886/01, 29.3.06 and eight other grand chamber judgments of the same date.

awarded, to simplify the procedure and to extend the scope of the remedy to include injunctions to expedite proceedings."[109]

In its most recent report on this question, the Committee of Ministers has stipulated that the following issues need to be resolved regarding the application of the Pinto Law. Firstly, adequate compensation must be paid by the courts, and the case-law of the European Court must be followed when applying the law. Secondly, there should be a reduction in court fees for applicants seeking a remedy via the Pinto Law, and, thirdly, the courts must ensure that compensation is paid within good time.[110] The position of the Prime Minister's Office as regards the failings in the Pinto Law are further discussed in Section 4.4.1.1 below.

A number of our respondents acknowledged that the pilot judgment procedure had been positive in the case of Italy, and that the process had enabled the Court of Cassation and Constitutional Courts to raise the status of the Convention with respect to domestic law. Some respondents, however, noted that the status of the Convention is still developing, but said that they hoped, and expected, that in a few years' time the Convention will be directly applicable in Italian law in all instances. We consider these issues in the next section.

4.3. THE EFFECT OF PILOT JUDGMENTS ON THE STATUS OF THE EUROPEAN CONVENTION ON HUMAN RIGHTS IN DOMESTIC LAW: CONSTITUTIONAL COURT JUDGMENTS 348 & 349

In the Italian domestic legal system, it is the Constitutional Court which is responsible for interpreting how judgments of the European Court of Human Rights should be reconciled with domestic law, whereas in contrast EU law has a higher status, and must be directly applied in the domestic legal system.[111] Andrea Saccucci confirmed that a judgment of the European Court of Human Rights

---

109 Committee of Ministers (2009), Interim Resolution CM/ResDH(2009)42 *Execution of the judgments of the European Court of Human Rights concerning the excessive length of judicial proceedings in Italy: Progress achieved and outstanding issues in the context of general measures to ensure compliance with the judgments of the European Court of Human Rights*, p. 3. https://wcd.coe.int/ViewDoc.jsp?Ref=CM/ResDH(2009)42&Language=lanEnglish&Ver=original&Site=CM&BackColorInternet=9999CC&BackColorIntranet=FFBB55&BackColorLogged=FFAC75.

110 Directorate General of Human Rights and Legal Affairs. *Execution of the Judgments of the European Court of Human Rights. Pending Cases. Current State of Execution, Italy*, pp. 23–24 at 7.10.09. http://www.coe.int/t/dghl/monitoring/execution/Reports/Current_en.asp.

111 Mercedes Candela Soriano (2008), 'The Reception Process in Spain and Italy' in Keller, Helen and Alec Stone Sweet (eds.), *A Europe of Rights*, pp. 393–450, p. 404.

cannot be invoked directly and applied as a precedent by judges in ordinary courts in assessing the constitutionality of the domestic law. When asked whether the Convention will ever attain the same status as EU law, (that is, directly applicable), Andrea Saccucci told us he believed that this was possible, in about twenty years, on the basis that this was how long it took for EU law to be recognised as such.[112] Nonetheless, judgments 348 and 349, issued by the Constitutional Court in 2007, appear to have raised the status of the Convention significantly with respect to the domestic law. The Constitutional Court Judge, Giuseppe Tesauro told us that:

> "Judgments 348 and 349 were the first step of a journey to have a satisfying system – a satisfying union between the Italian legal order and the European Convention. So this was only the first step and I think that there will be many developments – an evolution – ... to have ... the European Convention as our standard of protection."[113]

This development followed the *Scordino* (No.1) Grand Chamber judgment of March 2006, when in May and June 2006, the Palermo Court of Appeal and Court of Cassation held the 1992 Law regulating compensation for the expropriation of land[114] unconstitutional – under Articles 111 and 117 of the Constitution.[115] These provisions of the Italian Constitution stipulate the requirement to recognize international agreements. The Court of Cassation referred to the European Court's *Scordino* judgments and found the particular provisions of the 1992 law to be insufficient in upholding the rights enshrined in Article 6 and Article 1 of Protocol No. 1 to the European Convention. Subsequently the matter was referred to the Constitutional Court, which issued judgments 348 and 349 in October 2007, concerning the unconstitutionality of the laws regulating compensation for property expropriated by the state. In judgment 348 the Constitutional Court clarified the status of the Convention with respect to domestic law:

> "Compared to other international law treaties, the ECHR has the particular characteristic of having provided for the jurisdiction of a court, the European Court of Human Rights, which is charged with the role of interpreting the provisions of the Convention. In fact, Article 32(1) provides: 'The jurisdiction of the Court shall extend to all cases concerning the interpretation and application of the Convention and its Protocols which are referred to it in accordance with Articles 33, 34 and 47.'

---

112 Interview with Professor Andrea Saccucci, Rome, 9.6.09.

113 Interview with Giuseppe Tesauro, Constitutional Court, Rome, 8.6.09.

114 Article 5*bis*, paragraph 7*bis* of the 1992 law no. 333 – 'Urgent measures on the recovery of public finances'.

115 Constitutional Court. Judgment 348 of 22.10.07, section. 1; 1.4. http://www.cortecostituzionale.it/versioni_in_lingua/eng/attivitacorte/pronunceemassime/recent_judgments_2007.asp.

"Since legal norms live through the interpretation which is given to them by legal practitioners, and in the first place the courts, the natural consequence of Article 32(1) of the Convention is that the international law obligations undertaken by Italy in signing and ratifying the ECHR include the duty to bring its own legislation into line with the Convention, in line with the meaning attributed by the Court specifically charged with its interpretation and application. It is therefore not possible to speak of the jurisdiction of a court overlapping with that of the Italian courts, but of a pre-eminent interpretative role which the signatory states have recognised in the European Court, thereby contributing to clarifying their international law obligations in that particular area."[116]

At the same time, once the European Court has found an incompatibility between the Convention and Italian domestic law, this does not automatically mean that the law in question has been quashed and that the Convention ruling prevails:

"It is equally incorrect to maintain that the incompatibility between the national provision and the ECHR can be resolved by the ordinary courts simply setting aside the former. Assuming that this cannot be a result of the general communitisation of the ECHR, for the reasons already mentioned above, it is still necessary to consider whether it is possible to find that such provisions (and in particular Article 1 of the Additional Protocol) are directly effective, along the same lines and with the same implications as directly effective Community law, including in particular the ability of the national courts to apply them directly in the place of national legislation in conflict with them."[117]

The Constitutional Court also held that Article 117 of the Constitution, which refers to the binding nature of international agreements, must be applied within the context of the rest of the Constitution, and that the European Court's judgments are implemented within this framework:

"This court and the Strasbourg Court ultimately fulfil different roles, even though both share the same objective of protecting as effectively as possible the fundamental rights of man. The interpretation of the Rome Convention and of the Protocols is a matter for the Strasbourg Court, which only guarantees the application of a uniform level of protection throughout the member states. Where a question is raised over the constitutionality of a national provision in the light of Article 117(1) of the Constitution due to a breach – insurmountable through

116 Constitutional Court. Judgment 348 of 22.10.07, section 4.6. http://www.cortecostituzionale.it/versioni_in_lingua/eng/attivitacorte/pronunceemassime/recent_judgments_2007.asp.

117 Constitutional Court. Judgment 349 of 22.10.07, section 6.1. http://www.cortecostituzionale.it/versioni_in_lingua/eng/attivitacorte/pronunceemassime/recent_judgments_2007.asp.

> interpretation – of one or more ECHR provisions, this court is on the other hand charged with ascertaining the breach and, where one is found to exist, verifying whether the provisions of the ECHR, as interpreted by the Strasbourg Court, guarantee a protection of fundamental rights that is at least equivalent to the level guaranteed by the Italian Constitution. This does not entail calling into question the interpretation of the ECHR by the Strasbourg Court … but of verifying the compatibility of the ECHR provisions, as interpreted by the Court specifically charged with this task by the member states, with the relevant Constitutional provisions. In this way, a correct balance is struck between the need to guarantee respect for international obligations required by the Constitution and to prevent this also resulting in a breach of the Constitution itself."[118]

Although the 1992 Law was declared unconstitutional, the Constitutional Court held in judgment 348 that the Italian courts are not always bound to follow the principle of *restitutio in integrum* in accordance with the Strasbourg ruling in *Scordino*, and that the Strasbourg Court itself "is not unequivocal regarding the identification of the venal value of the property as the only criterion for calculating compensation admissible in the light of Article 1 of the First Protocol." The Constitutional Court found that, instead, the terms of compensation awarded by the Strasbourg Court under Article 41 are applicable only in the specific cases concerned, and that where land is expropriated in the public interest compensation may be determined by the Italian Government at an amount lower than the market value of the property.[119]

The 2008 annual report of the Prime Minister's office in accordance with the Azzolini law (see section 4.4.1 below), noted that, further to Constitutional Court judgments 348 and 349, and their effect on the status of the Convention with respect to national law, national jurisprudence has taken into consideration the provisions of the European Convention, as interpreted by the Strasbourg Court. Where it is difficult, or impossible, for the domestic law to be interpreted in compliance with the European Convention, the matter should be referred to the Constitutional Court.[120]

---

118 Constitutional Court. Judgment 349 of 22.10.07, section 6.2. http://www.cortecostituzionale.it/versioni_in_lingua/eng/attivitacorte/pronunceemassime/recent_judgments_2007.asp.

119 Constitutional Court. Judgment 348 of 22.10.07, section 1.5 http://www.cortecostituzionale.it/versioni_in_lingua/eng/attivitacorte/pronunceemassime/recent_judgments_2007.asp.

120 Italy. Presidenza del Consiglio dei Ministri (2008), *L'esecuzione delle pronunce della Corte europea dei diritti dell'uomo nei confronti dello stato italiano Legge 9 gennaio 2006, n. 12 : Relazione al Parlamento Anno 2008 = The execution of the decisions of the European Court of Human Rights with respect to the Italian State, law of 9 June 2006, no. 12 : Report to the Parliament, 2008*, p. 11. Translation by Federica Arisco.

We might surmise from this judgment, that in implementing the European Court's judgment, the rationale for doing so stemmed from a 'coincidence of interests' as between the Constitutional Court and the European Court (as we saw in Poland and Slovenia in chapters two and three) rather than through measures of enforcement as such.

As a direct result of this new, enhanced status for the European Convention in domestic law, the Italian Constitutional Court has since, for example, analysed Article 5 of the Convention, and the relevant European Court case law (including *Witold Litwa v Poland* and *N.C. v Italy*) when considering the right to freedom from arbitrary detention.[121]

Although, in theory, the Convention, as interpreted through Strasbourg judgments, is thus more directly applicable within the national system, the means by which the authorities monitor this process remains patchy, as we discuss in the next section.

4.4. MONITORING IMPLEMENTATION OF STRASBOURG JUDGMENTS

THE 'AZZOLINI LAW'

There is no independent mechanism responsible for monitoring the implementation of European Court judgments relating to Italy.[122] However, since 2006 the Prime Minister's Office[123] has been responsible for monitoring this process, by presenting a report each year to Parliament on the progress in the execution of European Court judgments, in accordance with the Azzolini Law (named after Claudio Azzolini, who was president of the Italian delegation to PACE from 2001 to 2006 and who presented the bill to Parliament).[124]

The Azzolini Law provides that the Prime Minister's Office should periodically review the case-law of the European Court with the aim of identifiying possible measures to ensure the implementation of European Court judgments. In

121 Italy. Corte Costituzionale. Judgment 219 of 11 June 2008. http://www.cortecostituzionale.it/versioni_in_lingua/eng/attivitacorte/pronunceemassime/recent_judgments_2007.asp
122 Interview with Pietro Marcenaro, the Senate, Rome, 9.6.09.
123 *La Presidenza del Consiglio dei Ministri.*
124 By an amendment made to the law 'Provisions on the execution of judgments of the European Court of Human Rights' on 9 June 2006. Disposizioni in materia di esecuzione delle pronunce della Corte europea dei diritti dell'uomo. http://gazzette.comune.jesi.an.it/2006/15/2.htm legge 9 gennaio 2006, no. 12.

accordance with this law, once identified, any incompatibility should then be reported to the Parliament.[125]

However, according to one interviewee, insufficient measures have been taken as a result of the Azzolini law.[126] Another interviewee stated that he was not sure who is monitoring the implementation of European Court judgments and expressed doubt that the authorities would in any case take any action as a result of such data.[127] When asked whether the Azzolini law has led to further implementation of Strasbourg judgments, Judge Tesauro suggested to us that it was probably beginning to do so.[128] In his *Juristras* report, Marcello Flores has argued that Parliament is not being regularly informed of the latest judgments:

> "The law is intended to permit Parliament to be regularly informed about judgments and to rapidly adopt legislative measures as they become necessary. However, it has not yet been implemented."[129]

The 2008 report by the Prime Minister's Office, published in July 2009, noted a significant rise in the number of new applications from Italy lodged at the Court in 2008 – from 41,700 in 2007 to 49,900, but a reduction of 0.5% in the number of violations.[130] Most of the judgments were clone cases in which a violation of Article 6(1) (right to a fair trial and a trial within a reasonable time) were found by the Court.[131] However, as the next sections discuss, the report appears to argue against Strasbourg rulings and attempts to justify the Government's stance regarding the implementation of the Pinto Law and the deportation of terrorist suspects.

4.4.1. REPORT ON THE PINTO LAW

In the 2008 annual report to Parliament, the Prime Minister's Office stated that problems with the implementation of the Pinto Law resulted from a lack

---

125 Marcello Flores [2009], *Supranational rights litigation, implementation and the domestic impact of Strasbourg Court jurisprudence: A case study of Italy, Juristras: final case study report*, p. 24. http://www.juristras.eliamep.gr/?cat=8.

126 Interview with Professor Andrea Saccucci, Rome, 9.6.09.

127 Interview with a civil servant, Rome. 9.6.09.

128 Interview with Giuseppe Tesauro, Constitutional Court, Rome, 8.6.09.

129 Marcello Flores [2009], *Supranational rights litigation, implementation and the domestic impact of Strasbourg Court jurisprudence: A case study of Italy, Juristras: final case study report*, p. 24. http://www.juristras.eliamep.gr/?cat=8.

130 Italy. Presidenza del Consiglio dei Ministri (2008), *L'esecuzione delle pronunce della Corte europea dei diritti dell'uomo nei confronti dello stato italiano Legge 9 gennaio 2006, n. 12 : Relazione al Parlamento Anno 2008 = The execution of the decisions of the European Court of Human Rights with respect to the Italian State, law of 9 June 2006, no. 12: Report to the Parliament, 2008*, p. 19. Translated by Federica Arisco.

131 *Ibid.*

of resources. It stated that, according to the Pinto Law, "the disbursement of compensation to those entitled takes place within the bounds of available resources", "meaning that the State will clear pending payments of compensation only if funds are available."[132] The report argues that the European Court had further burdened the Italian state with additional payments owing to claimants, which the Court of Cassation had characterised as being 'very serious and absurd'. In 2006 the total compensation paid in applying the Pinto Law was €51.5 million – by 2008 this had risen to €81.3 million and €36.6 million was still owing.[133]

4.4.2. REPORT ON THE RENDITION OF TERRORIST SUSPECTS: *SAADI V ITALY*

With reference to a series of cases concerning the 'rendition' of alleged terrorist suspects to Tunisia, the 2008 report referred to the case of *Saadi v Italy*[134] as being a 'real pilot judgment'.[135] There had been approximately 15 such cases in total,[136] and they therefore constituted a form of 'clone' case,[137] however, they were in fact neither 'full' pilot judgments nor 'quasi-pilot' judgments: there was no application of Article 46 of the Convention. There is no explanation in the report as to the interpretation of *Saadi* as a pilot judgment. What is common to each case, however, is that individual measures are specified in the operative part of the judgment, in order to prevent the applicant's deportation: "if the decision to deport the applicant to Tunisia were to be enforced, there would be a violation of Article 3 of the Convention."[138]

Instead of alerting Parliament to the issue of a persistent violation of the Convention, with a view to resolving the problem, the report criticised the Strasbourg judgment, arguing that the relevant individuals constituted a

---

132 *Ibid.*, p. 28.
133 *Ibid.*
134 *Saadi v Italy*, No. 37201/06, 28.2.08.
135 Presidenza del Consiglio dei Ministri (2008), *L'esecuzione delle pronunce della Corte europea dei diritti dell'uomo nei confronti dello stato italiano Legge 9 gennaio 2006, n. 12 : Relazione al Parlamento Anno 2008 = The execution of the decisions of the European Court of Human Rights with respect to the Italian State, law of 9 June 2006, no. 12 : Report to the Parliament, 2008*, p. 29. Translated by Federica Arisco.
136 See for example: *Saadi v Italy*, No. 37201/06, 28.2.08; *Sellem v Italy*, No. 12584/08, 5.5.09; *Bouyahia v Italy*, No. 46792/06, 24.3.09; *Darraji v Italy*, No. 11549/05, 24.3.09; *Soltana v Italy*, No. 37336/06, 24.3.09; *CBZ v Italy*, No.44006/06, 24.3.09; *Ben Salah v Italy*, No. 38128/06, 24.3.09; *Hamraoui v Italy*, No. 16201/07, 24.3.09; *Abdelhedi v Italy*, No. 2638/07, 24.3.09; *O. v Italy*, No. 37257/06, 24.3.09.
137 Presidenza del Consiglio dei Ministri (2008), *L'esecuzione delle pronunce della Corte europea dei diritti dell'uomo nei confronti dello stato italiano Legge 9 gennaio 2006, n. 12: Relazione al Parlamento Anno 2008 = The execution of the decisions of the European Court of Human Rights with respect to the Italian State, law of 9 June 2006, no. 12: Report to the Parliament, 2008*, p. 29.
138 See for example: *Saadi v Italy*, No. 37201/06, 28.2.08, operative provisions, para. 2.

recognised threat to the community and that the Court should not therefore prohibit the expulsion of such individuals. The report also cast doubt on the veracity of the various intelligence sources quoted in the Court's judgment as evidence that this category of individuals are systematically ill-treated following rendition.[139] Moreover, the report proposes the alternative measure of placing these individuals in forced-labour (criminal) detention centres for a year, with the possibility of further extension.[140]

In October 2009, the Committee of Ministers expressed its concern about the Italian authorities' failure to comply with interim measures indications, such that individuals had been deported in spite of the Court's prohibition:

> "... failure to comply with an interim measure in the context of a deportation constitutes an irreversible hindrance to the effective exercise of the right of individual petition of deported applicants. However, it is noted with regret that ... the applicant in the case of Ali Toumi ... had been deported to Tunisia ... despite the Court's request for an interim measure. For this reason, it is all the more important and urgent to take general measures to prevent such violations in the future."[141]

4.5. CONCLUSION

Many of our interviewees considered the pilot judgment procedure to be a positive way to bring about legislative change in Italy. None expressed the opinion that the Strasbourg Court is in any respect over-reaching its powers. As we have seen, one consequence of the application of the European Court's 'quasi-pilot' judgment procedure in *Scordino v Italy* was that the Constitutional Court has elevated the very status of the European Convention in domestic law. Furthermore, there is some evidence of alignment between the Italian Constitutional Court and the European Court, notably in respect of the expropriation legislation.

---

139 Presidenza del Consiglio dei Ministri (2008), *L'esecuzione delle pronunce della Corte europea dei diritti dell'uomo nei confronti dello stato italiano Legge 9 gennaio 2006, n. 12: Relazione al Parlamento Anno 2008 = The execution of the decisions of the European Court of Human Rights with respect to the Italian State, law of 9 June 2006, no. 12: Report to the Parliament, 2008*, p. 29. Translated by Federica Arisco.

140 *Ibid.*, p. 30.

141 Directorate General of Human Rights and Legal Affairs. Execution of the Judgments of the European Court of Human Rights. Pending Cases. Current State of Execution, Italy, p. 32 at 7.10.09. http://www.coe.int/t/dghl/monitoring/execution/Reports/Current_en.asp.

Andrea Saccucci has argued that a more prescriptive approach could be more effective:

> "I am sure that ... in future if the Strasbourg Court [gave] precise indications as to which measures the State should adopt in order to comply with the judgment, and these measures involve reform or an amendment of domestic law, the Constitutional Court will be able to accomplish the mission."

Nevertheless, questions remain about the extent of the familiarity of lawyers and judges in the lower courts with the European Convention, and European Court case law. Access to Strasbourg precedents in Italian is problematic.

Italy has been the subject of clone cases on a vast scale, notably in respect of the issue of the excessive length of legal proceedings. The Pinto legislation, which was introduced in an attempt to solve this problem, in practice gave rise to a new variety of clone cases in Strasbourg. Widespread violations of the Convention arising from the expropriation of property led to a Grand Chamber finding in 2006 that neither the existence nor the systemic nature of the problem had been acknowledged by the Italian judicial authorities.

We heard a number of concerns as to how the Italian authorities respond to Strasbourg judgments: that the executive and legislature are insufficiently aware of Strasbourg judgments and are ineffectual as regards the implementation of the Convention in Italian legislation. Amendments to the Criminal Procedure Code, to deal with problems relating to trial in absentia, were introduced in 2005 following the quasi-pilot judgment in *Sejdović*, but the problem had first been highlighted in the 1980s. The Italian Government has unsuccessfuly argued against the application of the pilot judgment procedure (or 'quasi-pilot' judgments) as lacking a legal basis in the Convention, as encroaching on the sovereignty of the state and usurping the role of the Committee of Ministers. Questions have been raised about the effectiveness of the Azzolini law, introduced in 2006, to establish a procedure for the monitoring of the implementation of Strasbourg judgments. Finally, the annual reports produced by the Prime Minister's Office have in some respects sought to challenge the European Court decisions.

CHAPTER 5

EXPANDING THE SCOPE OF THE PILOT JUDGMENT PROCEDURE

The experience of Russia, Ukraine, Moldova, Bosnia and Herzegovina, Turkey, Georgia and the United Kingdom

5.1. INTRODUCTION

In addition to the pilot (and 'quasi-pilot') judgments relating to our three 'target' countries (Poland, Slovenia and Italy), a small number of pilot judgments have been issued in respect of other Council of Europe states – and the Court is considering the suitability of the procedure in a number of pending cases. This chapter therefore considers the application of the pilot judgment procedure in these other states.

During the course of 2009, a further four 'full' pilot judgments were issued by the Court. The first, in January 2009, was *Burdov v Russia (No. 2)*.[1] The others were: *Olaru and others v Moldova*,[2] *Yuriy Nikolayevich Ivanov v Ukraine*[3] and *Suljagić v Bosnia and Herzegovina*.[4] In each of the pilot judgments against Russia, Ukraine and Moldova, the Court found a violation of Article 6 on account of the systemic failure to execute domestic court judgments. In *Suljagić v Bosnia and Herzegovina* the Court found a systemic violation of Article 1 of Protocol No. 1 to the Convention as a result of the government's failure to adequately reimburse applicants for lost foreign currency savings deposited in national banks in the former Yugoslavia before 1991. As had been the case in *Hutten-Czapska*, the respondent Governments in both *Ivanov* and *Suljagić* objected to the application

1 *Burdov v Russia (No. 2)*, No. 33509/04, 15.1.09.
2 *Olaru and others v Moldova*, Nos. 476/07, 22539/05, 17911/08 and 13136/07, 28.7.09.
3 *Ivanov (Yuriy Nikolayevich) v Ukraine*, No. 40450/04, 15.10.09.
4 *Suljagić v Bosnia and Herzegovina*, No. 27912/02, 3.11.09.

of the pilot judgment procedure, but nonetheless the Court issued 'full' pilot judgments, adjourning other similar cases pending before the Court.

Additionally the Court continues to issue a large number of 'quasi-pilot judgments' (or 'Article 46 judgments') (which we define in chapter one). Although too numerous to examine each in detail, we discuss two examples. The first is *Xenides-Arestis v Turkey,*[5] a case which arose in the particular circumstances of the ongoing dispute as regards the status of the northern part of Cyprus. It bears the hallmarks of a 'full' pilot judgment (including stipulations in the operative provisions as to general measures and the adjournment of other similar cases), although it was not classified as such by the Court itself. The second is *Manole v Moldova,*[6] concerning the Government's control over a major broadcaster. Finally, we also refer to two cases in which the Court has consulted the parties about the application of the pilot judgment procedure: *Bekoyeva v Georgia,*[7] (relating to the armed conflict between Russia and Georgia in August 2008) and *O'Donoghue v United Kingdom*[8] (concerning the Certificate of Approval Scheme aimed at reducing the number of 'sham marriages' involving immigrants).

5.2. THE FAILURE TO IMPLEMENT DOMESTIC COURT JUDGMENTS

In 2009, the Committee on Legal Affairs and Human Rights (CLAHR) of the Parliamentary Assembly of the Council of Europe noted that the failure to enforce domestic judicial decisions had given rise to a total of 445 European Court judgments issued against Russia and Ukraine.[9] The CLAHR report suggested that the mass of judgments is indicative of 'grave systemic problems' in both states that require urgent resolution.[10]

5.2.1. *BURDOV V RUSSIA*

Anatoliy Burdov has brought two cases to the European Court concerning the Russian state's failure to enforce court decisions. He first applied in 2000 to

5 *Xenides-Arestis v Turkey*, No. 46347/99, 22.12.05.

6 *Manole and others v Moldova*, No. 13936/02, 17.9.09.

7 *Bekoyeva (Elza Alikhanovna) v Georgia*, No. 48347/08 (communicated 26.1.09).

8 *O'Donoghue (Sinead) and others v UK*, No. 34848/07 (communicated 1.12.08).

9 Parliamentary Assembly of the Council of Europe. Committee on Legal Affairs and Human Rights (CLAHR) (2009), *Implementation of Judgements of the European Court of Human Rights*, Christos Pourgourides, AS/Jur (2009) 36 31 August 2009, pp. 17–18 http://assembly.coe.int/CommitteeDocs/2009/ejdoc36ADD_2009.pdf.

10 Parliamentary Assembly of the Council of Europe. Committee on Legal Affairs and Human Rights (CLAHR) (2009), *Implementation of Judgements of the European Court of Human Rights*, Christos Pourgourides, AS/Jur (2009) 36 31.8.09, pp. 18 http://assembly.coe.int/CommitteeDocs/2009/ejdoc36ADD_2009.pdf.

complain about the non-payment of benefits awarded to him on account of injury sustained through his work. Mr. Burdov had been engaged in emergency operations following the Chernobyl disaster between 1986 and 1987 and was consequently subjected to extensive radioactive emissions. He was entitled to benefits as a result of his illness, but did not actually receive them. In 1997 he brought proceedings against the Shakhty Social Security Service and the Shakhty City Court awarded him damages of nearly 24 million roubles. By 1999 the compensation had still not been paid to Mr. Burdov, and so the Shakhty Bailiff's Service instituted enforcement proceedings to recover the sum. The Bailiffs then informed Mr. Burdov that the Social Security Service was unable to pay the award because of insufficient funding. In 2000, the Rostov Regional Department of Justice informed Mr. Burdov that compensation for Chernobyl victims would be financed by the federal budget. In March 2001 (after Burdov had applied to the European Court) Mr. Burdov received the sum owed.[11] Nonetheless, the European Court decided that Mr. Burdov had not received adequate redress, in that the authorities had failed to acknowledge the violation of his Convention rights, and had only paid the outstanding sum after the European Court had communicated the *Burdov* case.[12] The European Court reiterated that lack of funds could not justify non-payment and held that Mr. Burdov's four year wait for payment constituted a violation of Article 6(1) of the Convention.[13] Furthermore the Court decided that denying Mr. Burdov income which he could reasonably have expected to receive also violated Article 1 of Protocol No. 1 to the Convention.[14] The *Burdov* judgment – in May 2002 – was the Court's first judgment in relation to Russia.

Since the first *Burdov* judgment in 2002, the non-enforcement of domestic court decisions has continued to be the most significant systemic human rights problem that Russia has faced (in terms of the number of applications to Strasbourg).[15] By 2007 such cases comprised about 40% of all admissible applications to the Court from Russia.[16] Between 2002 and March 2009 the Court delivered more than two

---

11 *Burdov v Russia*, No. 59498/00, 7.5.02, paras. 7–22.

12 *Ibid.*, para. 31.

13 *Ibid.*, paras. 34–38.

14 *Ibid.*, paras. 40–42.

15 See, *e.g.*, Philip Leach (2007), 'Strasbourg's oversight of Russia – an increasingly strained relationship' *Public Law*, Winter, pp. 643–645; Alexei Trochev (2009), 'All appeals lead to Strasbourg? Unpacking the impact of the European Court of Human Rights on Russia', *Demokratizatsiya*, Vol. 17, No. 2, pp. 145–178, Spring 2009, University of Winsconsin Legal Studies Research Paper No. 1082, available at: http://papers.ssrn.com/sol3/papers.cfm?abstract_id=1421342.

16 Committee of Ministers (2007), Information Documents CM/Inf/DH(2006)19 rev3. *Non-enforcement of domestic judicial decisions in Russia: general measures to comply with the European Court's judgments: Memorandum prepared by the Department for the execution of the European Court's judgments (Application of Article 46 of the ECHR) 4 June 2007*, Introduction, para. 4. https://wcd.coe.int/ViewDoc.jsp?Ref=CM/Inf/DH(2006)19&Language=lanEnglish&Ver=rev3&Site=CM&BackColorInternet=DBDCF2&BackColorIntranet=FDC864&BackColorLogged=FDC864.

hundred Russian judgments concerning the authorities' failure to execute judicial decisions against the state.[17]

There are a number of contributory causes of this problem, which the Committee of Ministers has acknowledged requires 'comprehensive and complex measures at the federal and local level.'[18] These comprise, firstly, administrative problems in the judiciary and enforcement agencies (such as inefficiencies within the bailiff system; a lack of coordination between enforcement agencies and the courts' failure to identify the debtor clearly). Secondly, there are problems with the disbursement of monies because of the relevant authorities' lack of funds and their confusion regarding administrative procedures to claim funds from the Ministry of Finance.[19]

The Russian Government has adopted a number of legislative and regulatory measures since 2005 to address these issues. These have included amendments to the Budgetary Code concerning the specific procedure for the execution of judicial decisions delivered against the state; the introduction (on 5 October 2007) of the new Federal Law on enforcement proceedings and, in April 2007, further amendments to the Budgetary Code in order to extend the Federal Treasury's control over budgetary institutions' accounts.[20] To improve regulatory mechanisms, the Ministry of Finance has introduced various administrative changes, including a new system to monitor daily how the Ministry deals with the execution of court decisions delivered against the state.[21] Modifications have been made to the form of the writ of execution to ensure that execution documents are

[17] Committee of Ministers (2009), Interim Resolution CM/ResDH(2009)43. *Execution of the judgments of the European Court of Human Rights in 145 cases against the Russian Federation relative to the failure or serious delay in abiding by final domestic judicial decisions delivered against the state and its entities as well as the absence of an effective* remedy CM/Inf/DH(2006)19 revised and CM/Inf/DH(2006)45, CM/Inf/DH(2006)19 revised. https://wcd.coe.int/ViewDoc.jsp?id=1423205&Site=CM&BackColorInternet=9999CC&BackColorIntranet=FFBB55&BackColorLogged=FFAC75.

[18] *Ibid.*

[19] Committee of Ministers (2007), Information Documents CM/Inf/DH(2006)19 rev3. *Non-enforcement of domestic judicial decisions in Russia: general measures to comply with the European Court's judgments: Memorandum prepared by the Department for the execution of the European Court's judgments (Application of Article 46 of the ECHR) 4 June 2007*, Introduction, para. 2. https://wcd.coe.int/ViewDoc.jsp?Ref=CM/Inf/DH(2006)19&Language=lanEnglish&Ver=rev3.

[20] Committee of Ministers (2009), Interim Resolution CM/ResDH(2009)43. *Execution of the judgements of the European Court of Human Rights in 145 cases against the Russian Federation relative to the failure or serious delay in abiding by final domestic judicial decisions delivered against the state and its entities as well as the absence of an effective remedy* CM/Inf/DH(2006)19 revised and CM/Inf/DH(2006)45, CM/Inf/DH(2006)19 revised. https://wcd.coe.int/ViewDoc.jsp?id=1423205&Site=CM&BackColorInternet=9999CC&BackColorIntranet=FFBB55&BackColorLogged=FFAC75.

[21] Ministry of Finance, Order No. 271, 15.8.06.

not returned to the claimants without execution.[22] The Federal Treasury has also introduced new rules to streamline the execution of court judgments and has set up a monitoring system.[23] Measures have been taken to improve accountability; firstly by an Order of the President, bailiffs have been entrusted with the role of coordinating the execution of court judgments.[24] Secondly, with respect to Chernobyl victims the specific authorities responsible for the execution of relevant judgments have been identified.[25] Nevertheless, these steps have clearly not been adequate, as demonstrated by the Court's pilot judgment in *Burdov* (No. 2) in January 2009.

5.2.1.1. Burdov v Russia (No. 2)

In 2004, Anatoliy Burdov applied for a second time to the Court – over the authorities' continued failure to comply with domestic court judgments between 2003 and 2007. In July 2008 the First Section decided to grant the case priority and informed the parties that it was considering the suitability of applying the pilot judgment procedure.[26] As we noted in chapter one, the Court applied the pilot judgment procedure on account of the fact that 200 judgments had already been issued with respect to the Russian authorities' failure to execute domestic court decisions in similar circumstances, including in relation to payment of social benefits (pensions and child allowances), compensation for damage sustained during military service or compensation for wrongful prosecution. There were also another 700 similar cases pending. Moreover, as in the case of *Burdov*, a number of applicants had already previously applied to the Court over the same violation,[27] which the Court considered to be indicative of the persistent and systemic nature of the problem. In its judgment, the European Court found a violation of Article 6, Article 1 of Protocol No. 1, and Article 13. In the operative part of the judgment, the Court required that the Russian Government should set up a remedy within 6 months to provide redress for the non-enforcement of court decisions, and froze all other similar clone cases, stipulating that they should receive compensation within a year.

---

22 Ministry of Finance, Resolution No 579 on the form of the writ of execution, 31.7.08.

23 Federal Treasury, Order No. 103, 24.4.08.

24 21.4.08.

25 Committee of Ministers (2009), Interim Resolution CM/ResDH(2009)43. *Execution of the judgements of the European Court of Human Rights in 145 cases against the Russian Federation relative to the failure or serious delay in abiding by final domestic judicial decisions delivered against the state and its entities as well as the absence of an effective remedy* CM/Inf/DH(2006)19 revised and CM/Inf/DH(2006)45, CM/Inf/DH(2006)19 revised. https://wcd.coe.int/ViewDoc.jsp?id=1423205&Site=CM&BackColorInternet=9999CC&BackColorIntranet=FFBB55&BackColorLogged=FFAC75.

26 *Burdov v Russia (No. 2)*, No. 33509/04, 15.1.09, para. 5. See also Chapter one, section 1.2.1.3.

27 See, *e.g.*, *Wasserman v Russia (No. 2)*, No. 21071/05, 10.4.08; *Kukalo v. Russia (No. 2)*, No. 11319/04, 24.7.08.

As we discuss above (and in Chapter One, Section 1.2.1.3), the Russian authorities have for many years been aware of problems relating to the enforcement of domestic judgments, and they have acknowledged the gravity of the issue. Indeed, President Medvedev spoke to the Federal Assembly in 2008 of the need for a mechanism to compensate people for unreasonable length of proceedings and for the authorities' failure to implement court decisions. He stated that the general failure to enforce court decisions was largely the result of a lack of accountability.[28] In his December 2008 address to the Congress of Judges, the President bemoaned the fact that judgments are not executed in as many as fifty percent of cases.[29] It therefore seems inexplicable that in the course of the *Burdov* (No. 2) case the Russian Government denied that there was any such systemic problem, a position which seemed to surprise (or exasperate) the Court: "their submissions in the present case appear to run against an almost undisputed recognition at both domestic and international level of the existence of structural problems in this field".[30]

According to two Moscow-based human rights lawyers whom we interviewed, the *Burdov* (No. 2) judgment has increased public awareness of the issue[31] as a systemic problem.[32] Olga Shepeleva, from the Public Interest Law Institute, was of the view, when interviewed in September 2009, that the main cause of the problem is the lack of accountability for the implementation of court judgments: the Supreme Court, the Supreme Court of Arbitration, the Justice Department at the Supreme Court, the Bailiff Service, the Ministry of Economy and Ministry of Finance are all responsible for ensuring the execution of court judgments, but in practice none of them takes the lead.[33] The 1997 Law on Enforcement Proceedings[34] clearly sets out a procedure by which bailiffs must arrange with defendants compliance with a court's writ of execution.[35] In practice, however, according to Shepeleva, in cases where public authorities are the defendants, the regional authorities do not prioritise the payment of compensation awarded to

---

28 *Burdov v Russia (No. 2),* No. 33509/04, 15.1.09, para. 38;See: Prezident Rossii. *Poslanie Federal'nomu Sobraniiu Rossiĭskoĭ Federatsii, 5.11.08 = Memorandum from the President of Russia to the Federal Assembly of the Russian Federation.* http://tours.kremlin.ru/appears/2008/11/05/1349_type63372type63374type63381type82634_208749.shtml.

29 *Medvedev rasskazal sud'iam o reforme: otkryto, ėffektivno, bezopasno = Medvedev told judges that reform should be transparent, effective and foolproof.* http://www.newsru.com/russia/02dec2008/medsud_print.html. The proportion of judicial decisions that are not enforced has remained around 50% at least since 2005 (see: European Commission for the Efficiency of Justice (CEPEJ), *Examination of problems related to the execution of decisions by national civil courts against the state and its entities in the Russian Federation* (CEPEJ(2005)8, 09.12.05, para. 11).

30 *Burdov v Russia (No.2),* No. 33509/04, 15.1.09, para. 132.

31 Interview with Olga Shepeleva, lawyer, Public Interest Law Institute, Moscow, 22.9.09.

32 Interview with Maria Voskobitova, lawyer, International Protection Centre, Moscow, 23.9.09.

33 Interview with Olga Shepeleva, lawyer, Public Interest Law Institute, Moscow, 22.9.09.

34 The Law on Enforcement Proceedings of 21 July 1997 (no. 119-ФЗ).

35 *Burdov v Russia (No. 2),* No. 33509/04, 15.1.09, para. 22.

claimants in court judgments.[36] The main reason for this, Shepeleva suggested, is that the regional authorities lack the necessary funds to pay these monies, as regional taxes are mostly channelled into the federal budget.[37]

The higher courts in Russia have handed down a number of judgments which arguably ought to have led to more effective legislative change. In 2005, the Constitutional Court judged the provisions specified in the law 'On the Federal Budget for 2005'[38] as being incompatible with Articles 8, 19 and 46 of the Russian Constitution in that they did not require the authorities to pay compensation for procedural delays within a fixed time limit.[39] This judgment cited the European Court's *Burdov* judgment of 2002 in support.[40]

In December 2007 the Supreme Court issued a judgment "On the length of judicial review of criminal, civil and administrative violations by the Russian courts" in which it found that the practice of procedural delays in the domestic courts constituted a violation of Articles 46 and 15(4) of the Constitution and Article 6(1) of the European Convention (guaranteeing the right to a fair trial within a reasonable time).[41] In September 2008 the Supreme Court decreed that the *Duma* should adopt a new law on the right to trial within a reasonable time.[42]

---

36 Interview with Olga Shepeleva, lawyer, Public Interest Law Institute, Moscow, 22.9.09.

37 *Ibid.*

38 Russia (Federation). Federal'noe Sobranie. Gosudarstvennaia Duma. *O federal'nom budzhete na 2005 god = On the federal budget for 2005.* http://www.budgetrf.ru/Publications/2005/Adoption/Federal/Npd/Budgetlaws/173fz231204/173fz231204000.htm.

39 Russian Federation. Konstitutsionnyĭ Sud. *Postanovlenie Konstitutsionnogo Suda RF ot 14 iiulia 2005 g. N 8-P "Po delu o proverke konstitutsionnosti otdel'nykh polozheniĭ federal'nykh zakonov o federal'nom biudzhete na 2003 god, na 2004 god i na 2005 god i postanovleniia Pravitel'stva Rossiĭskoĭ Federatsii "O poriadke ispolneniia Ministerstvom finansov Rossiĭskoĭ Federatsii sudebnykh aktov po iskam k kazne Rossiĭskoĭ Federatsii na vozmeshchenie vreda, prichinennogo nezakonnymi deĭstviiami (bezdeĭstviem) organov gosudarstvennoĭ vlasti libo dolzhnostnykh lits organov gosudarstvennoĭ vlasti" v sviazi s zhalobami grazhdan Ė.D. Zhukovitskogo, I.G. Poĭma, A.V. Poniatovskogo, A.E. Cheslavskogo i OAO "Khabarovskėnergo" = Decision of the Constitutional Court RF 14.07.05 g. N 8-P "On the matter of verifying the constitutionality of separate positions of the federal laws on the federal budget for 2003, 2004, 2005 and decisions of the Government of the Russian Federation "On the situation of how the Ministry of Finance of the Russian Federation is implementing court decisions against the Russian state to provide compensation for violations, unlawful acts (or failure to act) by state organs or authorities in connection with the complaints of citizens Ė.D. Zhukhovitskogo, I.G. Poĭma, A.V. Poniatovskogo, A.E. Cheslavskogo i OAO 'Khabarovskėnergo',* 1.1. *http://www.supcourt.ru/vscourt_detale.php?id=5491* or *http://ksportal.garant.ru:8081/SESSION/S__yUcOFK1X/PILOT/main.html.*

40 *Ibid.*, 2.1.

41 Russia (Federation). Verkhovnyĭ Sud. *Postanovlenie Plenuma Verkhovnogo Suda Rossiĭskoĭ Federatsii No. 52 ot 27 dekabria 2007 g. "O srokakh rassmotreniia sudami Rossiĭskoĭ Federatsii ugolovnykh, grazhdanskikh del i del ob administrativnykh pravonarusheniiakh" = Resolution of the Plenary session of the Supreme Court of the Russian Federation, No.52, 27 December 2007 "On the length of judicial review of criminal, civil and administrative offences in the courts of the Russian Federation."* http://www.supcourt.ru/vscourt_detale.php?id=5121.

42 Russia (Federation). Verkhovnyĭ Sud. *Postanovlenie Plenuma Verkhovnogo Suda Rossiĭskoĭ Federatsii No.16, O vnesenii v Gosudarstvennuiu Dumu Federal'nogo Sobraniia Rossiĭskoĭ Federatsii proektov federal'nogo konstitutsionnogo zakona "O vozmeshchenii gosudarstvom*

In December 2008, the Congress of judges similarly endorsed the proposal that Parliament should adopt such a law. In both the Supreme Court judgment and in the resolution of the Congress of Judges, measures were proposed to improve the administrative efficiency of the courts.[43]

There has been some pressure on this issue from the Commissioner for Human Rights of the Russian Federation, Vladimir Lukin, who stated in his 2007 Activities Report that there was still a widespread perception that domestic judgments were 'non-compulsory recommendations', and that Constitutional Court judgments were also treated as such. During meetings held with regional authorities and representatives of the Presidential administration, between 2006 and 2007, the idea emerged that a national mechanism should be developed to examine Convention complaints at the national level. The Commissioner concluded that this should serve as a way of eliminating the problem at its root, rather than a means of simply reducing the number of Strasbourg complaints.[44] What progress there has been, however, in developing such a mechanism is not clear.[45]

Another question which arises, is how significant is the role of the government agent? For example, Trochev has recently highlighted its pivotal role within government in the Russian context:

> "The office's main job is to inform the rest of the central government apparatus, including Russia's top courts and the procurator general, about all aspects of the litigation in Strasbourg, from the admissibility of applications to the

vreda, prichinennogo narusheniem prava na sudoproizvodstvo v razumnye sroki i prava na ispolnenie v razumnye sroki vstupivshikh v zakonnuiu silu sudebnykh aktov" i federal'nogo zakona "O vnesenii izmeneniĭ v otdel'nye zakonodatel'nye akty Rossiĭskoĭ Federatsii v sviazi s priniatiem Federal'nogo konstitutsionnogo prava na sudoproizvodstva v razumnye sroki i prava na ispolnenie v razumnye sroki vstupivshikh v zakonnuiu silu sudebnykh aktov" 26.09.08. = Resolution of the Plenary session of the Supreme Court of the Russian Federation No.16 to lay a federal constitutional bill with the State Duma of the Federal Assembly of the Russian Federation "On compensation for state violations of the right to trial within a reasonable time and the right to the execution of judgments that should have come into force" and the federal law "On amending individual legal acts of the Russian Federation in connection with the adoption of the Federal Constitutional law "On compensation for state violations of the right to trial within a reasonable time and the right to the execution of judgments that should have come into force"". 26.9.08. http://www.supcourt.ru/arxiv_out/TEXT.PHP?id_text=121232&i1text=разумные%20 сроки.

43 Russia (Federation). Sovet Sudeĭ Rossiĭskoĭ Federatsii. *Postanovlenie VII Vserossiĭskogo S"ezda Sudeĭ g. Moskva 04 dekabria 2008 g. O sostoianii sudebnoĭ sistemy rossiĭskoĭ federatsii i prioritetnykh napravleniiakh ee razvitiia i sovershenstvovaniia = Resolution of the VII All-Russian Congress of Judges, Moscow, 4 December, 2008 "On the current state of the judicial system in the Russian Federation and priorities for how to develop and improve it"*. www.oblsud.tsl.ru/siezd.files/siesd.doc.

44 *Burdov v Russia (No.2)*, No. 33509/04, 15.1.09, para. 25.

45 The research team were regrettably unable to secure an interview with the Commissioner during a trip to Moscow in September 2009, or to receive answers from him to subsequent questions by telephone or email.

> implementation of ECtHR judgments. Therefore, this office serves as a key source of information about the ECtHR for top Russian government officials and is, in large part, responsible for shaping their perceptions of the tribunal."[46]

Trochev argues that the transfer of this post from the presidential administration to the Ministry of Justice in 2007 was, in effect, a demotion of the office within the Russian bureaucratic hierarchy. Prior to that, the office's 'privileged status' within the presidential administration meant that it enjoyed more leverage over ministers and senior officials.[47]

5.2.1.2. The response to Burdov *(No. 2) from the executive, the judiciary and the legislature*

Although the Court affirmed in its judgment in *Burdov* (No. 2) that the most effective remedy in relation to delayed enforcement of court judgments would include a mechanism for expediting cases, it also acknowledged that a respondent state could decide simply to provide a compensatory mechanism.[48] Since the *Burdov* (No. 2) judgment the Russian authorities have proved willing to pay compensation to individuals in a similar situation, but legislative progress has been rather more problematic. In its decision in *Viktor Mikhaylovich Uskov (and 17 other applications) v Russia*, the Court struck out a series of similar applications (brought on behalf of 100 applicants) on the basis of compensation payments offered by the Russian authorities, together with their acknowledgment of the excessive duration of the enforcement of the applicants' judgments.[49]

The urgency of the task confronting Russia was highlighted by the Russian judge at the European Court, Anatoly Kovler, at a meeting with the Russian Constitutional Court in St Petersburg in February 2009, as reported in the *Kommersant* newspaper.[50] He reviewed Russia's results before the European Court in 2008 and suggested that if Russia failed to resolve the systemic problem of the non-implementation of court decisions within the following six months,

---

46 Alexei Trochev (2009), 'All appeals lead to Strasbourg? Unpacking the impact of the European Court of Human Rights on Russia' *Demokratizatsiya*, Vol. 17, No. 2, pp. 145–178, Spring 2009, University of Wisconsin Legal Studies Research Paper No. 1082 , p. 151, available at: http://papers.ssrn.com/sol3/papers.cfm?abstract_id=1421342.

47 *Ibid.*

48 *Burdov v Russia (No. 2), No.* 33509/04, 15.1.09, paras. 96–100.

49 *Uskov (Viktor Mikhaylovich) (and 17 other applications) v Russia*, Nos. 6394/05, 7144/05, 9464/05, 10542/05, 30006/06, 39119/06, 50742/06, 2229/07, 5951/07, 31624/07, 31698/07, 51340/07, 51342/07, 9463/08, 13132/08, 16251/08, 16849/08 and 39590/08, dec. 12.11.09. The compensation payments ranged from €1,400 to €3,350.

50 Anna Pushkarskaia 'Evropeĭskiĭ sud pozhalovalsia na Rossiiu Konstitutsionnomu: potrebovav ispolneniia sudebnykh reseheniĭ' *Kommersant* No.36P (4091) 2.3.09, at http://www.kommersant.ru/doc.aspx?DocsID=1128309; see also http://www.newsru.com/russia/02mar2009/eurosud_kovler.html.

it could lead to termination of Russia's membership of the Council of Europe. The most glaring tendency of 2008, Kovler argued, had been the lengthy non-execution of judgments of Russian courts and the absence of a mechanism for payment of damages by the government for unlawful actions of judges. Although in September 2008 the Supreme Court, on the proposal of President Medvedev, had submitted a draft constitutional law to the State Duma to remedy this problem, the draft had been 'cut to the roots' by bureaucrats, according to Judge Kovler (we discuss this draft law below). Indeed, the patience of the European Court had, said Judge Kovler, been exhausted by the case *Burdov v Russia (No.2)*. Kovler pointed out that the judgment of the Court would, if implemented, enable Strasbourg to get rid of about one thousand cases.

As noted above, in response to *Burdov (No. 2)*, a draft law to compensate those who have not received settlements resulting from court judgments,[51] was submitted by the Supreme Court, and registered with the State Duma, on 30 September 2008. The draft law contained no mechanism to expedite either the proceedings or the execution of court decisions (although, as we note above, this was not explicitly required by the *Burdov* (No. 2) judgment). Moreover, the State Duma Committee on Constitutional Legislation and Government structures scrutinised the draft law, and concluded in its report, which was presented to the Duma Council on 21 May 2009, that such a law is 'unnecessary'.[52] The State Duma Committee considered that the proposed new procedure would further lengthen court proceedings, that it contravened Article 46(3) of the Russian Constitution[53] and

---

51 Russia (Federation). Verkhovnyĭ Sud. *Vnositsia Verkhovnym Sudom Rossiĭskoĭ Federatsii Proekt Rossiĭskaia Federatsiia Federal'nyĭ Konstitutsionnyĭ zakon o vozmeshchenii gosudarstvom vreda, prichinennogo narusheniem prava na sudoproizvodstvo v razumnye sroki i prava na ispolnenie v razumnye sroki vstupivshikh v zakonnuiu silu sudebnykh aktov = The Supreme Court of the Russian Federation introduces a Russian Federation Constitutional Bill on compensation for state violations of the right to trial within a reasonable time and the right to the execution of judgments that should have come into force.* http://asozd.duma.gov.ru/work/dz.nsf/ByID/325C666567526F04C32574D50027E910/$File/текст0002.rtf?OpenElement.

52 Russia (Federation). Federal'noe Sobranie. Gosudarstvennaia Duma. Komitet Gosudarstvennoĭ Dumy po konstitutsionnomu zakonodatel'stvu i gosudarstvennomu stroitel'stvu Po porucheniu Soveta Gosudarstvennoĭ Dumy ot 21 maia 2009 goda (protocol No. 113, punkt 6) *Zakliuchenie po proektu federal'nogo konstitutsionnogo zakona No. 103575-5 "O vozmeshchenii gosudarstvom vreda, prichinennogo narusheniem prava na sudoproizvodstvo v razumnye sroki i prava na ispolnenie v razumnye sroki vstupivshikh v zakonnuiu silu sudebnykh aktov" vnesennomu Verkhovnym Sudom Rossiĭskoĭ Federatsii (pervoe chtenie)* = Committee of the State Duma on Constitutional legislation and state institutions, commissioned by the Council of the State Duma 21.5.09 (protocol no. 113, art. 6). *Conclusions on the project of the federal constitutional bill No. 103575-5 "On compensation for state violations of the right to trial within a reasonable time and the right to the execution of judgments that should have come into force", laid by the Supreme Court of the Russian Federation (first reading).* http://asozd.duma.gov.ru/work/dz.nsf/ByID/6A92F9F9B257A0F6C32575DA00213024/$File/0617103575-5.165.RTF?OpenElement.

53 *Ibid.*

that it would further reduce individuals' right to apply to the European Court, in violation of Article 34 of the Convention.[54]

The State Duma Committee was also critical that the draft law did not prescribe time limits to proceedings, nor clarify whether or not unsuccessful applicants need appeal to the Court of Cassation in order to exhaust domestic remedies.[55] According to Olga Shepeleva, interviewed in September 2009, the assessment of the draft law within the 'expert community' was that it was not properly prepared.[56] Another interpretation was that the draft law had been specifically written in an open-ended way to allow room for later amendments.[57]

In its interim resolution on the case, in December 2009, the Committee of Ministers noted "with satisfaction the Russian authorities' prompt and constructive response to the Court's pilot judgment and to the Committee of Ministers' Interim Resolution."[58] Indeed, a representative of the Russian Government Agent's Office in Strasbourg confirmed to us that they welcomed the Court's application of the pilot judgment procedure.[59] Furthermore, a Court Registry lawyer was hopeful about the implementation of the *Burdov (No. 2)* judgment, because of the apparent support from the Russian Government and judiciary:

> "I think that what makes me rather optimistic about this case is that it is common ground that there is a structural problem – that measures should be taken and some of them have already been taken … Of course there is some resistance on the part of certain officials in this case, saying that we don't have a structural problem, but if you look at the relevant domestic material the great majority accepts that there is such a problem, including the President of the Russian Federation, who has said [this] repeatedly."[60]

---

54 *Ibid.*

55 *Ibid.*

56 Interview with Olga Shepeleva, lawyer, Public Interest Law Institute, Moscow, 22.9.09. See also: Alexei Trochev (2009), 'All appeals lead to Strasbourg? Unpacking the impact of the European Court of Human Rights on Russia' *Demokratizatsiya*, Vol. 17, No. 2, pp. 145–178, Spring 2009, University of Wisconsin Legal Studies Research Paper No. 1082, pp. 155–156 http://papers.ssrn.com/sol3/papers.cfm?abstract_id=1421342.

57 Mark Ėntin, (2010), 'Nastoiashchee i budushchee Interlakenskogo protesessa' *Internet zhurnal Vsia Evropa*, No.1(40) = 'The Present and the Future of the Interlaken Process' *Internet Newspaper 'All Europe'* No.1(40). http://alleuropa.ru/index.php?option=com_content&task=view&id=1419#_ftnr.

58 Committee of Ministers (2009), Interim Resolution CM/ResDH(2009)158, *Execution of the pilot judgement [sic] of the European Court of Human Rights in the case Burdov No. 2 against the Russian Federation relative to the failure or serious delay in abiding by final domestic judicial decisions delivered against the state and its entities as well as the absence of an effective remedy* (Application No. 33509/04, judgment of 15.1.09, final on 4.5.09). An earlier interim resolution, CM/ResDH(2009) 43, was adopted on 19.3.09.

59 Interview with Vladislav Ermakov, Strasbourg, 25.3.09.

60 Interview with Court Registry lawyer, Strasbourg, 27.3.09.

However, in its interim resolution, the Committee of Ministers also noted that the Russian Government had failed to meet the deadline of 4 November 2009, by which date it should have introduced a new remedy. The Committee of Ministers therefore urged the Russian Government to prioritise resolution of the problem of non-enforcement, and continue with the initiated legislative reforms.[61]

Nonetheless, during 2009 the State Duma had, as shown above, discussed shortcomings in the judicial system, which could be interpreted as some progress in addressing some of the general structural problems which impede the smooth running of the judicial process. The discussion suggests that the legislature is aware of the need to streamline legislation concerning the judicial process and is willing, in principle, to take measures, even if not those contained in the draft law. At a session in September 2009, V.I. Iliukhin (a member of the Communist Party and Deputy Chairman of the Committee for Legislation and Construction of the State in the State Duma) said that problems in the judiciary constitute some of the most serious challenges for both state and society. In particular he criticised judges' partiality in arriving at decisions and the fact that in 2008 one third of judicial decisions had been overturned.[62]

Just at the time of going to press, in March 2010, a draft federal law was submitted by the Russian President to the Duma (and adopted by the Duma on 21 April 2010) whose aim is to provide compensation for both undue length of proceedings and the failure to enforce court judgments.[63] The bill does not however provide a remedy (under the Civil Procedure Code) to ensure the timely enforcement of a judgment (i.e. a 'preventive' remedy). Commenting on this draft law, Anton Burkov has already argued that the Bill may be another source of Article 6 cases against Russia arising from the non-execution of compensation awards.[64]

---

61 Committee of Ministers (2009), Interim Resolution CM/ResDH(2009)158, *Execution of the pilot judgement [sic] of the European Court of Human Rights in the case Burdov No. 2 against the Russian Federation relative to the failure or serious delay in abiding by final domestic judicial decisions delivered against the state and its entities as well as the absence of an effective remedy* (Application No. 33509/04, judgment of 15.1.09, final on 4.5.09).

62 Russia (Federation). Federal'noe Sobranie. Gosudarstvennaia Duma. *Sessiia GD 4-ia sessiia GD piatogo sozyva (osen´ 2009 g.) Presedatel´stvuiushchiĭ 11.09.09 = State Duma session, 4th session of the 5th Duma [2008–2011] (autumn 2009), 11.9.09.* http://www.cir.ru/docs/duma/302/2091794?QueryID=2872326&HighlightQuery=2872326

63 *O kompensatsii za narushenie prava na sudoproizvodstvo v razumnyĭ srok ili prava na ispolnenie sudebnogo akta v razumnyĭ srok = Law on Compensation to Citizens for Violation of the Right to a Fair Trial within a Reasonable Time or the Right to Execution of a Judgement within a Reasonable Time.* http://asozd2.duma.gov.ru/work/dz.nsf/ByID/894E7FFB99505EA5C325770C00208086/$File/%D1%82%D0%B5%D0%BA%D1%81%D1%82%203%20%D1%87%D1%82%D0%B5%D0%BD%D0%B8%D0%B520.04.doc?OpenElement (last accessed 22.4.10) See also electronic registration card http://asozd2.duma.gov.ru/main.nsf/(Spravka)?OpenAgent&RN=346759-5&02 (last accessed 22.4.10).

64 Burkov, Anton (2010), 'New Draft Law on Compensation for Citizens who do not receive a Fair Trial within a reasonable time' EU-Russia Centre, 13 April 2010 http://www.eu-russiacentre.

Ukraine has experienced similar endemic problems, as the case of *Ivanov* illustrates.

5.2.2. *YURIY NIKOLAYEVICH IVANOV V UKRAINE*

In October 2000 the applicant, Yuriy Ivanov, a Russian national, retired from the Ukrainian Army, and was consequently entitled to a lump sum retirement payment and compensation for his uniform. In 2001 he instituted civil proceedings at the Regional Military Court to seek recovery of the debt and he was awarded his claim in full. However, Ivanov was subsequently informed the following year, by the Ministry of Defence, that the necessary funds were not available for the sale of his uniform.[65] He was also informed by the bailiffs that they had frozen the debtor's bank account and that there were no funds.[66]

In 2008 the Committee of Ministers had issued an interim resolution in relation to 232 Ukrainian cases pending before the Court regarding the non-enforcement of domestic judgments, and Ukraine's continued non-compliance.[67] The resolution reiterated that in a number of these cases the Court had found that there was no effective domestic remedy and emphasised in this respect that the Ukrainian Government should comply with the Committee's 2004 Recommendation concerning such legislative provision.[68] According to one of our interviewees, the main reason for the non-execution of court decisions is simply that there is no specific budgetary allocation, so that in practice the authorities lack the necessary financial resources.[69]

---

org/our-publications/column/draft-law-compensation-citizens-receive-fair-trial-reasonable-time.html.

65 *Ivanov (Yuriy Nikolayevich) v Ukraine*, No. 40450/04, 15.10.09, para. 12.

66 *Ibid.*, paras. 26–29. The relevant law that specifies the procedure for the forcible execution of decisions of courts and of other competent authorities and officials ("judgments") is the 'Enforcement Proceedings Act' of 21.4.99. According to this law the enforcement of judgments (including those of the European Court) is entrusted to the State Bailiffs' Service, which forms part of the Ministry of Justice and which enjoys wide powers in enforcing this law.

67 Committee of Ministers (2008), *Interim Resolution* CM/ResDH(2008)1 *of the Committee of Ministers on the execution of the judgments of the European Court of Human Rights in 232 cases against Ukraine relative to the failure or serious delay in abiding by final domestic judicial decisions delivered against the state and its entities as well as the absence of an effective remedy, 6 March 2008.* https://wcd.coe.int/ViewDoc.jsp?id=1259451&Site=CM.

68 Committee of Ministers (2004), Recommendation Rec(2004)6 of the Committee of Ministers to member states on the improvement of domestic remedies *(adopted by the Committee of Ministers on 12 May 2004, at its 114th Session).* https://wcd.coe.int/ViewDoc.jsp?Ref=Rec(2004)6&Language=lanEnglish&Site=CM&BackColorInternet=C3C3C3&BackColorIntranet=EDB021&BackColorLogged=F5D383.

69 Telephone interview with Arkadiy Buschenko of the Kharkiv Human Rights Protection Group, 29.1.10. According to Mr. Buschenko there is, however, a budget earmarked for the execution of Strasbourg decisions, so that it is easier to secure compensation resulting from Strasbourg decisions than from judgments of the domestic courts.

The Ukrainian Government had informed the Court that it would introduce new legislation to resolve the problem[70] but at the time of writing, no such measures had been introduced.[71] In December 2009, the Committee of Ministers noted that the Ukrainian authorities had failed to take relevant measures concerning the execution of the Strasbourg judgments, and noted 'with grave concern that no concrete or visible progress [had] been made in this field since the adoption by the Committee of Ministers of its first Interim Resolution'. Moreover the Committee of Ministers underlined that it had been supervising the matter for more than five years. Using forceful language, the Committee of Ministers deplored

> "that, despite the urgency of the situation and the Committee's repeated calls to that effect, the Ukrainian authorities have continuously failed to give priority to finding effective solutions to the important problem of non-enforcement of domestic courts' decisions."[72]

As to the question of implementation, the Director of the Ukrainian Helsinki Human Rights Union told us that the organisation is to present a report on the Ukrainian Government's execution of Strasbourg judgments to the Council of Europe in May 2010.[73] There is clearly awareness of the *Ivanov* case among the human rights community in Ukraine, as is evident from a Ukrainian human rights portal in Kharkiv which has posted details of the Strasbourg judgment in the case and described the process of the pilot judgment procedure with reference to the analogous *Burdov v Russia* (No.2) and *Olaru v Moldova* cases.[74] However, human rights lawyers consider that there is little awareness of the case among the general public,[75] and we were told that the Government has done little to publicise the Strasbourg judgment.[76]

---

70 *On Amendments to Certain Legal Acts of Ukraine (on the protection of the right to pre-trial and trial proceedings and enforcement of court decisions within reasonable time).*

71 As at 29.1.10 (telephone interview with Dr Ganna Yudkivska of the International Protection Centre, Moscow).

72 Committee of Ministers (2009), *Interim Resolution CM/ResDH(2009)159, Execution of the judgments of the European Court of Human Rights in 324 cases against Ukraine concerning the failure or serious delay in abiding by final domestic courts' decisions delivered against the state and its entities as well as the absence of an effective remedy.* https://wcd.coe.int/ViewDoc.jsp?Ref=CM/ResDH(2009)159&Language=lanEnglish&Ver=original&Site=COE&BackColorInternet=DBDCF2&BackColorIntranet=FDC864&BackColorLogged=FDC864.

73 Telephone interview with Volodymyr Yavorskiy, Director, Ukrainian Helsinki Human Rights Union 29.1.10.

74 Ganna Yudkivska (2009), *IEvropeĭs'kyĭ sud z prav liudyny zobov'iazav Ukraïnu protiahom roku zaprovadyty efektyvnyĭ zasıb vıdshkoduvannia u razı nevykonannia abo zatrymky vykonannia sudovykh rıshen' natsıonal'nykh sudıv = The European Court of Human Rights held that Ukraine was to secure within one year sufficient redress for the non-enforcement or delayed enforcement of domestic decisions.* http://www.khpg.org/index.php?id=1256551783.

75 Telephone interview with Arkadiy Buschenko of the Kharkiv Human Rights Protection Group, 29.1.10.

76 Telephone interview with Volodymyr Yavorskiy, Director, Ukrainian Helsinki Human Rights Union 29.1.10.

The Government disputed the application of the pilot judgment procedure in *Ivanov*, arguing that the causes of the violations varied and that the application of the procedure by the Court in this way was inappropriate. The Court summarised the Government's position in this way:

> "The Government submitted that the problems impeding the enforcement of domestic decisions differed in particular cases. In some instances, domestic decisions remained un-enforced because of the lack of budgetary allocations, whereas in other cases this was due to shortcomings in national legislation and administrative practice, or, as in the present case, because of omissions or inaction on the part of the bailiffs. In their view, this case therefore did not concern a systemic problem. The Government further argued that the pilot-judgment procedure should not be applied in the present case as the measures aimed at resolving the problems of prolonged non-enforcement had already been determined by the Committee of Ministers in its Interim Resolution of 6 March 2008. They suggested that the application of such a procedure in the present case would amount to the performance of a supervisory function by the Court."[77]

The Court expressly rejected the Government's argument that its application of the pilot judgment procedure would tread on the toes of the Committee of Ministers, invoking its Article 19 *raison d'être*: "to ensure the observance of the engagements undertaken by the High Contracting Parties in the Convention and the Protocols thereto", and remarking that such a task was "not necessarily best achieved by repeating the same findings in large series of cases".[78]

Since the judgment only became final in mid-January 2010, the Ukrainian Government still has, at the time of writing, almost a year within which to establish an effective domestic remedy.[79] The Government is currently developing a strategy to provide redress for applicants which it will present in due course to the Committee of Ministers.[80] However, according to Arkadiy Buschenko, of the Kharkiv Human Rights Protection Group, the development of a remedy similar to the Italian Pinto Law[81] has been considered by the Government, but there have been concerns that such a remedy could further complicate the problem,

---

77 *Ivanov (Yuriy Nikolayevich) v Ukraine*, No. 40450/04, 15.10.09, para. 77.
78 *Ibid.*, para. 82.
79 In fact, the period of a year is the latest time by which Ukraine is required to comply with the judgment – it was required to do so "without delay".
80 Telephone interview with Dr Ganna Yudkivska of the International Protection Centre, Moscow, 29.1.10. Just at the point of going to publication, the Ukrainian Cabinet of Ministers issued a decree on 11.2.10 (Decree No. 222-r) stipulating that budgetary and legislative steps should be taken in 2010 and 2011 in response to the *Ivanov* judgment. See: http://minjust.gov.ua/0/24680 (last accessed 11.4.10).
81 See Chapter Four, Section 4.2.3.1.

as has been the case in Italy.[82] According to Volodymyr Yavorskiy, Director of the Ukrainian Helsinki Human Rights Union, the Supreme Court has expressed concern at the introduction of such a remedy because it considers there are insufficient resources to cope with expediting proceedings, and that setting time limits under such conditions is not feasible.[83]

When asked whether the application of the pilot judgment procedure was appropriate to the case of *Ivanov*, Dr. Ganna Yudkivska, of the International Protection Centre (Moscow) suggested that it was perhaps simply another way for the Court to reiterate to the Ukrainian Government the message of the Committee of Ministers' Resolution of 2004 that the Government must create a domestic remedy.[84] According to Dr Yudkivska the procedure is better suited to violations which stem from a simple legislative dysfunction rather than those which emanate from a combination of structural factors, such as administrative problems or malpractice.[85]

One interviewee suggested that there were those within the executive, including the Ukrainian Ministry of Justice, who were disappointed with the Court's pilot judgment because it did not give sufficiently specific directives as to how to resolve the issue, and because the Court's formulation of the requirements was too vague. We were told that they would prefer the Court to explain precisely to the Ukrainian Parliament and to the Government exactly what the problem constitutes and what is required of them.[86] Another respondent disagreed with this, suggesting that the Court was right not to have been any more prescriptive in its judgment, as this is the role of the Committee of Ministers.[87] Our respondents expressed divergent views concerning the appropriateness of the time-limits imposed by the Court in the pilot judgment procedure. One viewed the resolution of systemic problems within a year as being unrealistic,[88] another considered that it was not unreasonable to expect a solution by 2010 in light of the fact that

[82] Telephone interview with Arkadiy Buschenko of the Kharkiv Human Rights Protection Group, 29.1.10.

[83] Telephone interview with Volodymyr Yavorskiy, Director, Ukrainian Helsinki Human Rights Union 29.1.10.

[84] Telephone interview with Dr Ganna Yudkivska of the International Protection Centre, Moscow, 29.1.10.

[85] *Ibid.*

[86] Telephone interview with Arkadiy Buschenko of the Kharkiv Human Rights Protection Group, 29.1.10.

[87] Telephone interview with Dr Ganna Yudkivska of the International Protection Centre, Moscow, 29.1.10.

[88] Telephone interview with Volodymyr Yavorskiy, Director, Ukrainian Helsinki Human Rights Union 29.1.10.

the Court first informed the Ukrainian Government that there was no adequate domestic remedy in in 2004 in the case *Voytenko v. Ukraine*.[89]

In 2006, Ukraine introduced a law specifically designed to facilitate the speedy implementation of European Court judgments ('the 2006 Law').[90] This law sets out a series of specific, time-limited state obligations, in response to a Strasbourg judgment. Under the 2006 Law, within 3 days of a European Court judgment becoming final, the Government Agent is obliged to submit a summary of the judgment in Ukrainian for publication in the *Uriadovyi Kurier* and *Golos Ukrayiny* newspapers.[91] The Agent is also required to send the full judgment, and a summary, to the creditor, the Ombudsperson, and all state bodies, officials, and other persons directly affected by the judgment.[92] The state is obliged to translate and publish the full text of the judgment.[93] Furthermore, within a month of the judgment becoming final, the Government Agent is obliged to submit a "motion on general measures" to the Ukrainian Cabinet of Ministers.[94] This document must contain proposals for the settlement of any underlying systemic problem. Within the same period, the Government Agent must prepare an analytical review of the case for the Supreme Court, including proposals to bring the national courts' case law into line with the European Convention. Following receipt of the motion, the Prime Minister of Ukraine is required to "determine central executive bodies in charge of the execution of general measures and immediately provide them with relevant instructions". General measures must then be adopted and relevant draft laws submitted by the Cabinet of Ministers to the *Verkhovna Rada* (the Parliament) of Ukraine, within three months of the Prime Minister's instruction.[95]

Although strong on paper, respondents with whom we spoke, however, considered that the law is ineffective[96] because the Government Agent's Office does not in practice have sufficient authority to carry out its duties. It was suggested that the Government Agent's Office has not been given sufficient powers to deal effectively

---

89 No. 18966/02, 29.6.04. Telephone interview with Dr Ganna Yudkivska of the International Protection Centre, Moscow, 29.1.10.

90 Law No. 3477-IV of 23 February 2006. An unofficial translation of the 2006 Law is annexed to: *Implementation of judgments of the European Court of Human Rights*, Report, Committee on Legal Affairs and Human Rights – Rapporteur: Mr. Erik Jurgens, Netherlands, Socialist Group, Doc. 11020, 18 September 2006. It is also available at: http://sutyajnik.ru/rus/echr/etc/2006_law_ukraine.htm#_ftn1 (last accessed 11.4.10).

91 Article 4 of the 2006 Law.

92 Article 5 of the 2006 Law.

93 Article 6 of the 2006 Law.

94 Article 14 of the 2006 Law.

95 Article 15 of the 2006 Law.

96 Telephone interview with Dr Ganna Yudkivska of the International Protection Centre, Moscow, 29.1.10; Telephone interview with Arkadiy Buschenko of the Kharkiv Human Rights Protection Group, 29.1.10.

with Parliament, and also has ill-defined powers *vis-à-vis* the Government, which limit its capacity to initiate the required legislative changes in accordance with Strasbourg judgments. Its designated role as coordinator between various Government agencies was described to us as untenable.[97]

In Moldova, although the problem of the non-enforcement of court decisions has been widespread, by contrast, this problem is mainly contained within the specific area of social housing provision for public employees, as we discuss in the next section.

5.2.3. *OLARU AND OTHERS V MOLDOVA*

The *Olaru* case originated in four applications to the Court which complained of the non-enforcement of court judgments with regard to the applicants' entitlements to social housing. All the applications related to the Chişinau and Edineţ municipal councils' failure to provide the applicants with housing which was subsequently upheld in the respective district court judgments. As a police officer, Vasile Olaru should have been provided with housing after three years' employment.[98] Similarly, as a former judge, Artur Lungu was entitled to housing.[99] The third applicant, Vera Gusan complained of the non-enforcement of a court judgment which granted her housing provision after the housing block in which her apartment was situated was returned to its former owner, under a law relating to the rehabilitation of victims of political repression.[100] The fourth applicant, Simion Racu, applied to the Court as a result of the Moldovan authorities' failure to enforce a court judgment allocating him housing as an internally displaced person, following his forced migration from Transdniestria to Chişinau.[101]

In its judgment the European Court stated that the Government did not dispute that the problem of non-enforcement of domestic judgments awarding social housing disclosed the existence of a 'systemic problem'. Consequently, the Government expressed "their willingness to have the applicants' cases examined

---

97 Telephone interview with Arkadiy Buschenko of the Kharkiv Human Rights Protection Group, 29.1.10.

98 In accordance with Section 35 of Law no. 416 on Police Forces. See: *Olaru and others v Moldova*, Nos. 476/07, 22539/05, 17911/08 and 13136/07, 28.7.09, paras. 6, 25.

99 According to Section 30 of the Law No. 544 on the Status of Judges.

100 In accordance with Law No. 1225-XII "on the rehabilitation of the victims of the political repression committed by the totalitarian communist occupying regime".

101 Decision no. 658 "on housing for persons forced to quit their houses in the eastern region of Moldova".

within the framework of a 'pilot procedure'".[102] As to the causes, the Court noted that:

> "the problems at the root of the violations ... stem from the provisions in Moldovan law granting social housing to numerous categories of persons at the expense of local governments without providing adequate funding for such social projects. The Court notes that the Government admitted that this situation was also contrary to the principle of local autonomy and decentralisation ..."[103]

and that:

> "... local governments are placed in a situation where they have to choose between fulfilling their normal duties such as, for instance, providing community services and operating schools and kindergartens or using the funds for building accommodation for judges, police officers, prosecutors and others."[104]

Furthermore, the Court noted that fifty percent of non-enforcement cases from Moldova fell into this category, and that local authorities simply did not have the means to comply with their obligations to provide social housing, because of a chronic lack of funds. The Court also found that the Government's failure to provide local authorities with the necessary funds amounted to a breach of the principle of local autonomy as guaranteed by Article 9 of the European Charter of Local Self-Government.[105] The Court's judgment therefore acknowledged that the proposal to cancel rights to free social housing for 23 categories of people would solve the problem in the future.[106] As we noted in chapter one, what is therefore unusual in the case of *Olaru* is that the Court expressed its approval of a solution which essentially takes away a substantive right from a sector of the population (a form of 'levelling down'). The Court adjourned all other similar pending cases and specified general measures in the operative part of the judgment. Within six months the Government was required to have set up an effective domestic remedy and within a year to have granted redress to all victims of non-enforcement or unreasonably delayed enforcement of social housing final judgments.[107]

---

102 *Olaru and others v Moldova*, Nos. 476/07, 22539/05, 17911/08 and 13136/07, 28.7.09, paras. 47–48.
103 *Ibid.*, para. 57.
104 *Ibid.*, para. 55.
105 *Ibid.*, para. 44.
106 *Ibid.*, paras. 55–57.
107 *Ibid.*, operative provisions, paras. 4–6.

The new legislation, which passed its first reading in the Moldovan Parliament on 27 November 2009, and was adopted on 4 December 2009, accordingly withdraws the right to social housing for certain categories of public sector employees.[108] Attached to the draft bill is an explanation of the European Court judgment in *Olaru* and its requirement that the Moldovan Government find a remedy to the problem within 6 months.[109] The legislation proposes to remunerate these sectors of employees to supplement their income accordingly.[110]

The 'forces' within the state 'in favour' of the pilot judgment procedure

Before the Court's communication of the *Olaru* case to the Moldovan Government on 3 July 2008, the Ministry of Justice had already drafted a bill designed to deal with the problem, which was sent to various branches of the Government for approval in November 2008.[111] According to Vladislav Gribincea, of Lawyers for Human Rights (the NGO that represented the applicants in the *Olaru* case), this bill was essentially the same as the bill that was subsequently presented to Parliament in November 2009.[112] In November 2008, when the bill was first presented, the Communist Party was in a majority in the Parliament and, according to Gribincea, the Government was concerned that the new legislation would adversely affect the Party's prospects in the imminent 2009 elections, as it ran counter to their general social welfare policies.[113] Although the Government did not publicise the matter, there was evidently some public awareness of the draft bill, especially among those who would have been affected by it: in particular the police, judges and prosecutors. In anticipation of the bill's endorsement by Parliament, some 300 public employees filed similar cases in Chişinau to claim compensation for their housing entitlement. Many of these applications preceded the European Court's judgment in July 2009.[114]

Gribincea suggested to us that the Moldovan Government Agent and the Minister of Justice were in favour of the Court's application of the pilot judgment procedure,

---

[108] Including members of the police force, certain sectors of the military, certain individuals who have suffered from radioactive emissions from the Chernobyl disaster, parliamentary deputies, fire-fighters, judges, those working in penitentiary institutions, customs officers, members of the diplomatic service, veterans, employees of the Service for Civil Protection and Emergency Situations, security service officers, employees of the Service for Maintaining Peace in the State and employees of the Procuracy.

[109] Moldova. Parlamentul (2009), *Cu privire la aprobarea proiectului de lege pentru modificarea unor acte legislative = Regarding the approval of the project on the law amending a number of legislative acts* no. 1232, 2009, approved by the Government 7.10.09. http://www.parlament.md/download/drafts/ro/1232.2009.doc (last accessed 11.4.10).

[110] *Ibid.*

[111] Olaru and others v Moldova, Nos. 476/07, 22539/05, 17911/08 and 13136/07, 28.7.09, para 31.

[112] Telephone interview with Vladislav Gribincea, Lawyers for Human Rights, Chişinău, 16.12.09.

[113] *Ibid.*

[114] Telephone interview with Vladislav Gribincea, Lawyers for Human Rights, Chişinău, 27.1.10.

as a means of pressuring the Government to adopt the Ministry of Justice's legislation to withdraw social housing provision.[115] According to Gribincea, the Ministry of Justice developed the bill in 2008 in response to the European Court judgments – the initiative was not designed with the aim of countermanding Communist Party policy *per se*. Instead, Gribincea suggested that the former political culture among the ruling elite was to follow the lead of Moscow, and that after the break-up of the Soviet Union, the Moldovan elite has, by analogy, been strongly influenced by international bodies such as the Council of Europe in the development of its domestic policy. We might therefore infer that within the executive there is some political will to comply with Strasbourg rulings in a way that transcends party politics.[116]

The Communist Party's opposition to the legislation was apparent from the debate during the first Parliamentary reading of the bill. At the session in November 2009, Inna Şupac, of the Communist Party, asked whether public employees no longer required housing, and said that she and her colleagues would monitor how the law was implemented.[117] Valentin Guznac, also of the Communist Party, stated that the cause of the problem was the municipal authorities' lack of funds, and complained about the Government's arrogance.[118]

5.3. COMPENSATION FOR LOST FOREIGN CURRENCY SAVINGS AFTER THE BREAK-UP OF YUGOSLAVIA: *SULJAGIĆ V BOSNIA AND HERZEGOVINA*

The case of *Suljagić* concerned citizens' rights to compensation for foreign currency savings that had been frozen since the socialist era. Mustafa Suljagić applied to the European Court in 2002 because of his inability to withdraw hard-currency savings earned and deposited in a Bosnian bank in the former Yugoslavia ('SFRY'). During the 1970s and 1980s he had worked abroad as a postman, handyman and construction worker and had deposited his savings in a bank in Tuzla in accordance with the SFRY's Foreign-Currency Transactions Act

115 Telephone interview with Vladislav Gribincea, Lawyers for Human Rights, Chişinău, 16.12.09.

116 Telephone interview with Vladislav Gribincea, Lawyers for Human Rights, Chişinău, 27.1.10.

117 Moldova. Parlamentul (2009), *Dezbateri parlamentare. Parlamentul Republicii Moldova de legislatura a XVIII-a Sesiunea I ordinară – Noiembrie 2009. Şedinţa din ziua de 27 noiembrie 2009. Stenograma Sumar.* Inna Şupac, PCRM. http://www.parlament.md/news/plenary-records/29.11.2009/.

118 Moldova. Parlamentul (2009), *Dezbateri parlamentare. Parlamentul Republicii Moldova de legislatura a XVIII-a Sesiunea I ordinară – Noiembrie 2009. Şedinţa din ziua de 27 noiembrie 2009. Stenograma Sumar.* Valentin Guznac, PCRM. http://www.parlament.md/news/plenary-records/29.11.2009/.

1977.[119] The terms of access to these savings changed in 1985 when banks placed restrictions on the withdrawal of foreign-currency savings as an emergency measure to support the economy during the monetary crisis of the 1980s. After Bosnia and Herzegovina's declaration of independence from the SFRY, war broke out in 1992. During that time, banks based in Bosnia and Herzegovina were effectively nationalised, and foreign-currency savings remained inaccessible. In 1995 the Dayton Peace Agreement recognised the independent status of Bosnia and Herzegovina, and in 1997 the banks were privatised. During this process Bosnia and Herzegovina assumed liability for the 'old' foreign-currency savings in the local banks. Although withdrawal of the savings was still impossible, provision was made to allow residents to purchase state-owned flats where they were living, and state-owned companies, using the foreign-currency. However, the scheme led to abuses: the savings were 'sold' in some instances for as little as 3% of their nominal value. In 2000, the Human Rights Commission within the Constitutional Court (the legal successor to the Human Rights Chamber in Bosnia) held that the legislation was incompatible with Article 1 of Protocol No. 1 to the Convention.[120] Consequently, in 2004, the authorities amended the legislation and set up a repayment scheme to recompense 'old' foreign-currency savers in cash and government bonds.[121]

After several failed attempts to withdraw his savings, Mustafa Suljagić complained to the Human Rights Commission within the Constitutional Court which found the legislation still to be incompatible with Article 1 of Protocol No. 1 to the Convention (on account of the lack of a fair balance between the relevant interests).[122] Additionally, because of the frequent incidence of delays in reimbursement, the Human Rights Commission found the legislation violated Article 6 of the Convention[123] on account of the lack of procedural guarantees. On 14 April 2006 the Old Foreign Currency Savings Act came into force, which provided the relevant account holders with the right to partial compensation in Euros and the remainder in government bonds.[124] In accordance with this law, in December 2006 the state verification agency assessed Mustafa Suljagić's 'old' foreign-currency savings at 269,275.21 Bosnian Convertible Marks ('BAM'). However, at the time of the European Court's judgment in November 2009, the applicant had only received BAM 4,237.44, and was still waiting for the government bonds which had been due in March 2008.[125]

---

119 *Suljagić v Bosnia and Herzegovina*, No. 27912/02, 3.11.09, paras. 9, 21.
120 *Suljagić v Bosnia and Herzegovina*, No. 27912/02, dec. 20.6.06, p. 5.
121 *Suljagić v Bosnia and Herzegovina*, No. 27912/02, 3.11.09, paras 10–19.
122 Decision CH/98/375, 6.4.05.
123 *Suljagić v Bosnia and Herzegovina*, No. 27912/02, dec. 20.6.06.
124 *Suljagić v Bosnia and Herzegovina*, No. 27912/02, 3.11.09, para. 27.
125 *Ibid.*, paras 22–25.

In light of the fact that at the time of the judgment, 1,350 other similar cases were pending before the Court, and that the number of people who had 'old' foreign currency savings was estimated at more than 1 million,[126] the Court decided to adopt the pilot judgment procedure, in spite of the Government's objection, as the body of other clone cases represented "a serious threat to the future effectiveness of the Convention machinery".[127]

The length of proceedings of the *Suljagić* case in Strasbourg was quite considerable; originally lodged with the Court in July 2002, the judgment was published in November 2009. Indeed, the issue of foreign currency savings has been a domestic concern for a number of years, as is apparent from Parliamentary debates since February 2007.[128] Proposed amendments to the 2006 Law were examined at the Parliamentary session of 30 July 2007 but were rejected on the advice of the Parliamentary Committee on Finance and the Budget. Representing this parliamentary committee, Božo Rajić, of the Croatian Democratic Union, told Parliament that the existing 2006 Law, which remained unenforced, was introduced just before the 2006 elections and that it was nothing more than an illusory remedy. Rajić emphasised that amending the law was essential, not only for the sake of compensating people for their lost savings, but also in the interests of 'Euro-atlantic integration'. The main problem, according to Rajić, was that although the amended bill promised to provide sufficient redress for lost savings, it would in practice result in the state's financial collapse.[129] In December 2007 a Provisional Joint Committee was formed to try to resolve the issue. Some months before the pilot judgment was issued, in March 2009, the Provisional Joint Committee stated that any resolution of the problem would have to be in keeping with the standards of the European Convention.[130] The new amended bill was presented to Parliament in September 2008 together with the comments from the Committee on Finance and the Budget. The minutes of the parliamentary session state that there was no discussion of the matter and that there was simply

---

126 *Suljagić v Bosnia and Herzegovina*, No. 27912/02, 3.11.09, para. 63. The Court's judgment cites the following source for this information: *Bosnia and Herzegovina: Selected Economic Issues*, IMF Country Report No. 04/54, March 2004, p. 26.

127 *Suljagić v Bosnia and Herzegovina*, No. 27912/02, 3.11.09, para. 63.

128 Bosnia and Herzegovina. Parlamentarna Skupština. Vijesti. *Razgovori članova kolegija predstavničkog doma sa premijerom R. Slovenije, Janezom Janšom = [News] Discussions held between members of the College of the lower house of Parliament [of Bosnia and Herzegovina] with the [visiting] Prime Minister of Slovenia Janez Janša*, 19.02.07. http://www.parlament.ba/vijesti/1/0/23.html.

129 Bosnia and Herzegovina. Parlamentarna Skupština. Dom Naroda. *Transkript 7. sjednice Doma Naroda Parlamentarne Skupštine Bosne i Hercegovine, održane 30.07.07. = Transcript of the 7th Session of the People's House of the Parliamentary Assembly of Bosnia and Herzegovina*, 30.7.07. http://www.parlament.ba/sjednica/1/0/60.html.

130 Bosnia and Herzegovina. Parlamentarna Skupština. Vijesti. *Održana sjednica privremene zajedničke komisije za utvrđivanje stare devizne štednje građana BiH* = [News:] *Session held of the provisional joint Committee for fixing old foreign currency savings for citizens of Bosnia and Herzegovina*, 10.3.09. http://www.parlament.ba/vijesti/1/0/860.html.

a vote on whether to endorse the committee's advice to reject the bill, with which 28 members agreed, 10 members voted against and one abstained.[131] As of the end of December 2009, a revised bill had not been presented again to the Parliament.

5.4. QUASI-PILOT JUDGMENTS & COMMUNICATED CASES

We have also selected for discussion in this chapter four cases concerning diverse issues: the 'quasi-pilot' judgments of *Xenides-Arestis v Turkey* and *Manole and others v* Moldova, and two cases, *O'Donoghue v United Kingdom* and *Bekoyeva v Georgia* in which, at the point of their communication to the respondent Government, the Court asked the parties their views as to the application of the pilot judgment procedure. Both *Xenides-Arestis* and *Bekoyeva* arose from inter-state conflict. *Xenides-Arestis* concerns the applicant's loss of access to, and use of, her property following the Turkish occupation of northern Cyprus, and *Bekoyeva* relates to the armed conflict between Georgia and Russia in August 2008. Legislative deficiencies were in issue in both *O'Donoghue v UK* (a scheme intended to reduce the number of 'sham marriages' involving immigrants) and in *Manole* (legislation dealing with broadcasting during an election). These examples arguably illustrate the flexibility of the pilot judgment procedure in the context of very different domestic situations.

5.4.1. *XENIDES-ARESTIS V TURKEY*

This case concerns the widespread violations of the Convention in respect of property owned by Greek Cypriots in the 'Turkish Republic of Northern Cyprus'. Mrs Myra Xenides-Arestis applied to the Court regarding the Turkish Government's failure to provide compensation for the continuing occupation of her home in Famagusta, which she had been forced to abandon as a result of the Turkish military invasion in 1974.[132] In its judgment of December 2005 the Court found violations of Article 8 and Article 1 of Protocol No. 1 (as it had done in a series of cases since the *Loizidou* judgment of 1996).[133] It also found deficiencies in the law introduced by the Turkish Government in 2003 to provide redress to Greek Cypriots who owned property in the occupied territories – the Law on

---

[131] Bosnia and Herzegovina. Parlamentarna Skupština. *Zakonodavstvo: Neusvojeni Zakoni; Prijedlog zakona o izmjenama i dopunama Zakona o izmirenju obaveza po osnovi računa stare devizne štednje = Legislation: laws that have been rejected: proposed law on amending and executing the Law on Foreign Currency Savings.* Bill laid on 1.9.08; rejected at the 42nd Session of the House of Representatives,17.12.08. http://www.parlament.ba/nzakoni/1/0/0.html.

[132] *Xenides-Arestis v Turkey*, No. 46347/99, 7.12.06, paras. 10–11.

[133] *Loizidou v Turkey*, No. 15318/89, 18.12.96.

Compensation for Immovable Properties Located within the Boundaries of the Turkish Republic of Northern Cyprus (TRNC) ('Law no. 49/2003').[134] Moreover, the Court noted the 1,400 similar pending cases concerning property disputes against Turkey, and that the violations were caused "as a matter of 'TRNC' policy or practice".[135] Applying Article 46, the Court required Turkey to provide a remedy not only for the applicant in that case, but also for the applicants in all similar pending cases, which were adjourned.[136]

By the time that *Xenides-Arestis* came back before the Court a year later in order to adjudicate on the applicant's just satisfaction claim under Article 41, a new compensation law (Law No. 67/2005) had been introduced in the TRNC ('the 2005 Law'). The amended law included provision that applications should be assessed by a supervisory body (the Immovable Property Commission – the IPC) and that the terms of restitution should be set by this Commission.[137] The Court indicated in its 2006 judgment that the new compensation and restitution mechanism 'in principle, has taken care of the requirements of the decision of the Court'.[138]

Although the 'pilot judgment procedure' was not expressly applied, as such, in *Xenides-Arestis,* it has the main hallmarks of a 'full' pilot judgment:[139] general measures were indicated in the operative part of the 2005 judgment, and pending clone cases were adjourned. The case has also been described by various commentators as being akin to a pilot judgment.[140] According to Erik Fribergh, 'one sees elements of the pilot judgment procedure' applied in *Xenides-Arestis.*[141] Although Frowein did not characterise *Xenides-Arestis* as a pilot judgment, he noted that the Court's requirements in the operative provisions were similar to those in the *Broniowski* judgment, such that both governments were required to

---

134 *Xenides-Arestis v Turkey,* No. 46347/99, dec. 14.3.05 & 22.12.05, para. 40.

135 *Xenides-Arestis v Turkey,* No. 46347/99, 22.12.05, para. 38.

136 The remedy was required to be available within 3 months of the date of delivery of the judgment, and redress was to be provided three months thereafter. See: *Xenides-Arestis v Turkey,* No. 46347/99, 22.12.05, paras. 40 & 50.

137 *Xenides-Arestis v Turkey,* No. 46347/99, 7.12.06, paras. 10–11. The IPC comprised 5–7 members, two of whom were foreign: Hans-Christian Krüger (the former Secretary to the European Commission of Human Rights and former Deputy Secretary General of the Council of Europe) and Daniel Tarschys (the former Secretary General of the Council of Europe).

138 *Xenides-Arestis v Turkey,* No. 46347/99, 7.12.06, para. 37.

139 See Chapter One, Section 1.2.1.7. In fact in the later admissibility decision in the *Demopoulos* case, the Grand Chamber does state that the pilot judgment procedure was applied in *Xenides-Arestis.* See: *Demopoulos and others v Turkey,* Nos. 46113/99, 3843/02, 13751/02, 13466/03, 10200/04, 14163/04, 19993/04, 21819/04, dec. 1.3.10 (GC), para. 82.

140 See, for example, Costas Paraskeva (2007), 'Human Rights protection begins at home: the Pilot Judgment Procedure developed by the European Court of Human Rights' *Human Rights Law Commentary* v. 3, pp. 8–9. https://portal2.nottingham.ac.uk/shared/shared_hrlcpub/Paraskeva.pdf.

141 See Erik Fribergh (2008), 'Pilot judgments from the Court's perspective', Stockholm Colloquy, 9–10 June 2008.

take measures to remedy the systemic dysfunction by amending legislation.[142] Degener and Mahoney described *Xenides-Arestis* as one of a number of other judgments where the Court had 'taken a lead from Broniowski'.[143] Unlike the case of *Broniowski*, however, in which the Polish Government acknowledged a structural problem, the Turkish Government has never conceded responsibility for any violation of the Convention in *Xenides-Arestis*.[144] As noted above, we have charaterised the case as a 'quasi-pilot' judgment, which is akin to *Lukenda v Slovenia* (which we discuss in Chapter three).[145]

The effectiveness of the 2005 Law

Since the *Xenides-Arestis* case, in the course of its consideration of a number of similar cases,[146] the Court has sought to assess the implementation of the 2005 Law – in the cases of *Demopoulos and others v Turkey*.[147] The Court explicitly asked the Turkish Government to inform the Court of any changes to the 2005 Law and provide concrete information about cases resolved by the IPC.[148]

At the hearing of the *Demopoulos* cases, the Turkish Government argued that the changes stipulated in the Court's judgment in *Xenides-Arestis* had indeed been adequately addressed by the 2005 Law, and accordingly that the applicants had failed to exhaust domestic remedies as they had not applied to the IPC. In their observations, the Government of the Republic of Cyprus argued that the Turkish Government had failed to abide by the Court's decision in not implementing the general measures specified, and that, unlike the Polish Government's response to

---

142 See: Jochen Frowein (2007), 'The binding force of ECHR judgments and its limits' in Breitenmoser, Stephan (ed.), *Human Rights, Democracy and the Rule of Law: Liber Amicorum Luzius Wildhaber*, Nomos, pp. 264–266.

143 See: Renata Degener and Paul Mahoney (2007), "The prospects for a Test-Case Procedure in the European Court of Human Rights" in Hanno Hartig (ed.), *Trente Ans De Droit Européen Des Droits De L'homme – Etudes À La Mémoire De Wolfgang Strasser*, Droit et Justice 74, pp. 173–208.

144 Webcast of ECtHR hearing in *Demopoulos and others v Turkey*, 18.11.09. Legal representative on behalf of the applicants in *Demopoulos and others v Turkey*, Nos. 46113/99, 3843/02, 13751/02, 13466/03, 14163/04, 10200/04, 19993/04, 21819/04. http://www.echr.coe.int/ECHR/EN/Header/Press/Multimedia/Webcasts+of+public+hearings/webcastEN_media?&p_url=20091118-1/en/ (last accessed 11.4.10).

145 Although in the case of *Lukenda*, unlike *Xenides-Arestis*, other clone cases were not adjourned.

146 There were 1,475 similar pending applications at the Court, Webcast of ECtHR hearing in *Demopoulos and others v Turkey* Nos. 46113/99, 3843/02, 13751/02, 13466/03, 14163/04, 10200/04, 19993/04, 21819/04. 18.11.09 http://www.echr.coe.int/ECHR/EN/Header/Press/Multimedia/Webcasts+of+public+hearings/webcastEN_media?&p_url=20091118-1/en/ (last accessed 11.4.10).

147 *Demopoulos and others v Turkey*, Nos. 46113/99, 3843/02, 13751/02, 13466/03, 10200/04, 14163/04, 19993/04, 21819/04, dec. 1.3.10 (GC).

148 See for example, Statement of Facts, *Chrisostomou (née Savvopoulou) v Turkey*, No. 21819/04 (communicated 6.3.08).

the *Broniowski* judgment, the remedy provided was inadequate.[149] The applicants claimed that the remedy was still inadequate, and that the Turkish Government lacked the political will to provide redress, which they argued was apparent from the fact that Mrs. Xenides-Arestis had still not received the compensation due to be paid to her (by the time of the hearing in *Demopoulos* in November 2009).[150] Moreover, according to the applicants, redress was in practice applied in a discretionary manner by the IPC, any compensation offered was derisory and its independence was questionable.[151] Although the applicants could have contested a decision of the IPC at the High Administrative Court of the TRNC, they argued that this did not constitute an effective remedy as they had been pressured into accepting settlements 'offered' by the IPC because of the prospect that appeals to the High Court could take as long as ten years to process.[152] It was also argued on the applicants' behalf that applications to the IPC were obstructed because application forms were not available in the Greek language and applicants were required to obtain a visa for admission to the occupied territory (and visas expired after three months).[153] Immediate restitution of property was said to be only feasible in 4% of cases, and, according to the applicants, such a course of action had been vitiated by the Turkish Government's sale to third parties of some 40,000 of the occupied properties in Northern Cyprus. Only 0.02% of victims had had their property returned to them. According to the applicants those were the reasons why only a small percentage of potential claimants had applied to the IPC. The applicants also argued that Turkey had failed to introduce a remedy for claims of violations of Article 8 of the Convention (the right to respect for the home) and that the IPC could not deal with such complaints. The Turkish

149 Observations of the Government of the Republic of Cyprus, In the European Court of Human Rights, Takis, Eleni & Elpida Demopoulos, *46113/99;Evoulla Chrysostomi, 3843/02; Lordos & A. Lordou Anastasiadou, 13751/02; Eliadou & 3 Others, 13466/03; Thoma Kilara Sotiriou & Thoma Kilara Moushoutta, 14163/04; Stylas, 10200/04; Charalambou Onoufriou & 3 Others, 19993/04; Chrysostomou (nee Savvopoulos), 21819/04 v Turkey*, paras. 14–19.

150 Webcast of ECtHR hearing in *Demopoulos and others v Turkey*, 18.11.09, Nos. 46113/99, 3843/02, 13751/02, 13466/03, 14163/04, 10200/04, 19993/04, 21819/04 http://www.echr.coe.int/ECHR/EN/Header/Press/Multimedia/Webcasts+of+public+hearings/webcastEN_media?&p_url=20091118-1/en/ (last accessed 11.04.10). The failure to pay the Court's award to Mrs Xenides-Arestis was noted by the Committee of Ministers in December 2009: Committee of Ministers (2009), CM/Del/Dec(2009)1072 7 December 2009 1072nd (DH) meeting, 1–3 December 2009 Decisions adopted at the meeting.

151 Webcast of ECtHR hearing in *Demopoulos and others v Turkey* 18.11.09, Nos. 46113/99, 3843/02, 13751/02, 13466/03, 14163/04, 10200/04, 19993/04, 21819/04 http://www.echr.coe.int/ECHR/EN/Header/Press/Multimedia/Webcasts+of+public+hearings/webcastEN_media?&p_url=20091118-1/en/ (last accessed 11.4.10).

152 Webcast of ECtHR hearing in *Demopoulos and others v Turkey*, 18.11.09, Nos. 46113/99, 3843/02, 13751/02, 13466/03, 14163/04, 10200/04, 19993/04, 21819/04 http://www.echr.coe.int/ECHR/EN/Header/Press/Multimedia/Webcasts+of+public+hearings/webcastEN_media?&p_url=20091118-1/en/ (last accessed 11.4.10).

153 Webcast of Court hearing in *Demopoulos and others v Turkey*, 18.11.09, Nos. 46113/99, 3843/02, 13751/02, 13466/03, 14163/04, 10200/04, 19993/04, 21819/04 http://www.echr.coe.int/ECHR/EN/Header/Press/Multimedia/Webcasts+of+public+hearings/webcastEN_media?&p_url=20091118-1/en/ (last accessed 11.4.10).

Government argued that the low number of applications was the result of the Greek Cypriot authorities' intimidation of potential claimants.[154]

In March 2010 the Grand Chamber declared the *Demopoulos* cases inadmissible, finding that the 2005 Law provided an accessible and effective framework of redress which the applicants had failed to utilise. The Court relied on the following statistics, as regards the extent of the redress provided by the IPC: 433 cases had been brought; 85 had been concluded (the vast majority by friendly settlement); restitution and compensation had been ordered in four cases; in two cases exchange of property was agreed; in one case the applicant agreed to restitution on resolution of the Cyprus problem; in more than 70 cases, compensation had been awarded (a total of approximately €47 million); and 361,493 square metres of property had been restituted. Nevertheless, clearly the context of the long-running political dispute over northern Cyprus was critical to the Court's decision:

> "In the present applications, some thirty-five years have elapsed since the applicants lost possession of their property in northern Cyprus in 1974. Generations have passed. The local population has not remained static. Turkish Cypriots who inhabited the north have migrated elsewhere; Turkish-Cypriot refugees from the south have settled in the north; Turkish settlers from Turkey have arrived in large numbers and established their homes. Much Greek-Cypriot property has changed hands at least once, whether by sale, donation or inheritance.
>
> Thus, the Court finds itself faced with cases burdened with a political, historical and factual complexity flowing from a problem that should have been resolved by all parties assuming full responsibility for finding a solution on a political level. This reality, as well as the passage of time and the continuing evolution of the broader political dispute must inform the Court's interpretation and application of the Convention which cannot, if it is to be coherent and meaningful, be either static or blind to concrete factual circumstances".[155]

5.4.2. *MANOLE AND OTHERS V MOLDOVA*

In its 'quasi-pilot' judgment in *Manole and others v Moldova,* the Court found a systemic violation of Article 10 on account of the Communist Party Government's control over the most popular television channel in the Republic of Moldova,

---

[154] Webcast of ECtHR hearing in *Demopoulos and others v Turkey*, 18.11.09, Nos. 46113/99, 3843/02, 13751/02, 13466/03, 14163/04, 10200/04, 19993/04, 21819/04 http://www.echr.coe.int/ECHR/EN/Header/Press/Multimedia/Webcasts+of+public+hearings/webcastEN_media?&p_url=20091118-1/en/ (last accessed 11.4.10).

[155] *Demopoulos and others v Turkey*, Nos. 46113/99, 3843/02, 13751/02, 13466/03, 10200/04, 14163/04, 19993/04, 21819/04, dec. 1.3.10 (GC), paras. 84–85.

and the censorship of certain topics broadcast. This included a significant bias towards reporting on the activities of the President and Government, restricting television coverage of opposition parties and allowing only circumscribed discussion of particular sensitive issues, such as human rights violations perpetrated during the Soviet era. The Court found the legislative framework to be flawed, as it did not provide sufficient safeguards against the control of the broadcaster's senior management, and its editorial policy, by the Government. The Court accordingly concluded that legal reform was required to resolve the issue (applying Article 46) – for the first time in relation to an Article 10 case:

> "... the Court ... has found a violation of Article 10 arising *inter alia* out of deficiencies in ... [the] ... legislative framework. It considers that the respondent State is under a legal obligation under Article 46 to take general measures at the earliest opportunity to remedy the situation which gave rise to the violation of Article 10. In the light of the deficiencies found by the Court, these general measures should include legislative reform, to ensure that the legal framework complies with the requirements of Article 10 and takes into account the Committee of Ministers' Recommendation no. R(96)10 ..."[156]

In this instance the Constitutional Court had scrutinised and approved the legislation in 2007 following a constitutional complaint brought by a group of deputies from the liberal opposition bloc.[157] According to the human rights lawyer Vladislav Gribincea, who acted as legal representative for the applicants, this Constitutional Court judgment may in part be explained by the fact that the Court is heavily influenced by the Government.[158]

The Government's response to the European Court's *Manole* judgment has been remarkably swift. A remedy was introduced two months before the judgment was made final in December 2009. In September 2009 the Court issued the judgment, and a draft bill to remedy the problem was debated in the Parliament in October 2009 and endorsed the same month. The eagerness of the Government to remedy the violation may be explained by the fact that there had been a change of ruling party from Communist to liberal coalition. Since the judgment condemned the existing legislation for failing to ensure balanced television coverage of opposition parties, it is hardly surprising that the topic received considerable discussion in the parliament. During the debate, Vitalie Nagacevschi, of the Liberal Democratic

---

156 *Manole and others v Moldova*, No. 13936/02, 17.9.09, para. 117.

157 Moldova. Monitorul Oficial al Republicii Moldova (2006), *Acte ale Curții Constituționale a Republicii Moldova Hotărîre pentru controlul constituționalității unor prevederi din Codul audiovizualului al Republicii Moldova nr. 260-XVI din 27 iulie 2006 = Act of the Constitutional Court of the Republic of Moldova. Decision on the constitutionality of the Audiovisual Code of the Republic of Moldova.*

158 Telephone interview with Vladislav Gribincea, Lawyers for Human Rights, Chişinău, 16.12.09.

Party of Moldova and also the legal representative for *Manole and others*, explained the significance of the application of Article 46 of the Convention by the Court:

> "... Article 46 ... obliges the government to comply with the judgments of the European Court of Human Rights ... there is a European Court judgment which states that the current legislation which regulates the activities of the Audiovisual Public Institutions 'Teleradio-Moldova', is insufficient. For this we have been judged."[159]

Grigore Petrenco of the Communist Party expressed concern at the provisions in the bill and asked whether the draft legislation had been scrutinised by a Council of Europe expert,[160] in accordance with the 2002 Recommendation by the Parliamentary Assembly to Moldova, which had been reiterated in the *Manole* judgment.[161] The amendments to the law designate Parliament to select (by a majority vote) the supervisory board, after consulting with the Committee on Appointments and the Committee on Matters of the Right to Appointment and Immunity.[162] Since the new law lowers the required threshold for this majority vote from 2/3 of Parliament to a simple majority in favour, Gribincea suggested that this therefore favours whichever party or coalition happens to be in a majority, essentially making it an executive decision.[163] It would appear, therefore, that executive control over broadcasting has remained intact, despite a change of government in the summer of 2009 from the Communists to a liberal coalition.

159 Moldova. Parlamentul (2009), *Dezbateri parlamentare, Parlamentul Republicii Moldova de legislatura a XVIII-a, Sesiunea I ordinară, octombrie 2009, Şedinţa din ziua de 15 octombrie 2009, Stenograma Sumar = Parliamentary debates of the Republic of Moldova's legislature of the 18th ordinary session, October 2009, Stenographic summary of the session of 15 October.* http://www.parlament.md/news/plenaryrecords/15.10.2009/.

160 *Ibid.*

161 On 24 April 2002 the Parliamentary Assembly adopted Resolution 1280(2002) on "The functioning of democratic institutions in Moldova" which stated that the "Assembly calls upon the Moldovan authorities to co-operate fully with the Council of Europe and its bodies, and in particular: ... ii. to submit for Council of Europe expert appraisal the future bills for the reform broadcasting and transform the state company Teleradio Moldova into an independent public service corporation ...".

162 Moldova. Monitorul Oficial al Republicii Moldova (2009), *Zakon o vnesenii izmenenii v Kodeks televideniia i radio Respublika Moldova No. 260-XVI ot 27 iiulia 2006 goda N 42-XVIII ot 20.10.2009 Monitorul Ofichial N 157/442 ot 22.10.09 = The law on introducing amendments to the Republic of Moldova's Code on Television and Radio No. 260-XVI of 27.07.06, N 42-XVIII, 20.10.09. N 157/442, 'Monitorul Oficial', 22.10.09.*

163 Telephone interview with Vladislav Gribincea, Lawyers for Human Rights, Chişinău, 16.12.09. See: Moldova. Monitorul Oficial al Republicii Moldova (2009), *Zakon o vnesenii izmenenii v Kodeks televideniia i radio Respublika Moldova No. 260-XVI ot 27 iiulia 2006 goda N 42-XVIII ot 20.10.2009 Monitorul Ofichial N 157/442 ot 22.10.09 = The law on introducing amendments to the Republic of Moldova's Code on Television and Radio No. 260-XVI of 27.07.06, N 42-XVIII, 20.10.09. N 157/442, 'Monitorul Oficial', 22.10.09.*

5.4.3. *BEKOYEVA V GEORGIA*

This is one of seven cases communicated by the Court in January 2009, concerning the Russia-Georgia conflict in August 2008.[164] This particular case concerns the circumstances surrounding the death of the applicant's daughter during the conflict. Mrs. Bekoyeva is a Russian national of Ossetian origin, who lived in Tskhinvali, Georgia. She complained that, during the shelling of Tskhinvali between 7 and 8 August 2008, Mrs. Bekoyeva, her fourteen year old daughter and a number of others hid in the basement of their apartment building, with nothing to eat or drink. On the evening of 9 August Mrs. Bekoyeva's brother attempted to drive his sister, her daughter and three others out of Tskhinvali. Their car came under fire and the passengers fled, but Mrs. Bekoyeva's daughter was shot and killed by a sniper. The remaining passengers hid in a nearby cemetery, but were unable to return for Mrs. Bekoyeva's daughter because of the continued gunfire. Later they managed to escape in the car, but were unable to retrieve Mrs. Bekoyeva's daughter because of renewed gunfire.[165] Mrs. Bekoyeva applied to the Court complaining of a violation of Article 2 regarding her daughter's death, Article 3 with respect to the inhuman conditions while hiding in the basement, Article 13 because of the lack of an effective domestic remedy, and Article 14 on account of the discrimination she experienced because of her nationality.[166]

When communicating the case to the Georgian Government, the Court asked the parties whether the case was suitable for the application of the pilot judgment procedure given that more than 3,300 similar applications had been filed with the Court.[167]

The application of the pilot judgment procedure in such a context would represent a departure from the Court's previous practice. The circumstances arising in a case like *Bekoyeva* are quite different from the usual systemic targets,[168] resulting from legislative deficiencies, budgetary deficits or administrative practice (or a combination of the three). Indeed, the Court has tended assiduously to treat

---

164 See: 'Seven applications against Georgia concerning hostilities in South Ossetia', European Court of Human Rights, Press Release, 14.1.09.

165 *Bekoyeva (Elza Alikhanovna) v Georgia*, No. 48347/08 (communicated 26.1.09).

166 *Ibid.*

167 "In view of the nature of the situation which gave rise to the present case and given that more than 3,300 applications having the same situation for their background were lodged with the Court, is the present application suitable for the "pilot judgment" procedure? The parties are invited to make their comments in the light of the Court's case-law ..." *Bekoyeva (Elza Alikhanovna) v Georgia*, No. 48347/08 (communicated 26.1.09).

168 See for example the comments of Levan Meskhoradze, the Georgian Government Agent, in Wołąsiewicz, Jakub (ed.), *Pilot Judgment Procedure in the European Court of Human Rights and the future development of Human Rights standards and procedures : Third informal seminar for government agents and other institutions, Warsaw 14–15 May, 2009*, Kontrast, Warsaw, 2009, pp. 131–132.

cases arising from situations of conflict as individual cases (for example, rejecting complaints of systemic discrimination in the cases brought by Kurdish victims of conflict in Turkey in the 1990s). The sheer number of cases is a significant factor: more than 3,300 cases brought against Georgia arising from the August 2008 conflict (not to mention the pending cases against Russia).[169] The Court may also be reacting to its experience of having to adjudicate in recent years on hundreds of individual cases from south-east Turkey and Chechnya.[170] In any event, we would welcome the application of the procedure to conflict and post-conflict situations, which may of course feature large-scale, systematic violations of the Convention, and indeed violations which could be characterised as being systemic, such as treatment that is discriminatory and a state's failure to investigate complaints of egregious human rights violations. A pilot judgment in such a context could place greater leverage on the state to respond appropriately to, and seek to resolve, such large-scale and serious violations.

5.4.4. *O'DONOGHUE V UNITED KINGDOM*

The European Court has proposed the application of the pilot judgment procedure in the case of *O'Donoghue* which concerns the unlawfulness of the Certificate of Approval Scheme that had been introduced by the UK Government in 2005, nominally to reduce the number of 'sham marriages' involving immigrants. According to this scheme, all couples where one or both parties were subject to immigration control (*i.e.* non-EEA nationals) were required to apply for permission to marry from the Home Office. In successive judgments between 2006 and 2008 the High Court, Court of Appeal and House of Lords found that the legislation did not serve the purpose for which it was nominally designed, in that the scheme did not investigate the genuineness of the marriage, and that, as such, the authorities were not in a position to decide whether or not a couple had the right to marry. As Lord Bingham, in the House of Lords' judgment, stated:

> "This means that the authorities are not free simply to disregard those marriages which they believe have been entered into purely in order to gain some perceived immigration advantage. No doubt such marriages do take place. No doubt also they are difficult to detect, not least because of the difficulty of unpicking the variety of reasons why two people might choose to marry one another. There are

169 See, for example, *Georgians take Russia to European Court of Human Rights over August 2008 armed* conflict, Press Release, European Human Rights Advocacy Centre, 10.2.10 (concerning 32 groups of applications on behalf of 134 Georgian citizens) – available at: http://www.londonmet.ac.uk/londonmet/fms/MRSite/Research/HRSJ/EHRAC/Press%20releases/EHRAC%20Press%20Release%2062%20Russia-Georgia%20conflict%20apps%20lodged%2010_2_10.pdf.

170 See, for example, Philip Leach (2008), 'The Chechen Conflict: Analysing the Oversight of the European Court of Human Rights' *European Human Rights Law Review* 6, pp. 732–761.

many perfectly genuine marriages which may bring some immigration advantage to one or both of the parties depending on where for the time being they wish to make their home. That does not make them 'sham' marriages."[171]

In its judgment, the House of Lords ruled that the Certificate of Approval scheme constituted an interference with the right to marry (Article 12 of the Convention) and that the scheme discriminated against those wishing to marry under faiths other than the Church of England (Article 14 of the Convention).[172] In August 2007 the responsible Minister confirmed to the Joint Committee on Human Rights (JCHR) that the Government intended to remedy the incompatibility with Article 14 of the Convention 'as soon as practicable' by extending the scheme to Church of England marriages. The Government then decided to wait for the House of Lords' judgment, to avoid wasting resources on a scheme which could be declared unlawful.[173]

When communicating the *O'Donoghue* case to the UK Government, the Court asked the parties whether they considered it concerned a systemic defect that could give rise to numerous other applications. In their observations, the UK Government stated that it was aware of only 30 cases pending in the UK courts concerning the Certificate of Approval scheme and that, in contrast, by the time the *Broniowski* case was communicated to the Polish Government there were already 167 similar cases pending before the European Court.[174] Furthermore, the Government suggested it was unlikely that other similar cases would come to Strasbourg, as appropriate changes had been made to the Certificate of Approval scheme. In particular, the Government had introduced provision for refunding the application fee for all those individuals who could prove financial hardship.[175] The applicant's representative, Nuala Mole, considers that the number of applicants eligible for a refund according to the Government's criteria is negligible. It was suggested on behalf of the applicant that there are potentially as many as 50,000 similar cases.[176]

---

171 *R (On the application of Baiai and others) v Secretary of State for the Home Department* [2008] UKHL 53 30.07.08, para. 35. http://www.publications.parliament.uk/pa/ld200708/ldjudgmt/jd080730/rhome-1.htm.

172 *Ibid.*, para. 26.

173 United Kingdom. Parliament. Joint Committee on Human Rights. *Thirty-First Report, Declarations on Incompatibility, Religious discrimination in sham marriages regime (Baiai v Secretary of State for the Home Department)* paras. 96–106. http://www.publications.parliament.uk/pa/jt200708/jtselect/jtrights/173/17308.htm.

174 UK Government's Observations and annexes on the admissibility of the *O'Donoghue v United Kingdom* application (34848/07), Derek Walton, Agent for the Government of the UK, 28.4.09, para. 29.

175 *Ibid.*, para. 20.

176 Interview with Nuala Mole, the AIRE Centre, London, 27.11.09.

In any event the Government subsequently informed the Court that it had decided to bring forward a remedial order under Section 10 of the Human Rights Act 1998 to repeal the Certificate of Approval Scheme.[177] Instead of amending the Certificate of Approval scheme, it was stated that the intention was to introduce a series of new measures designed to strengthen the authorities' consideration of applications for residence in the UK on the basis of marriage to a British citizen or EEA national, by identifying marriages of convenience before immigration status is granted on the basis of marriage. This would involve more face to face interviews and enhanced identity verification of individuals and the introduction of civil penalties for those making false statements to the UK Border Agency or who knowingly fail to notify the Agency if their circumstances change.[178] According to Nuala Mole, these measures and the existing scheme for refunding certain applicants do not address the situation of thousands of individuals who have already been affected by the scheme. Therefore the applicant in *O'Donoghue* has argued that the pilot judgment procedure should be applied, in order to ensure effective supervision by the Committee of Ministers of the measures taken by the Government in these cases (such as the provision of compensation and other redress for those individuals who had applied to the Home Office through the scheme).[179] Moreover, according to Nuala Mole there has been no 'wide consultation' on the matter as the Government had promised.[180]

It remains to be seen how the Court responds, although as discussed in Chapter One, Section 1.4.1, this case again demonstrates evidence in support of the proposition that the Court is more likely to initiate the pilot judgment procedure in those cases where there is 'support' for systemic change from the higher domestic courts, or from within the legislature.

5.5. CONCLUSION

5.5.1. THE RESPONSE OF THE EXECUTIVE TO THE PILOT JUDGMENT PROCEDURE

As we have seen, the pilot judgment procedure has been brought into play *vis-à-vis* endemic deficiencies in the implementation of domestic court judgments, with mixed results. The cases discussed in this chapter have revealed varied responses

---

177 Letter to European Court from Derek Walton, Foreign and Commonwealth Office, 12.11.09.
178 *Ibid.*
179 Interview with Nuala Mole, the AIRE Centre, London, 27.11.09.
180 *Ibid.* See also: Joint Committee on Human Rights (JCHR): *Enhancing Parliament's role in relation to human rights judgments*, HL Paper 85, HC 455, 26.3.10, paras. 145–155. http://www.publications.parliament.uk/pa/jt200910/jtselect/jtrights/85/85.pdf.

from the respondent Governments. In the case of *Burdov v Russia (No. 2),*[181] there has been pressure from the higher domestic courts in effecting change, and as was the case with the 'full' pilot judgments in *Broniowski* and *Hutten-Czapska*, there was acknowledgement from elements of the respondent government that the violation was systemic. According to interviewees, the Russian Government consented to the application of the procedure, but at the time of writing has not yet introduced a remedy, as we discuss in Section 5.2.1 above. The Moldovan Government Agent and Ministry of Justice were in favour of the Court's application of the pilot judgment procedure in *Olaru v Moldova*, but the Moldovan Government was concerned how the relevant bill would affect its chances of re-election. By the time the Court issued the judgment, the Communist Party was no longer in a parliamentary majority, and a new social housing policy has since been presented to Parliament and endorsed. In *Manole v Moldova*, which highlighted defects in the legislative regulation of broadcasting, there was a swift response from the executive to the Strasbourg judgment, following the change in Government.

By contrast, in the *Ivanov* and *Suljagić* cases the Ukrainian and Bosnian Governments objected to the application of the procedure. Nevertheless, the Court invoked the procedure, in part possibly because the sheer number of similar clone cases represented a threat to the Court's future operation.

5.5.2. DIFFERING DOMESTIC PRESSURES IN FAVOUR OF ARTICLE 46 JUDGMENTS

In the case of *O'Donoghue v UK*, in which the Court has proposed to apply the pilot judgment procedure, there was pressure from the higher courts and from the legislature (the JCHR) to repeal the Certificate of Approval scheme. This pattern mirrors Article 46 judgments issued to Poland, Slovenia and the case of *Scordino v Italy*, where in each case the Constitutional Court issued judgments advocating legislative change. This factor was emphasised in the Court's communication of the *O'Donoghue* case to the UK Government. The Government has since responded by promulgating changes to the Certificate of Approval scheme and proposing the introduction of a different set of measures aimed specifically at investigating sham marriages. Although the Government acknowledged that the Certificate of Approval scheme was discriminatory, it has not, according to the legal representative for Sinead O'Donoghue, acknowledged the need to provide redress to those that have suffered as a result of the scheme. Whether the Court will be satisfied by the Government's measures, or instead apply the pilot judgment procedure, remains to be seen.

[181] No. 33509/04, 15.1.09.

5.5.3. THE EFFICACY OF THE PILOT JUDGMENT PROCEDURE

The case of *Xenides-Arestis v Turkey* is one which concerns entrenched political differences between Cyprus and Turkey, in that the Court is essentially adjudicating on a post-conflict settlement between the two states. Although neither *Xenides-Arestis* nor *Demopoulos and others v Turkey* were 'inter-state' cases, the role of the Greek Cypriot authorities as an intervening third party indicates the significance of these cases for both states. *Xenides-Arestis* was akin to a 'full' pilot judgment, as general measures were stipulated in the operative part of the judgment, and pending clone cases were adjourned. Like *Burdov* and *Ivanov*, and unlike *Broniowski* or *Hutten-Czapska*, the problem exemplified by the case had been the subject of many previous Strasbourg decisions.

With respect to *Burdov (No. 2)*, the Russian Government failed to comply with the Court's requirement to provide a remedy by the deadline of 4 November 2009. In its 2009 resolution, the Committee of Ministers strongly urged the Russian Government to adopt legislative reform. This is the first instance of a state clearly failing to comply with a pilot judgment, within the timescale laid down by the Court. The *Suljagić* case has also proved problematic. In 2006 the Government amended the existing law concerning the right to compensation for 'old' frozen, foreign currency savings, but should this law be widely enforced, then in practice, according to some parliamentarians, it could bankrupt the state.

Only one state – Ukraine- has introduced a law that is specifically aimed at improving, and indeed systematising, the state's response to European Court judgments. However, there are real questions about its implementation in practice.

The application of the pilot judgment procedure in such a range of cases exemplifies the flexibility of the mechanism, but again shows that it is not a 'panacea' as a number of interviewees at the Court reminded us.[182] There is evidence to suggest that the procedure is better suited to violations arising from a more straightforward legislative dysfunction (like *Manole*) rather than those which result from a variety of structural factors. The mechanism may, however, initiate an iterative process of legislative change as new cases are examined and amendments introduced following the original pilot judgment are evaluated by

[182] Interview with Judge Lech Garlicki, Strasbourg, 25.3.09; Interview with Santiago Quesada, Strasbourg, 26.3.09.

the Court as still being problematic, in the light of new evidence, as was noted in Italian, Polish and Slovenian cases.[183] Finally, the suggestion that the pilot judgment procedure could be applied in the context of cases arising from armed conflict between two Council of Europe states (as we saw with *Bekoyeva*) could herald a more dynamic and interventionist stage in its development.

183 For example as we discussed in the cases of *Broniowski*, *Kudła*, *Lukenda* and *Bottazzi* in chapters 2, 3 and 4.

CHAPTER 6

CONCLUSIONS AND RECOMMENDATIONS

6.1. THE ORIGINS AND OBJECTIVES OF THE PILOT JUDGMENT PROCEDURE

The European Court's pilot judgment procedure was developed in the early 2000s as a result of the ever-growing backlog of cases at the Court, caused in part by the enlargement of the Council of Europe through the accession of a number of central and eastern European states in the 1990s. It was a response to the increasing number of repetitive violation judgments that were being issued by the Court, whose root cause was a systemic problem. It can also be seen as an indicator that the process of the supervision of the enforcement of judgments by the Committee of Ministers has not been working effectively. The concept was developed through the Court's 2003 *Position Paper* and the Committee of Minister's 2004 Resolution, and was first applied in the case of *Broniowski v Poland* in 2004. Its rationale was supported by the Group of Wise Persons in its 2006 report to the Committee of Ministers.

The main purpose of the procedure is to ensure the enforcement of the Court's judgment by inducing states to find a remedy to systemic violations. It also seeks, in the longer term, to ensure that victims of Convention violations can obtain redress more quickly at the national level (thus implementing the principle of subsidiarity), and to ease the burden of cases at the European Court. It is a form of judicial management which is intended to be flexible and adaptable.

6.2. DEFINING PILOT JUDGMENTS, QUASI-PILOT JUDGMENTS AND OTHER SYSTEMIC CASES

There is a substantial degree of uncertainty as to what exactly constitutes a 'pilot judgment', and how it is defined. Accordingly, we have proposed a typology with three tiers, constituting:

(i) 'full' pilot judgments;

(ii) 'quasi-pilot' (or 'Article 46') judgments; and

(iii) Other judgments addressing systemic issues

6.2.1. (I) 'FULL' PILOT JUDGMENTS

By January 2010, the Court had issued six 'full' pilot judgments: *Broniowski v Poland* (2004), *Hutten-Czapska v Poland* (2006), *Burdov v Russia (No. 2)* (2009), *Olaru and others v Moldova* (2009), *Yuriy Nikolayevich Ivanov v Ukraine* (2009) and *Suljagić v Bosnia and Herzegovina* (2009).

The criteria that we suggest define a pilot judgment are as follows:

(a) the explicit application by the Court of the pilot judgment procedure;

(b) the identification by the Court of a systemic violation of the Convention;

(c) the fact that general measures are stipulated in the operative part of the judgment in order that the respondent state should resolve the systemic issue (which may be subject to specific time limits).

A pilot judgment *may* also adjourn all other cases arising from the same systemic issue, either for a particular period of time, or, more generally, pending the resolution of the issue by the state.

The core systemic problem in the 'full' pilot judgments is alternatively described by the Court as being 'widespread' (*Broniowski*) or 'structural' (*Olaru*). In three cases, the cause was the 'malfunctioning' of domestic legislation or practice, or the 'deficient implementation' of legislation (*Broniowski*, *Hutten-Czapska* and *Suljagić*). The particular problem of the non-enforcement of domestic court judgments accounts for three of the judgments (*Burdov (No. 2), Olaru, Ivanov*).

The sheer numbers of people affected is evidently an important consideration in applying the pilot judgment procedure, not only because of the implications for the victims, and the state, but also for the Court itself.

The stipulation of general measures in the operative part of the judgment, rather than just the body of the judgment, is critical. In some decisions, the Court is more prescriptive in setting out the general measures required (e.g. *Suljagić*) than in other cases (e.g. *Burdov (No. 2)*).

6.2.2. (II) 'QUASI-PILOT' JUDGMENTS

In 'quasi-pilot judgments', like 'full' pilot judgments, the Court identifies a widespread or systemic dysfunction in legislation or practice and invokes Article 46 of the Convention to remind the respondent state in question that they are bound to remedy the violation holistically. However, they can be distinguished from 'full' pilot judgments for a number of reasons. Firstly, the Court itself does not describe them as pilot judgments. Secondly, although the Court does identify a systemic issue that has arisen and requires the state to take appropriate steps to resolve the problem, it does not go on to prescribe general measures in the operative part of the judgment. Thirdly, in 'quasi-pilot' judgments, other similar cases are usually not adjourned.

There are, however, rare exceptions to the second and third parts of this definition of 'quasi-pilot' judgments. In cases such as *Lukenda v Slovenia* and *Xenides-Arestis v Turkey* the respondent states *were* required by the operative provisions to take remedial measures, and in *Xenides-Arestis* similar pending cases were adjourned.

6.2.3. (III) OTHER JUDGMENTS ADDRESSING SYSTEMIC ISSUES

In this study, we have also included analysis of a 'third tier' of judgments which address systemic violations of the European Convention on Human Rights. In these judgments, there is no explicit application of Article 46, as such, but the Court notes that the problem which the case raises is systemic or widespread, and that holistic measures need to be taken to resolve the problem at its root. Some of the 'third tier' cases which we discuss pre-date the introduction of the pilot judgment procedure (such as *Bottazzi v Italy* (1999) and *Kudła v Poland* (2000)). A number of the cases we consider have been treated by the respondent Government as raising a systemic issue, even though the judgment itself does not characterise the case as such.

6.3. THE SELECTION OF CASES FOR THE APPLICATION OF THE PILOT JUDGMENT PROCEDURE

It has not always been evident why the pilot judgment procedure has been applied to some systemic situations, and not others.

The selection of cases for the application of the procedure will depend upon practical and political considerations, as well as legal factors. The question of whether a state is likely to be co-operative has been a significant factor – the Court Registry gauges the domestic political will to implement change. Concerns have been expressed that the state's non-co-operation may discredit the procedure. However, a state's consent is *not* a prerequisite for the application of the procedure. Indeed, in a number of cases, respondent states have expressly objected to the application of the procedure.

In a number of situations, an issue which has been the subject of several Court judgments has previously been identified by the Committee of Ministers as being systemic, and the Court has then issued a pilot judgment (e.g. *Ivanov*). In that respect, there is a symbiosis between the Court and the Committee of Ministers.

6.4. THE PRACTICE AND PROCEDURE OF THE COURT IN PILOT JUDGMENT CASES

The development by the Court of the pilot judgment procedure has been slow and gradual, in part because the Court has been concerned not to be over-ambitious.

The early practice was for the Grand Chamber to issue pilot judgments, but the Sections now also do so.

In a case where the Court is considering applying the pilot judgment procedure, at the stage when it is communicated to the respondent government, the parties will be asked whether or not they consider that the case is suitable for the application of the pilot judgment procedure. This is a process of consultation only – the parties do not have a 'right of veto'.

Cases which are symptomatic of a new systemic issue will be prioritized by the Court.

The Court is actively considering expanding the application of the pilot judgment procedure, for example, to conflict situations (such as the Georgia-Russia conflict of August 2008).

The Court Registry has adopted a relatively new practice of conducting in-country visits in order to discuss the range of systemic issues arising in pending cases before the Court.

6.5. QUESTIONS ARISING FROM THE APPLICATION BY THE COURT OF THE PILOT JUDGMENT PROCEDURE

What is its legal basis?

Concerns raised early on about the legal basis of the procedure (it is not expressly provided for in the Convention or in the Court Rules) have not inhibited the Court from developing its practice, invoking Article 46(1) of the Convention, according to which the Contracting States "undertake to abide by the final judgment of the Court in any case to which they are parties".

Reliance has also been placed on Article 1 (the general obligation on Contracting States to respect human rights) – reflecting the principle of subsidiarity – and Article 19 (the function of the Court to ensure states' observance of the Convention). This treaty basis is also underpinned by the political support of the Committee of Ministers through its Resolution Res(2004)3 on judgments revealing an underlying systemic problem.

Stipulating general measures: the respective roles of the Court, the Committee of Ministers and the respondent state

Some respondents questioned whether the Court has the means to assess whether a particular problem is systemic or not (in other words, that such an assessment might require a broader 'fact-finding' capacity going beyond the boundaries of an individual case).

Some observers have suggested that the procedure risks compromising the role of the Court by straying into the arena of the Committee of Ministers. It has been suggested that it is problematic for the Court both to adjudicate on a case and then subsequently to seek to verify the compatibility of new legislation with the Convention (in the course of deciding whether follow-on cases should be referred back in order to exhaust a new domestic mechanism of redress).

However, there is also a widespread view that the system of supervision of the enforcement of European Court judgments by the Committee of Ministers needs reforming. It has been argued that the Committee of Ministers' process lacks the necessary authority, or rigour, to entreat states to comply fully with the Court's judgments, or that, like the Court, the process is too overburdened with cases.[1] Its monitoring of implementation may be too heavily reliant on respondent states for the supply of data, which, as we have seen in relation to some states, is insufficient. Although there is now provision for the Committee of Ministers to take into

[1] See, e.g., Philip Leach (2009), 'Opinion: On reform of the European Court of Human Rights' *European Human Rights Law Review* 6, pp. 725–735.

account data submitted by NGOs and human rights institutions, it is not clear that these channels of information are being maximised. The Secretary General of the Council of Europe has recently signaled the need for a review of the role and working methods of the Committee of Ministers as regards its supervisory function.[2]

The Court may be taking a more assertive, or interventionist position, vis-à-vis respondent states, but a number of respondents considered this to be necessary as regards the most intractable problems.

Time limits
The imposition in pilot judgments of specific time limits on the implementation by the state of general measures is to be welcomed.

It was acknowledged that it may be more difficult for states to resolve endemic problems within a matter of a few months.

Assessing a state's response
Questions have been raised about the Court's competence to assess legislative (and other) measures introduced by the national authorities in response to a pilot judgment. Does the Court have the capacity, and the requisite information available, to make such an assessment? Some have suggested this is properly the realm of the Committee of Ministers.

The adjournment of similar cases
A significant element of the procedure is the adjournment of cases similar to the pilot judgment, which are pending before the European Court. Such cases can subsequently be referred back to the state once it has introduced a remedy in compliance with the pilot judgment. If the state's response is insufficient, the adjourned cases could be re-opened by the Court. However, similar, pending cases will not always be adjourned – this is a matter of discretion for the Court, depending on all the relevant circumstances. Cases will not be adjourned, for example, when an applicant's safety or well-being is at stake. The adjournment of cases may cause uncertainty for applicants and lead to substantial delays in the processing of their cases.

The position of the individual applicant
Does the application of the pilot judgment procedure represent a further stage in the 'constitutionalisation' of the Court, and is there an inherent conflict between individual justice and the Court's 'constitutional' role? There are clearly

---

2 *Contribution of the Secretary General of the Council of Europe to the Preparation of the Interlaken Ministerial Conference*, SG/Inf(2009)20, 18.12.09, para. 38.

differing views. Some respondents suggested that there is no such conflict; instead, Strasbourg is supporting domestic 'forces in favour' to bring about what represents a coincidence of interests between the Court and the domestic actors.

However, various concerns about the procedure have been expressed on behalf of applicants, including the consequential delays in adjudicating on similar cases pending before the Court, and that insufficient attention is given to investigating other 'clone' cases.

Concerns were expressed that a settlement figure is likely to be lower for a large number of clone cases, than for a 'one-off' case.

However, we also heard the view that some applicants may be prepared to take part in the procedure for the 'greater good', rather than for personal gain, in the understanding that a state's resources (financial or otherwise) are limited and may need to be shared.

6.6. THE EFFECTIVENESS OF THE PILOT JUDGMENT PROCEDURE

Our 'national' respondents (the executive, judiciary, academics, NGOs) were broadly in favour of pilot judgments as being a useful and effective mechanism, and one which reduces the burden on the Court.

The procedure has been applied both to particular problems affecting an identifiable group of people (such as the Polish 'Bug River' applicants who were not compensated for property which they had lost during World War II), and also to more endemic problems (such as the non-enforcement of domestic court decisions and the excessive length of domestic legal proceedings). There is some evidence to suggest that the application of the procedure is more effective vis-à-vis 'specific' problems and to systemic problems caused by relatively simple legislative deficiencies, than to more complex endemic problems which have multiple causes.

What a number of 'full' pilot judgments and 'quasi-pilot' judgments share in common is an *a priori* recognition by the state's constitutional court (or other higher court) that the existing law or practice in question violates the Convention, and that there has been a failure on the part of the executive or the legislature to respond adequately to such findings (e.g. *Broniowski*, *Lukenda*, *Hutten-Czapska*, *Scordino* (concerning compensation for expropriated property) and *Burdov (No.2)*). These are the domestic 'forces in favour' with which the European

Court judgment becomes aligned. The extent of the 'co-operation' between the constitutional and European Courts can be pivotal in the pilot judgment process.

There is evidence that the application of the procedure in the case of endemic problems (such as length of proceedings) is problematic as it results in the movement back and forth of cases between the national courts and Strasbourg, and in a long-term process of 'haggling' over the effectiveness of domestic remedies. Nevertheless, the procedure may initiate an iterative process of legislative change.

The application of the pilot judgment procedure in a range of different situations exemplifies the flexibility of the mechanism, but shows that it is not a panacea.

There are questions about its effectiveness in the context of entrenched inter-state disputes (as for example with the *Xenides-Arestis* case).

6.7. HOW STATES RESPOND TO PILOT JUDGMENTS

The application of the pilot judgment procedure to cases such as *Broniowski*, *Hutten-Czapska* and *Lukenda* is broadly considered to have been relatively successful,[3] because they have led to legislative changes aimed at resolving the structural problem. However, there have been other instances where the state's response has been inadequate, and this has been clearly signalled by the Court or the Committee of Ministers (for example, *Burdov (No. 2)* and *Ivanov*).

A state's non-compliance with a pilot judgment may be the result of 'voluntary' resistance (where there is a conscious decision not to execute the judgment) or 'involuntary' resistance (where there is political will to implement the judgment, but the state is simply not able to bring about the requisite changes). Involuntary resistance seems to be more frequent than voluntary resistance.

We were told by respondents that the monitoring of Strasbourg judgments by respondent states is generally insufficient. States have not developed a systematic response mechanism in respect of European Court judgments. The one exception which we encountered was the Ukrainian law of 2006, which we heard in practice has not been implemented adequately.

---

3 See, for example: Erik Fribergh, *Bringing Rights Home or How to deal with repetitive applications in the future*, Round Table, Bled, Slovenia, 21–22.9.09, para. 21.

There are multiple factors which influence the nature of a state's response, including the extent of the political will to resolve a systemic problem, the domestic political agenda, the status of the Convention in national law, reputational pressures, technical capacity and financial burdens. Also critical is the extent of awareness and in-depth understanding of the European Convention within the judiciary, Parliament, civil society and the media.

The role played by the Government agent is an important feature of the state's response – someone who is thoroughly engaged in the process, who understands the need for change, and who adopts a proactive approach, can be an effective catalyst. The extent of a Government agent's authority vis-à-vis domestic institutions is a significant factor in facilitating an appropriate response to Strasbourg judgments. The higher their status, the more successful they are likely to be in communicating with the relevant Ministries and public bodies, and in persuading them of the need to respond adequately to a European Court judgment. The Government agent needs to be in a position to enable the Council of Europe to engage with a sufficiently broad range of interlocutors.

In our case studies we heard little evidence to suggest that national Parliamentarians are engaging effectively in the process of ensuring compliance with human rights standards, either in 'auditing' draft legislation or in responding to judgments of the European Court of Human Rights. This represents a significant lacuna, as there is evidence to suggest that active Parliamentary involvement is crucial for the effective implementation of European Court judgments.

There is little or no evidence to suggest that states have established a means for the systematic monitoring of legislation which is introduced in response to pilot judgments. As a result, it is difficult to assess the adequacy of states' responses.

The continuing unavailability of European Court judgments in the national language remains a significant problem.

Our conclusions as regards each of the three 'target' countries are set out below:

6.7.1. POLAND

We were informed about a developing public awareness in Poland in respect of the European Court of Human Rights, but its decisions are not widely reported in the media.

There remain concerns that the Polish authorities are failing to respond adequately to the decisions of both the Constitutional Court and the Strasbourg Court. There is little evidence of rigorous Parliamentary engagement either in the 'auditing' of draft legislation according to human rights standards, or in the follow up to European Court judgments concerning Poland.

Legislation was introduced reasonably rapidly in response to the Court's two 'full' pilot judgments against Poland (although there remain concerns about the effectiveness of their implementation in practice). Respondents acknowledged the importance of the proactive role played by the Polish Government Agent.

Significant pressure for change has been brought about by the strong degree of correlation between the judgments of the Polish Constitutional Court and the European Court.

Beyond the issues raised in *Broniowski* and *Hutten-Czapska*, other 'systemic' issues, such as the length of legal proceedings, excessive periods of pre-trial detention and poor prison conditions have continued to cause problems.

There is no systematic national monitoring of the effectiveness of measures introduced in response to European Court decisions highlighting structural problems.

6.7.2. SLOVENIA

The sheer number of cases submitted against Slovenia concerning violations of the right to a trial within a reasonable time was the main reason why the Court issued a 'quasi-pilot' judgment in the case of *Lukenda*.

The problem of the excessive length of legal proceedings has plagued Slovenia for a number of years. The amendments made to the 2006 Law in accordance with the European Court's decisions arguably demonstrate a degree of willingness on the part of the Slovenian Government to comply with Strasbourg over this issue. However, problems remained even with the 2006 Law which was introduced in the wake of *Lukenda*.

In respect of systemic problems which have arisen in Slovenia, there is evidence of a correlation as between the judgments of the Slovenian Constitutional Court and the European Court.

Parliament has failed to implement certain Constitutional Court judgments adequately, and there have been substantial delays before laws which have been declared unconstitutional are subsequently amended. We were told about a lack of awareness about human rights issues amongst Parliamentarians.

It was not evident that there is systematic national monitoring of the effectiveness of the legislative changes introduced in response to European Court judgments.

6.7.3. ITALY

Many interviewees considered the pilot judgment procedure to be a positive way to bring about legislative change in Italy. Nevertheless, questions remain about the extent of the familiarity of lawyers and judges in the lower courts with the European Convention, and European Court case law. Access to Strasbourg precedents in Italian is problematic.

One consequence of the European Court's 'quasi-pilot' judgment in *Scordino* was that the Constitutional Court has elevated the very status of the European Convention in domestic law.

There is some evidence of alignment between the Italian Constitutional Court and the European Court – in respect of the expropriation legislation.

Italy has been the subject of clone cases on a vast scale, notably in respect of the issue of the excessive length of legal proceedings. The *Pinto* legislation, which was introduced in an attempt to solve this problem, in practice gave rise to a new variety of clone cases in Strasbourg. Widespread violations of the Convention arising from the expropriation of property led to a Grand Chamber finding in 2006 that neither the existence nor the systemic nature of the problem had been acknowledged by the Italian judicial authorities.

We heard a number of concerns as to how the Italian authorities respond to Strasbourg judgments: that the executive and legislature are insufficiently aware of Strasbourg judgments and are ineffectual as regards the implementation of the Convention in Italian legislation. The Italian Government has unsuccessfuly argued against the application of the pilot judgment procedure (or 'quasi-pilot' judgments) on the grounds that it lacks a legal basis in the Convention, encroaches on the sovereignty of the state and that the Court is therefore usurping the role of the Committee of Ministers.

Questions have been raised about the effectiveness of the Azzolini law, introduced in 2006, to establish a procedure for the monitoring of the implementation of Strasbourg judgments. The annual reports produced by the Prime Minister's Office have in some respects sought to challenge the European Court decisions.

6.8. THE CONTRIBUTION OF OTHER COUNCIL OF EUROPE ENTITIES

A number of other bodies within the Council of Europe have an essential role to play in assisting states to end systemic human rights violations.[4] These include the Commissioner for Human Rights,[5] the Parliamentary Assembly (the Committee on Legal Affairs and Human Rights),[6] the European Commission for Democracy through Law (Venice Commission),[7] and the European Commission for the Efficiency of Justice (CEPEJ).[8] The various entities maintain both formal and informal contacts.

Our understanding is that the Office of the Commissioner for Human Rights is cautious about becoming involved in litigation (for example as a third party intervenor), being mindful of the specific roles stipulated in the European Convention for both the Court and the Committee of Ministers.[9] Nevertheless, respondents told us that it is critical that the Commissioner raises systemic issues in the course of his in-country missions. Another avenue is the Commissioner's ongoing co-operation with ombudsmen and national human rights institutions. The Commissioner has alluded to the potential role which his office could play vis-à-vis pilot judgments.[10] There are already instances of the Court relying on the Commissioner's reports for broader, contextual information about a problem (as was the case, for example, in *Kauczor v Poland*, concerning pre-trial detention).

The Committee on Legal Affairs and Human Rights of the Parliamentary Assembly of the Council of Europe (CLAHR) has become increasingly engaged in recent

---

4 See, generally, Rick Lawson (2009), *How to maintain and improve mutual trust amongst EU Member States in police and judicial cooperation in criminal matters? Lessons from the functioning of monitoring mechanisms in the Council of Europe*, University of Leiden, 31.8.09.

5 http://www.coe.int/t/commissioner/default_en.asp.

6 http://assembly.coe.int/Main.asp?link=/Committee/JUR/role_E.htm.

7 http://www.venice.coe.int/site/main/Presentation_E.asp.

8 http://www.coe.int/T/dghl/cooperation/cepej/default_en.asp.

9 See I. Kitsou-Milonas (2009), 'A possible role for the Commissioner for Human Rights in the pilot judgment procedure', in Wołąsiewicz, Jakub (ed.), *Pilot Judgment Procedure in the European Court of Human Rights and the future development of Human Rights standards and procedures: Third informal seminar for government agents and other institutions, Warsaw 14–15 May, 2009*, Kontrast, Warsaw, pp. 94–98.

10 "I believe that, with the assistance of NHRIs, the Commissioner could assist the Court in identifying cases that should give rise to a pilot judgment, in defining the domestic measures required by the execution of a judgment in such a pilot case and in understanding the difficulties preventing the national authorities from taking such measures. The Commissioner and his partners could help the Court to formulate realistic, inventive and precise prescriptions of the measures expected from the States concerned, not only the States party to the proceedings but also third States concerned by the substance of the judgment" – T. Hammarberg, 'Alternative or complementary means of resolving disputes and other issues broached by the Wise Persons' Report', Colloquy *The Future of the European Court of Human Rights in the light of the Wise Persons' report*, San Marino, 22–23.3.07, CommDH/Speech(2007)4 REV, 23.3.07.

years in following up states' non-implementation of European Court judgments. It focuses on judgments not fully implemented after five years, the most urgent and important cases, and those which raise important implementation issues. The CLAHR has published six reports on the implementation of judgments (since 2000).[11] A seventh report is due in June 2010. Critical to the work of the CLAHR are its Parliamentary links – it is able to take advantage of the possibilities for a dialogue with national legislators. There is evidence to suggest that national Parliamentary involvement and oversight is critical to the effective implementation of the European Convention standards and European Court judgments.

6.9. RECOMMENDATIONS

6.9.1. CONTRACTING STATES

1. Take further steps to publicise and disseminate key European Court judgments (and their particular implications for the domestic system)

2. Develop a more formalised system and practice in order to respond to pilot judgments[12]

3. Respond more quickly and efficiently to pilot judgments by drafting, consulting on and publicising action plans

4. State bodies to which a pilot judgment is applicable should respond, as soon as is practicable, to the European Court's new requirements within the limits of their existing competencies (for example by changing their policies or practices).

5. Review the status and role of the Government Agent so that they are in a position to ensure a sufficient response from the various authorities within the state

6. Take the necessary steps to ensure the active and efficacious involvement of parliament in responding to pilot judgments

---

11 See: *Implementation of judgments of the European Court of Human Rights – Progress Report (Rapporteur: Mr Christos Pourgourides)*, Committee on Legal Affairs and Human Rights, AS/Jur (2009)36, 31.8.09.

12 See, inter alia, Recommendation CM/Rec(2008)2 of the Committee of Ministers to member states on efficient domestic capacity for rapid execution of judgments of the ECtHR *(Adopted by the Committee of Ministers on 6 February 2008 at the 1017th meeting of the Ministers' Deputies)* https://wcd.coe.int/ViewDoc.jsp?id=1246081&Site=CM.

7. Foster the active involvement of civil society (and national human rights institutions) in devising responses to pilot judgments

8. Develop a dialogue between the higher national courts and the European Court on systemic violations

9. Develop and maintain a means of independently monitoring the effectiveness of the state's response to a pilot judgment (i.e. by monitoring the effectiveness of consequential changes to the law)

10. Actively review judgments in cases against other states relating to systemic issues and formulate an appropriate response

6.9.2. CIVIL SOCIETY

1. Actively engage with state bodies in the formulation of a state's response to a pilot judgment

2. Engage directly with the Committee of Ministers as to the general measures required to resolve systemic problems (utilising Rule 9 of the Committee of Ministers' Rules)

3. Intervene as a third party in cases before the European Court of Human Rights which raise systemic issues (to provide the Court with a broader context)

6.9.3. COUNCIL OF EUROPE

1. Ensure greater understanding of the pilot judgment procedure, and greater transparency, by developing relevant rules or a practice direction

2. Give further consideration to broadening the breadth and scope of pilot judgments

3. Actively engage with state authorities over systemic issues, including expanding the Court Registry's programme of in-country visits to discuss pending cases

4. Develop closer co-operation between the Court, the Court's Department for Execution of Judgments and the Committee of Ministers in respect of

the identification of systemic issues, the diagnosis of consequential general measures required and the state's implementation of pilot judgments

5. Develop dialogues on systemic problems with higher national courts

6. Take steps to promote the *erga omnes* application of pilot judgments

7. Give high priority to fast-tracking the supervision of the implementation of pilot judgments

8. Develop a more rigorous scrutiny of the implementation of pilot judgments (for example by putting more resources into consulting a broader range of interlocutors)

9. Provide technical support and assistance to civil society to engage with the Council of Europe as to the general measures required to resolve a systemic problem (for example, under Rule 9 of the Committee of Ministers' Rules). Prioritise assistance to civil society in states where systemic problems are most prevalent.

10. Consider further how to combine the expertise and resources of various Council of Europe bodies in tackling structural problems: the Commissioner for Human Rights; Committee on Legal Affairs and Human Rights (of the Parliamentary Assembly); CEPEJ; and the Venice Commission.

11. Consider instigating a relevant inquiry by the Secretary General of the Council of Europe (under Article 52 of the Convention)

12. Conduct or commission further research into systemic violations and how they can be resolved at the national level

LIST OF CASES

Abdelhedi v Italy, No. 2638/07, 24.3.09
Apicella v Italy, No. 64890/01, 29.3.06 (GC)
Bączkowski v Poland, No. 1543/06, 3.5.07
Bekoyeva (Elza Alikhanovna) v Georgia, No. 48347/08 (communicated 26.1.09)
Belinger v Slovenia, No. 42320/98, dec. 2.10.01; 13.6.02
Belvedere Alberghiera S.r.l. v Italy, No. 31524/96, 30.5.00
Ben Khemais v Italy, No. 246/07, 24.2.09
Ben Salah v Italy, No. 38128/06, 24.3.09
Berková v Slovakia, No. 67149/01, 24.3.09
Boboc v Moldova, No. 27581/04, 4.11.08
Bottazzi v Italy, No. 34884/97, 28.7.99 (GC)
Bouyahia v Italy, No. 46792/06, 24.3.09
Broniowski v Poland, No. 31443/96, 22.6.04 (GC); 28.9.05 (GC)
Brumărescu v Romania, No. 28342/95, 28.10.99 (GC)
Burdov v Russia, No. 59498/00, 7.5.02
Burdov v Russia (No. 2), No. 33509/04, 15.1.09
Butolen (Boris) v Slovenia, No. 41356/08, dec. 9.6.09
Case Relating to Certain Aspects of the Laws on the Use of Languages in Education in Belgium v Belgium, Nos. 1474/62, 1677/62, 1691/62, 1769/63, 1994/63, 2126/64, 23.7.68
Cat Berro v Italy, No. 34192/07, dec. 25.11.08
C.B.Z. v Italy, No. 44006/06, 24.3.09
Carbonara and Ventura v Italy, No. 24638/94, 30.5.00
Charzyński (Piotr) v Poland, No. 15212/03, dec. 1.3.05
Cocchiarella v Italy, No. 64886/01, 29.3.06 (GC)
Colozza v Italy, No. 9024/80, 12.2.85 (GC)
Darraji v Italy, No. 11549/05, 24.3.09
Demopoulos (Takis) and others v Turkey, Nos. 46113/99, 3843/02, 13751/02, 13466/03, 10200/04, 14163/04, 19993/04, 21819/04, dec. 1.3.10 (GC)
Doğan v Turkey, Nos. 8803-8811/02, 8813/02 and 8815-8819/02, 29.6.04
Donnadieu v France (No. 2), No. 19249/02, 7.2.06
Driza v Albania, No. 33771/02, 13.11.07
E.G. v Poland (and 175 other Bug River applications), No. 50425/99, dec. 23.9.08
Elia S.r.l. v Italy, No. 37710/97, 2.8.01
Faimblat v Romania, No. 23066/02, 13.1.09
Grzinčič v Slovenia, No. 26867/02, 3.5.07

Guiso-Gallisay v Italy, No. 58858/00, 21.10.08; 22.12.09 (GC)
Hamraoui v Italy, No. 16201/07, 24.3.09
Hutten-Czapska v Poland, No. 35014/97, 22.2.05; 19.6.06 (GC); 28.4.08 (GC)
İçyer v Turkey, No. 18888/02, dec. 12.1.06
Ilić v Serbia, No. 30132/04, 9.10.07
Ivanov (Yuriy Nikolayevich) v Ukraine, No. 40450/04, 15.10.09
Karamitrov and others v Bulgaria, No. 53321/99, 10.1.08
Katz v Romania, No. 29739/03, 20.1.09
Kauczor v Poland, No. 45219/06, 3.2.09
Klass v Germany, No. 5029/71, 6.9.78
Korenjak (Matej) v Slovenia, No. 463/03, dec. 15.5.07
Kounov v Bulgaria, No. 24379/02, 23.5.06
Krawczak v Poland, No. 40387/06, 8.4.08
Kudła v Poland, No. 30210/96, 26.10.00 (GC)
Kukalo v Russia, No. 11319/04, 24.7.08
Lesjak (Robert) v Slovenia, No. 33946/03, 21.7.09
Loizidou v Turkey, No. 15318/89, 18.12.96
Lukenda v Slovenia, No. 23032/02, 6.10.05
Majewski v Poland, No. 52690/99, 11.10.05
Makuc (Milan) and others v Slovenia, No. 26828/06, dec. 31.5.07
Manole and others v Moldova, No. 13936/02, 17.9.09
Matko v Slovenia, No. 43393/98, 2.11.06
Mostacciuolo (Giuseppe) v Italy (No. 1), No. 64705/01, 29.3.06 (GC)
Mostacciuolo (Giuseppe) v Italy (No. 2), No. 65102/01, 29.3.06 (GC)
Musci v Italy, No. 64699/01, 29.3.06 (GC)
Musiał (Sławomir) v Poland, No. 28300/06, 20.1.09
O. v Italy, No. 37257/06, 24.3.09
O'Donoghue (Sinead) and others v UK, No. 34848/07 (communicated 1.12.08)
Olaru and others v Moldova, Nos. 476/07, 22539/05, 17911/08 and 13136/07, 28.7.09
Papamichalopoulos v Greece, No. 14556/89, 31.10.95 (GC)
Pasculli v Italy, No. 36818/97, 4.12.07
Pizzati (Riccardi) v Italy, No. 62361/00, 29.3.06 (GC)
Procaccini (Giuseppina and Orestina) v Italy, No. 65075/01, 29.3.06 (GC)
R.R. v Italy, No. 42191/02, 9.6.05
Ramadhi and 5 others v Albania, No. 38222/02, 13.11.07
Rehbock v Slovenia, No. 29462/95, 28.11.00
Rossitto v Italy, No. 7977/03, 26.5.09
Saadi v Italy, No. 37201/06, 28.2.08 (GC)
Scordino v Italy (No. 1), No. 36813/97, 29.07.04; 29.3.06 (GC)
Scordino v Italy (No. 2), No. 36815/97, 15.7.04
Scordino v Italy (No. 3), No. 43662/98, 6.3.07
Sejdović v Italy, No. 56581/00, 10.11.04; 1.3.06 (GC)
Sellem v Italy, No. 12584/08, 5.5.09

Šilih v Slovenia, No. 71463/01, 9.4.09 (GC)
Simaldone v Italy, No. 22644/03, 31.1.09
Soltana v Italy, No. 37336/06, 24.3.09
Somogyi v Italy, No. 67972/01, 18.5.04
Suljagić v Bosnia and Herzegovina, No. 27912/02, dec. 20.6.06; 3.11.09
Sürmeli v Germany, No. 75529/01, 8.6.06 (GC)
Szott-Medyńska and others v Poland, No. 47414/99, dec. 9.10.03
Terazzi SRL v Italy, No. 27265/95, 17.10.02
Tur v Poland, No. 21695/05, 23.10.07
Tysiąc v Poland, No. 5410/03, 20.3.07
Uskov (Viktor Mikhaylovich) (and 17 other applications) v Russia, Nos. 6394/05, 7144/05, 9464/05, 10542/05, 30006/06, 39119/06, 50742/06, 2229/07, 5951/07, 31624/07, 31698/07, 51340/07, 51342/07, 9463/08, 13132/08, 16251/08, 16849/08 and 39590/08, dec. 12.11.09
Viaşu v Romania, No. 75951/01, 9.12.08
Voytenko v Ukraine, No. 18966/02, 29.6.04
Witkowska-Toboła (Genowefa) v Poland, No. 11208/02, dec. 4.12.07
Wolkenberg (Andrzej) and others v Poland, No. 50003/99, dec. 4.12.07
Xenides-Arestis v Turkey, No. 46347/99, 22.12.05; 7.12.06
Zullo (Ernestino) v Italy, No. 64897/01, 29.3.06 (GC)
Žunič (Branko) v Slovenia, No. 24342/04, dec. 18.10.07
Zwoźniak v Poland, No. 25728/05, 13.11.07

All decisions are available on the European Court's HUDOC database: http://cmiskp.echr.coe.int/tkp197/search.asp?skin=hudoc-en.

The communicated cases can be located by searching the 'communicated cases collection' on HUDOC.

BIBLIOGRAPHY

Anagnostou, Dia and Mungiu-Pippidi, Alina (2009), *Why Do States Implement Differently the European Court of Human Rights Judgments? The Case Law on Civil Liberties and the Rights of Minorities*, JURISTRAS Project, April 2009, available at: http://www.juristras.eliamep.gr/wp-content/uploads/2009/09/why-do-states-implement-differently-the-european-court-of-human.pdf (last accessed 8.4.10).

Blitz, Brad (2006) 'Statelessness and the Social (De)Construction of Citizenship: Political Restructuring and Ethnic Discrimination in Slovenia' *Journal of Human Rights* 5, pp. 453–479.

Bodnar, Adam (2009), 'Shaping the Freedom of Assembly: Counter-Productive Effects of the Polish Road towards Illiberal Democracy' in András Sajó (ed.), *Free to Protest: Constituent Power and Street Demonstration*, Issues in Constitutional Law v.5, Eleven International Publishing, pp. 165–187.

Bosnia and Herzegovina. Parlamentarna Skupština. Dom Naroda. *Transkript 7. sjednice Doma Naroda Parlamentarne Skupštine Bosne i Hercegovine, održane 30.07.07. = Transcript of the 7th Session of the People's House of the Parliamentary Assembly of Bosnia and Herzegovina*, 30.07.07. http://www.parlament.ba/sjednica/1/0/60.html (last accessed 11.4.10).

Bosnia and Herzegovina. Parlamentarna Skupština. Predstavnički Dom. *Stenogram 42. sjednice Predstavničkog Doma Parlamentarne Skupštine BiH, 17.12.08. = Stenographic report of the 42nd Session of the House of Representatives of the Parliamentary Assembly of Bosnia and Herzegovina*. 17.12.07. http://www.parlament.ba/sjednica/1/0/111.html (last accessed 11.4.10).

Bosnia and Herzegovina. Parlamentarna Skupština. Vijesti. *Održana sjednica privremene zajedničke komisije za utvrđivanje stare devizne štednje građana BiH* = [News:] *Session held of the provisional joint Committee for fixing old foreign currency savings for citizens of Bosnia and Herzegovina*. 10.03.09 http://www.parlament.ba/vijesti/1/0/860.html (last accessed 11.4.10).

Bosnia and Herzegovina. Parlamentarna Skupština. Vijesti. *Razgovori članova kolegija predstavničkog doma sa premijerom R. Slovenije, Janezom Janšom = [News] Discussions held between members of the College of the lower house of Parliament [of Bosnia and Herzegovina] with the [visiting] Prime Minister of Slovenia Janez Janša*, 19.02.07 http://www.parlament.ba/vijesti/1/0/23.html (last accessed 11.4.10).

Bosnia and Herzegovina. Parlamentarna Skupština. *Zakonodavstvo: Neusvojeni Zakoni; Prijedlog zakona o izmjenama i dopunama Zakona o izmirenju obaveza po osnovu računa stare devizne štednje = Legislation: laws that have been rejected: proposed law on amending and executing the Law on Foreign Currency Savings*. Bill laid on 24.5.06

rejected at the 7th Session of the People's House, 30.07.07. http://www.parlament.ba/nzakoni/1/0/0.html (last accessed 17.2.10).

Bosnia and Herzegovina. Parlamentarna Skupština. *Zakonodavstvo: Neusvojeni Zakoni; Prijedlog zakona o izmjenama i dopunama Zakona o izmirenju obaveza po osnovi računa stare devizne štednje = Legislation: laws that have been rejected: proposed law on amending and executing the Law on Foreign Currency Savings*. Bill laid on 01.09.08; rejected at the 42nd Session of the House of Representatives, 17.12.08 http://www.parlament.ba/nzakoni/1/0/0.html (last accessed 17.2.10).

Bultrini, Antonio (2008), 'Le sentenze 348 e 349/2007 della Corte costituzionale: l'inizio di una svolta?' = 'The Constitutional Court judgments 348 and 349: the beginning of a turning point?' *Diritto Pubblico Comparato ed Europeo* = Comparative public rights and Europe.

Burkov, Anton (2010), ''New Draft Law on Compensation for Citizens who do not receive a Fair Trial within a reasonable time' EU-Russia Centre ,13 April 2010 http://www.eu-russiacentre/org/ourpublications/column/draft-law-compensation-citizens-receive-fair-trial-reasonable-time.html.

Byers, Michael (2006), Custom, power and the power of rules: international relations and customary international law, CUP.

Colandrea, Valerio (2007), 'On the power of the European Court of Human Rights to order specific non-monetary measures: some remarks in light of the Assandize, Broniowski and Sejdović cases' *Human Rights Law Review* 2, pp. 396–411.

Costa, Jean-Paul (2007), 'Comments on the Wise Persons' Report from the perspective of the European Court of Human Rights' in "Future developments of the European Court of Human Rights in the light of the Wise Persons' Report", San Marino, 22.03.07, pp. 34–43. http://www.coe.int/t/e/human_rights/cddh/1._publications/SanMarino_en.pdf (last accessed 8.4.10).

Degener, Renata and Paul Mahoney (2007), 'The prospects for a Test-Case Procedure in the European Court of Human Rights' in Hanno Hartig (ed.), *Trente ans de droit européen des droits de l'homme – Études à la mémoire de Wolfgang Strasser*, Droit et Justice 74, Emile Bruylant, pp. 173–208.

Della Cananea, Giacinto (2008), 'The Italian Constitutional Court and the European Court of Justice: From Separation to Interaction?' *European Public Law* 14:4, pp. 523–531.

Drzemczewski, Andrew and James Gaughan (2010), 'Implementing Strasbourg Court Judgments: the Parliamentary Dimension', in W. Benedek, W. Karl and A. Mihr (eds.), *European Yearbook on Human Rights 2010*, Vol. II, European Academic Press, 2010, pp. 247–258 (forthcoming).

Drzemczewski, Andrew and Marek Nowicki (2001), 'Poland' in Robert Blackburn and Jurg Polakiewicz (eds.), *Fundamental Rights in Europe: the European Convention on Human Rights and its member states, 1950–2000*, OUP, pp. 657–79.

Dzialuk, Igor (2009), 'Quasi-Pilot Judgments: comments from the perspective of Poland (cases Musiał and Kauczor)' in Wołąsiewicz, Jakub (ed.), *Pilot Judgment Procedure in the European Court of Human Rights and the development of Human Rights standards and procedures : Third informal seminar for government agents and other institutions, Warsaw 14–15 May, 2009*, Kontrast, pp. 107–112.

Ėntin, Mark (2010), 'Nastoiashchee i budushchee Interlakenskogo protesessa' *Internet zhurnal Vsia Evropa*, No.1(40) = 'The Present and the Future of the Interlaken Process' *Internet Newspaper 'All Europe'* No.1(40) http://alleuropa.ru/index.php?option=com_content&task=view&id=1419#_ftnr (last accessed 17.2.10).

European Commission (1997) *Agenda 2000 – Commission Opinion on Slovenia's Application for Membership of the European Union*, http://ec.europa.eu/enlargement/archives/pdf/dwn/opinions/slovenia/sn-op_en.pdf (last accessed 11.4.10).

European Human Rights Advocacy Centre (HRSJ, London Metropolitan University) (2010), Press Release. *Georgians take Russia to European Court of Human Rights over August 2008 armed conflict*, 10 February 2010 (concerning 32 groups of applications on behalf of 134 Georgian citizens) http://www.londonmet.ac.uk/londonmet/fms/MRSite/Research/HRSJ/EHRAC/Press%20releases/EHRAC%20Press%20Release%2062%20Russia-Georgia%20conflict%20apps%20lodged%2010_2_10.pdf (last accessed 17.2.10).

Flores, Marcello [2009], Supranational rights litigation, implementation and the domestic impact of Strasbourg Court jurisprudence: A case study of Italy, *Juristras: final case study report*, http://www.juristras.eliamep.gr/wp-content/uploads/2008/09/casestudyitaly.pdf (last accessed 9.4.10).

Fribergh, Erik (2008), 'Pilot judgments from the Court's perspective' *Stockholm Colloquy, 9–10 June 2008.*

Fribergh, Erik (2009), *Bringing Rights Home or How to deal with repetitive applications in the future'*, Round Table, Bled, Slovenia, 21–22.9.09.

Frowein, Jochen (2007), 'The binding force of ECHR judgments and its limits' in Breitenmoser, Stephan *et al.* (ed.), *Human Rights, Democracy and the Rule of Law: Liber Amicorum Luzius Wildhaber*, Nomos, pp. 261–269.

Garlicki, Lech (2007), 'Broniowski and After: On the Dual Nature of Pilot Judgments' in *Lucius Caflisch ed. (et al.) Liber amicorum Luzius Wildhaber: Human Rights, Strasbourg views*, N.P. Engel, pp. 177–192.

Gattini, Andrea (2007), 'Mass claims at the European Court of Human Rights' in *Stephan Breitenmoser ed. (et al.) Human Rights, Democracy and the Rule of Law: Liber Amicorum Luzius Wildhaber*, Nomos, pp. 271–294.

Georgians take Russia to European Court of Human Rights over August 2008 armed conflict, Press Release, European Human Rights Advocacy Centre, 10 February 2010 (concerning 32 groups of applications on behalf of 134 Georgian citizens) - available at: http://www.londonmet.ac.uk/londonmet/fms/MRSite/Research/HRSJ/EHRAC/Press%20releases/EHRAC%20Press%20Release%2062%20Russia-Georgia%20conflict%20apps%20lodged%2010_2_10.pdf (last accessed 11.4.10).

Goldsmith, Jack and Eric A. Posner (2005), *The Limits of International Law*, OUP.

'Government suspends sham marriage rules' *The Guardian*, 10.04.06. http://guardian.co.uk/society/2006/apr/10/asylum.politics/print (last accessed 19.2.10).

Grabbe, Heather (2006), *The EU's transformative power: Europeanization through conditionality in Central and Eastern Europe*, Palgrave.

Hammarberg, Thomas (2006), *Statement by Thomas Hammarberg, Commissioner for Human Rights at Press Conference in Ljubljana*, http://www.dosta.org/en/node/159 (last accessed 9.4.10).

Hammarberg, Thomas (2007), *'Alternative or complementary means of resolving disputes and other issues broached by the Wise Persons' Report'*, Colloquy "The Future of the European Court of Human Rights in the light of the Wise Persons' report", San Marino, 22–23 March 2007, CommDH/Speech(2007)4 REV, 23 March 2007.

Imbert, Pierre Henri (2004), 'Follow-up of the Committee of Ministers' Recommendations on the implementation of the Convention at the domestic level and the Declaration on 'Ensuring the effectiveness of the implementation of the European Convention on Human Rights at national and European levels', Speech by M. Pierre-Henri Imbert, *High Level Seminar on Reform of the European Human Rights System*, 18.10.04, Oslo, Norway.

Italy. Constitution (1948), http://www.servat.unibe.ch/icl/it00000_.html (last accessed 9.4.10).

Italy. Presidenza del Consiglio dei Ministri (2008), *L'esecuzione delle pronunce della Corte europea dei diritti dell'uomo nei confronti dello stato italiano Legge 9 gennaio 2006, n. 12 : Relazione al Parlamento Anno 2008=The execution of the decisions of the European Court of Human Rights with respect to the Italian State, law of 9 June 2006, no. 12 : Report to the Parliament, 2008.*

Kitschelt, Herbert, Zdenka Mansfeldová, Radoslaw Markowski and Gábor Tóka (1999), *Post-Communist Party Systems: competition, representation, and inter-party cooperation*, CUP.

Koh, Harold Hongju (1997), 'Review essay: Why do Nations obey International Law?' *Yale Law Journal* v.106, pp. 2599–2659, p. 2603.

Kowalska, Katarzyna (2009), 'Effective remedies for excessive length of proceedings' in Wołąsiewicz, Jakub (ed.), *Pilot Judgment Procedure in the European Court of Human Rights and the development of Human Rights standards and procedures : Third informal seminar for government agents and other institutions, Warsaw 14–15 May, 2009*, Kontrast, pp. 164–168.

Kozminski, Andrzej (1997), 'Restitution of private property: reprivatization in Central and Eastern Europe' *Communist and Post-Communist Studies* 30:1, pp. 95–106.

Krzyżanowska-Mierzewska, Magda (2008), 'Sprawy mienia zabużańskiego przed ETPCz' *Europejski Przegląd Sądowy* 12, pp. 20–25 = 'Property issues of the Bug River Region inhabitants before the ECtHR' *European Court Review* 12, pp. 20–25.

Krzyżanowska-Mierzewska, Magda (2008), 'The Reception Process in Poland and Slovakia' in Keller, Helen and Alec Stone Sweet (eds.), *A Europe of Rights: the Impact of the ECHR on National Legal Systems*, OUP, pp. 531–602.

Lagoutte, Stéphanie (2007), 'The Future of the European Human Rights Control System: Fighting With its Back to the Wall' in *Stéphanie Lagoutte, Hans-Otto Sano, Peter*

Scharff Smith, Human Rights in Turmoil, Facing Threats, Consolidating Achievements, Martinus Nijhoff Publishers, pp. 25–48.

Lambert-Abdelgawad, Elisabeth (2005), “Le protocole 14 et l’exécution des arrêts de la Cour européenne des droits de l’homme” in Cohen-Jonathan, Gérard and Jean-François Flauss, *La Réforme du système de contrôle contentieux de la Convention européenne des droits de l’homme*, Droit et Justice, Vol. 61, Bruylant, pp. 79-114.

Lawson, Rick (2009), ‘How to maintain and improve mutual trust amongst EU Member States in police and judicial cooperation in criminal matters? Lessons from the functioning of monitoring mechanisms in the Council of Europe’, University of Leiden, 31 August 2009.

Leach, Philip (2009), ‘Opinion: On reform of the European Court of Human Rights’ *European Human Rights Law Review* 6, pp. 725–735

Leach, Philip (2008), ‘The Chechen Conflict: Analysing the Oversight of the European Court of Human Rights’ *European Human Rights Law Review* 6, pp. 732–761.

Leach, Philip (2007), ‘Strasbourg’s oversight of Russia – an increasingly strained relationship’ *Public Law*, Winter, pp. 640–654.

Leach, Philip (2005), *Taking a Case to the European Court*, OUP, 2nd Ed.

Leach, Philip (2005), ‘Beyond the Bug River: a new dawn for redress before the European Court of Human Rights?’ *European Human Rights Law Review* 2, pp. 148–164.

Lewis, Paul and Zdenka Mansfeldová (2006), *The European Union and Party Politics in Central and Eastern Europe*, Palgrave.

Lewocki, Grzegorz (2008), ‘Kauczor et al. Strasburg o przeludnieniu w polskich więzieniach’ = ‘Kauczor et al.: Strasbourg on the issue of overcrowding in Polish prisons’ *Rzeczpospolita* 04.09.08. http://new-arch.rp.pl/artykul/804354.html (last accessed 9.4.10).

Mavčič, Arne (2001), ‘Slovenia’ in *Robert Blackburn and Jörg Polakiewicz, Fundamental Rights in Europe: the European Convention on Human Rights and its member states*, OUP, pp. 781–808.

Medvedev rasskazal sud’iam o reforme: otkryto, ėffektivno, bezopasno = Medvedev told judges that reform should be transparent, effective and foolproof http://www.newsru.com/russia/02dec2008/medsud_print.html (last accessed 11.4.10).

Michniewicz-Wanik, Krystyna (2008), *Mienie Zabużańskie: Prawne podstawy realizacji roszczeń*, Nortom = *Property of the Bug River Region: the legal basis of how claims are paid.*

Moldova. Parlamentul (2009), *Dezbateri parlamentare, Parlamentul Republicii Moldova de legislatura a XVIII-a, Sesiunea I ordinară, octombrie 2009, Şedinţa din ziua de 15 octombrie 2009, Stenograma Sumar = Parliamentary debates of the Republic of Moldova’s legislature of the 18th ordinary session, October 2009, Stenographic summary of the session of 15 October* http://www.parlament.md/news/plenaryrecords/15.10.2009/ (last accessed 11.4.10).

Moldova. Parlamentul (2009), *Dezbateri parlamentare. Parlamentul Republicii Moldova de legislatura a XVIII-a Sesiunea I ordinară – Noiembrie 2009. Şedinţa din ziua de*

27 noiembrie 2009. Stenograma Sumar. http://www.parlament.md/news/plenary-records/29.11.2009/ (last accessed 11.4.10).

Momot, Stanisław (2008), *Badania aktowe spraw, w których czas trwania tymczasowych aresztowań przekroczył 2 lata*, Instytut Wymiaru Sprawiedliwości = *Research into cases where pre-trial detention has exceeded 2 years.*

Moravcsik, Andrew (2000), 'The Origins of Human Rights Regimes: Democratic delegation in Postwar Europe' *International Organization* 54:2, pp. 217–52.

North, Douglass (1990), *Institutions, Institutional Change and Economic Performance*, CUP.

O'Boyle, Michael (2008), 'On reforming the operation of the European Court of Human Rights' *European Human Rights Law Review* 1, pp. 1–11.

Palombella, Gianluigi (2009), 'The rule of law beyond the state: failures, promises and theory' *International Journal of Constitutional Law* 7:3, pp. 442–467.

Paraskeva, Costas (2007), 'Human Rights protection begins at home: the Pilot Judgment Procedure developed by the European Court of Human Rights' *Human Rights Law Commentary* 3. https://portal2.nottingham.ac.uk/shared/shared_hrlcpub/Paraskeva.pdf (last accessed 11.4.10).

Pavlin, Peter (2006), *Overview of the contents of the protection of the right to a trial without undue delay act of the Republic of Slovenia of 2006*, Slovenian Ministry of Justice.

Poland. Ministerstwo Skarbu Państwa. Realizacja wypłat rekompensat. Komunikat nr 2/2010 w sprawie wypłat rekompensat z tytułu pozostawienia nieruchomości poza obecnymi granicami Rzeczypospolitej Polskiej, 5.2.10 = Poland. Ministry of the State Treasury. Implementing the disbursement of compensation. Communication nr 2/2010 over the issue of disbursing compensation for those properties left abroad by the Polish government, published 5.2.10. http://msp.gov.pl/portal/pl/118/8820/Komunikat_nr_22010_w_sprawie_wyplat_rekompensat_z_tytulu_pozostawienia_nieruchom.html (last accessed 9.4.10).

Poland. Kancelaria Sejmu, Biuro Komisji Sejmowych (2007), *Biuletyn*, nr. 2224/V kad. 5.7.07.

Poland. Kancelaria Sejmu, Biuro Komisji Sejmowych (2008), *Biuletyn*, nr. 506/VI kad. 9.4.08.

Poland. Ministry of Foreign Affairs (2005), *Broniowski v. Poland: Memorandum of the Polish Government*, Warsaw 14 November 2005.

Pollicino, Oreste (2008), 'Italy – Constitutional Court at the crossroads between constitutional parochialism and co-operative constitutionalism. Judgments No. 348 and 349 of 22 and 24 October 2007' *European Constitutional Law Review* 4, pp. 363–382.

Pushkarskaia, Anna (2009) 'Evropeĭskiĭ sud pozhalovalsia na Rossiiu Konstitutsionnomu: potrebovav ispolneniia sudebnykh resehenii̇̃' *Kommersant* No.36P (4091) 2.3.09, at http://www.kommersant.ru/doc.aspx?DocsID=1128309.

Russian Federation. Federal'noe Sobranie. Gosudarstvennaia Duma. Komitet Gosudarstvennoĭ Dumy po konstitutsionnomu zakonodatel'stvu i gosudarstvennomu stroitel'stvu Po porucheniu Soveta Gosudarstvennoĭ Dumy ot 21 maia 2009 goda (protocol No.113, punkt 6) *Zakliuchenie po proektu federal'nogo konstitutsionnogo zakona No. 103575-5 "O vozmeshchenii gosudarstvom vreda, prichinennogo narusheniem prava na sudoproizvodstvo v razumnye sroki i prava na ispolnenie v razumnye sroki vstupivshikh v zakonnuiu silu sudebnykh aktov" vnesennomu Verkhovnym Sudom Rossiĭskoĭ Federatsii (pervoe chtenie)* = Committee of the State Duma on Constitutional legislation and state institutions, commissioned by the Council of the State Duma 21.05.09 (protocol no. 113, article 6). *Conclusions on the project of the federal constitutional bill No. 103575-5 "On compensation for state violations of the right to trial within a reasonable time and the right to the execution of judgments that should have come into force", laid by the Supreme Court of the Russian Federation (first reading)* http://asozd.duma.gov.ru/work/dz.nsf/ByID/6A92F9F9B257A0F6C32575DA00213024/$File/0617103575-5.165.RTF?OpenElement (last accessed 11.4.10).

Russia (Federation). Federal'noe Sobranie. Gosudarstvennaia Duma. *Sessiia GD 4-ia sessiia GD piatogo sozyva (osen' 2009 g.) Presedatel'stvuiushchiĭ 11.09.09 = State Duma session, 4th session of the 5th Duma [2008–2011] (autumn, 2009), 11.09.09.* http://www.cir.ru/docs/duma/302/2091794?QueryID=2872326&HighlightQuery=2872326 (last accessed 10.4.10).

Russian Federation. *Prezident Rossii. Poslanie Federal'nomu Sobraniiu Rossiĭskoĭ Federatsii, 05.11.08 = Memorandum from the President of Russia to the Federal Assembly of the Russian Federation* http://tours.kremlin.ru/appears/2008/11/05/1349_type63372type63374type63381type82634_208749.shtml (last accessed 11.4.10).

Russian Federation. Sovet Sudeĭ Rossiĭskoĭ Federatsii *Postanovlenie VII Vserossiĭskogo S"ezda Sudeĭ g. Moskva 04 dekabria 2008 g. O sostoianii sudebnoĭ sistemy rossiĭskoĭ federatsii i prioritetnykh napravleniiakh ee razvitiia i sovershenstvovaniia = Resolution of the VII All-Russian Congress of Judges, Moscow, 4 December, 2008 "On the current state of the judicial system in the Russian Federation and priorities for how to develop and improve it"* www.oblsud.tsl.ru/siezd.files/siesd.doc (last accessed 11.4.10).

Russian Federation. Verkhovnyĭ Sud. *Vnositsia Verkhovnym Sudom Rossiĭskoĭ Federatsii Proekt Rossiĭskaia Federatsiia Federal'nyĭ Konstitutsionnyĭ zakon o vozmeshchenii gosudarstvom vreda, prichinennogo narusheniem prava na sudoproizvodstvo v razumnye sroki i prava na ispolnenie v razumnye sroki vstupivshikh v zakonnuiu silu sudebnykh aktov = The Supreme Court of the Russian Federation introduces a Russian Federation Constitutional Bill on compensation for state violations of the right to trial within a reasonable time and the right to the execution of judgments that should have come into force* http://asozd.duma.gov.ru/work/dz.nsf/ByID/325C666567526F04C32574D50027E910/$File/текст0002.rtf?OpenElement (last accessed 10.4.10).

Sadurski, Wojciech (2008), 'Partnering with Strasbourg: Constitutionalization of the European Court of Human Rights, the Accession of Central and East European States to the Council of Europe and the idea of Pilot Judgments', *EUI Working Papers Law* 2008/33.

Salamun, Michaela (2007), 'The laws on the organization of the administration in the Czech Republic, Hungary, Poland and Slovakia: A comparative analysis in the Context of European Integration' *Review of Central & East European Law* 32, pp. 267–301.

Schmitter, Philippe (2009), 'The changing politics of organised interests' in Goetz, Klaus H., Peter Mair and Gordon Smith (eds.), *European Politics: Pasts, presents, futures*, Routledge, pp. 199–203.

Seminara, Letizia (2009), *Les effets des arrêts de la Cour interaméricaine des droits de l'homme*, Droit et Justice 85, Emile Bruylant.

Slovenia. Constitution (1990), http://www.dz-rs.si/index.php?id=351&docid=25&showdoc=1 (last accessed 9.4.10).

Slovenia. Government Communication Office. News. 09.05.09. 'Amended Attorney's Act Takes Effect' http://www.ukom.gov.si/en/news/newsletter_slovenia_news/news/article/393/147/f210e94b84/?tx_ttnews%5Bnewsletter%5D=7 (last accessed 9.4.10).

Slovenia. Državni Svet. *Magnetogram 12. izredne seje Državnega sveta Republike Slovenije. 29.09.09 = minutes of the 12th extraordinary session of the National Council RS* http://www.ds-rs.si/?q=dejavnost/seje&CategoryID=95 (last accessed 17.2.10).

Slovenia. Državni Zbor. *Nadaljevanje 8. seje (15. julij 2009) = [Minutes of the Slovenian National Assembly] continuation of Session 8, 15 July 2009* http://www.dz-rs.si/index.php?id=97&cs=1&st=s&vt=15&fts=julija&unid=SZA|AAE1930FB30A1C00C1257632003892FE&showdoc=1 (last accessed 9.4.10).

Slovenia. Državni Zbor. *Odbor Državnega zbora Republike Slovenije za notranjo politiko, javno upravo in pravosodje. 1. nadaljevanje 6. seja*, 1.7.09 = *[Minutes of the] Committee on domestic politics, public management of justice, National Assembly of the Republic of Slovenia, 1 July 2009* http://www.dz-rs.si/index.php?id=97&cs=7&vt=15&fts=zvpsbno&unid=PMT|665FD5521ECE60C7C12575E700207487&showdoc=1 (last accessed 9.4.10).

Soriano, Mercedes Candela (2008), 'The Reception Process in Spain and Italy' in Keller, Helen and Alec Stone Sweet (eds.), *A Europe of Rights*, pp. 393–450.

Stawecki, Tomasz, Wiesław Staśkiewicz, Jan Winczorek (2008), *Między policentrycznością a fragmentaryzacją: wpływ Trybunału Konstytucyjnego na Polski porządek prawny*, Sprawne Państwo = *Between polycentrism and fragmentation: the impact of the Constitutional Court on the Polish legal system.*

Trochev, Alexei (2009), 'All appeals lead to Strasbourg? Unpacking the impact of the European Court of Human Rights on Russia' *Demokratizatsiya*, Vol. 17, No. 2, pp. 145–178, Spring 2009, University of Wisconsin Legal Studies Research Paper No. 1082, p. 151. http://papers.ssrn.com/sol3/papers.cfm?abstract_id=1421342 (last accessed 10.4.10).

United Kingdom. Parliament. Joint Committee on Human Rights. *Monitoring the Government's Response to Human Rights Judgments: Annual Report 2008*, HL Paper 173, HC 1078, 31 October 2008 http://www.publications.parliament.uk/pa/jt200708/jtselect/jtrights/173/17302.htm (last accessed 8.4.10).

United Kingdom. Parliament. Joint Committee on Human Rights (JCHR): Enhancing Parliament's role in relation to human rights judgments, HL Paper 85, HC 455, 26

March 2010. http://www.publications.parliament.uk/pa/jt200910/jtselect/jtrights/85/85.pdf (last accessed 21.4.10).

United Kingdom. Parliament. Joint Committee on Human Rights. *Thirty-First Report, Declarations on Incompatibility, Religious discrimination in sham marriages regime (Baiai v Secretary of State for the Home Department)*, paras. 96–106. http://www.publications.parliament.uk/pa/jt200708/jtselect/jtrights/173/17308.htm.

United Kingdom. *Pilot Judgments – Categorisation of Cases*, UK Government Paper produced at the request of the Reflection Group (DH-S-GDR), 2008 (unpublished).

Wildhaber, Luzius (2004), 'Consequences for the ECtHR of Protocol No. 14 and the Resolution on Judgments Revealing an Underlying Systemic Problem- Practical Steps of Implementation and Challenges' in *Applying and Supervising the ECHR-Reform of the European Human Rights System, Proceedings of the high-level seminar*, Oslo, 18 October 2004, pp. 23–32. http://www.coe.int/T/E/Human_rights/prot14e.asp; http://www.coe.int/t/e/human_rights/1reformeurhrsystem_e.pdf (last accessed 8.4.10).

Wildhaber, Luzius (2002), 'A Constitutional Future for the European Court of Human Rights?' *Human Rights Law Journal* 23, pp. 161–165.

Wołąsiewicz, Jakub (ed.) (2009), *Pilot Judgment Procedure in the European Court of Human Rights and the development of Human Rights standards and procedures: Third informal seminar for government agents and other institutions, Warsaw, 14–15 May*, Kontrast

Yudkivska, Anna (2009), *IEvropeĭs'kyĭ sud z prav liudyny zobov'iazav Ukraïnu protiahom roku zaprovadyty efektyvnyĭ zasıb vıdshkoduvannia u razı nevykonannia abo zatrymky vykonannia sudovykh rıshen' natsıonal'nykh sudıv = The European Court of Human Rights held that Ukraine was to secure within one year a sufficient redress for the non-enforcement or delayed enforcement of domestic decisions*, http://www.khpg.org/index.php?id=1256551783 (last accessed 11.4.10).

Zagorc, Saša (2005), "Dvojna Predramitev za slovensko oblast: odprava kršitev pravice do sojenja v razumnem roku – kako naprej? = Double wake-up call for Slovenian authorities effective legal remedies for the violation of the right to trial within a reasonable time – now what?" *Revus* 5, pp. 45–53.

COUNCIL OF EUROPE DOCUMENTS

Committee of Ministers (2006), 116th Session of the Committee of Ministers (Strasbourg, 18–19 May 2006) *Rules of the Committee of Ministers for the supervision of the execution of judgments and of the terms of friendly settlements (Adopted by the Committee of Ministers on 10 May 2006 at the 964th meeting of the Ministers' Deputies).* https://wcd.coe.int/ViewDoc.jsp?Ref=CM(2006)90&Language=lanEnglish&Site=COE&BackColorInternet=9999CC&BackColorIntranet=FFBB55&BackColorLogged=FFAC75 (last accessed 8.4.10).

Committee of Ministers (2006), CM(2006)203. *Report of the Group of Wise Persons to the Committee of Ministers*, 15 November 2006, 979bis Meeting https://wcd.coe.int/ViewDoc.jsp?id=1063779&BackColorInternet=9999CC&BackColorIntranet=FFBB55&BackColorLogged=FFAC75 (last accessed 9.4.10).

Committee of Ministers (2009), CM/Del/Dec(2009)1072 7 December 2009 1072nd (DH) meeting, 1–3 December 2009 *Decisions adopted at the meeting.* https://wcd.coe.int/ViewDoc.jsp?Ref=CM/Del/Dec(2009)1072&Language=lanEnglish&Ver=immediat&Site=COE&BackColorInternet=DBDCF2&BackColorIntranet=FDC864&BackColorLogged=FDC864 (last accessed 11.4.10).

Committee of Ministers (2009), *Final Resolution* CM/ResDH(2009)89 *Execution of the judgments of the European Court of Human Rights Broniowski against Poland*, 30 September 2009 http://cmiskp.echr.coe.int/tkp197/view.asp?item=6&portal=hbkm&action=html&highlight=Broniowski&sessionid=50829028&skin=hudoc-en (last accessed 8.4.10).

Committee of Ministers (2010), *High Level Conference on the Future of the European Court of Human Rights, Interlaken Declaration*, 19 February 2010, available at: http://www.eda.admin.ch/etc/medialib/downloads/edazen/topics/europa/euroc.Par.0133.File.tmp/final_en.pdf (last accessed 22.2.10).

Committee of Ministers (2007), Information Documents CM/Inf/DH(2006)19 rev3. *Non-enforcement of domestic judicial decisions in Russia: general measures to comply with the European Court's judgments: Memorandum prepared by the Department for the execution of the European Court's judgments (Application of Article 46 of the ECHR) 4 June 2007.* https://wcd.coe.int/ViewDoc.jsp?Ref=CM/Inf/DH(2006)19&Language=lanEnglish&Ver=rev3 (last accessed 10.4.10).

Committee of Ministers (2009), *Interim Resolution* CM/ResDH(2009)43. *Execution of the judgements of the European Court of Human Rights in 145 cases against the Russian Federation relative to the failure or serious delay in abiding by final domestic judicial decisions delivered against the state and its entities as well as the absence of an effective remedy* CM/Inf/DH(2006)19 revised and CM/Inf/DH(2006)45, CM/Inf/DH(2006)19 revised. https://wcd.coe.int/ViewDoc.jsp?id=1423205&Site=CM&BackColorInternet=9999CC&BackColorIntranet=FFBB55&BackColorLogged=FFAC75 (last accessed 10.4.10).

Committee of Ministers (2009), *Interim Resolution* CM/ResDH(2009)158. *Execution of the pilot judgement of the European Court of Human Rights in the case Burdov No.*

2 against the Russian Federation relative to the failure or serious delay in abiding by final domestic judicial decisions delivered against the state and its entities as well as the absence of an effective remedy. Adopted by the Committee of Ministers on 3 December 2009 at the 1072nd meeting of the Ministers' Deputies. https://wcd.coe.int/ViewDoc.jsp?id=1554569&Site=CM#P4094_273861.

Committee of Ministers (2009), *Interim Resolution* CM/ResDH(2009)159, *Execution of the judgments of the European Court of Human Rights in 324 cases against Ukraine concerning the failure or serious delay in abiding by final domestic courts' decisions delivered against the state and its entities as well as the absence of an effective remedy.* https://wcd.coe.int/ViewDoc.jsp?Ref=CM/ResDH(2009)159&Language=lanEnglish&Ver=original&Site=COE&BackColorInternet=DBDCF2&BackColorIntranet=FDC864&BackColorLogged=FDC864 (last accessed 11.4.10).

Committee of Ministers (2009), *Interim Resolution* CM/ResDH(2009)43 *Execution of the judgements of the European Court of Human Rights in 145 cases against the Russian Federation relative to the failure or serious delay in abiding by final domestic judicial decisions delivered against the state and its entities as well as the absence of an effective remedy.* https://wcd.coe.int/ViewDoc.jsp?id=1423205&Site=CM&BackColorInternet=9999CC&BackColorIntranet=FFBB55&BackColorLogged=FFAC75 (last accessed 11.4.10).

Committee of Ministers (2009), *Interim Resolution* CM/ResDH(2009)42 *Execution of the judgments of the European Court of Human Rights concerning the excessive length of judicial proceedings in Italy: Progress achieved and outstanding issues in the context of general measures to ensure compliance with the judgments of the European Court of Human Rights.* https://wcd.coe.int/ViewDoc.jsp?Ref=CM/ResDH(2009)42&Language=lanEnglish&Ver=original&Site=CM&BackColorInternet=9999CC&BackColorIntranet=FFBB55&BackColorLogged=FFAC75 (last accessed 9.4.10).

Committee of Ministers (2008), *Interim Resolution* CM/ResDH(2008)1 *of the Committee of Ministers on the execution of the judgments of the European Court of Human Rights in 232 cases against Ukraine relative to the failure or serious delay in abiding by final domestic judicial decisions delivered against the state and its entities as well as the absence of an effective remedy, 6 March 2008.* https://wcd.coe.int/ViewDoc.jsp?id=1259451&Site=CM (last accessed 10.4.10).

Committee of Ministers (2007), *Interim Resolution* CM/ResDH(2007)3 *Systemic violations of the right to the peaceful enjoyment of possessions through 'indirect expropriation' by Italy* (adopted by the Committee of Ministers on 14 February 2007 at the 987th meeting of the Ministers' Deputies). https://wcd.coe.int/ViewDoc.jsp?id=1095781&Site=CM&BackColorInternet=9999CC&BackColorIntranet=FFBB55&BackColorLogged=FFAC75 (last accessed 10.4.10).

Committee of Ministers (2007), *Interim Resolution* CM/ResDH(2007)75 *concerning the judgments of the European Court of Human Rights in 44 cases against Poland relating to the excessive length of detention on remand, 6 June 2007.* https://wcd.coe.int/ViewDoc.jsp?id=1146407&Site=CM (last accessed 9.4.10).

Committee of Ministers (2004), *Recommendation* Rec(2004)6 of the Committee of Ministers to member states on the improvement of domestic remedies *(adopted by the Committee of Ministers on 12 May 2004, at its 114th Session).* https://wcd.coe.int/ViewDoc.jsp?Ref=Rec(2004)6&Language=lanEnglish&Site=CM&BackColorInternet=C3C3C3&BackColorIntranet=EDB021&BackColorLogged=F5D383 (last accessed 8.4.10).

Committee of Ministers (2008), Recommendation CM/Rec (2008)2 of the Committee of Ministers to the member states on efficient domestic capacity for rapid execution of judgements of the ECtHR *(Adopted by the Committee of Ministers on 6 February 2008 at the 1017th meeting of the Ministers' Deputies)* https://wcd.coe.int/ViewDoc.jsp?id=1246081&Site=CM (last accessed 21.4.10).

Committee of Ministers (2005), ResDH(2005)55. *Resolution concerning the judgments of the European Court of Human Rights relating to the monitoring of prisoners' correspondence and the right to an effective remedy (case of Calogero Diana against Italy and 6 other cases) Adopted by the Committee of Ministers on 5 July 2005 at the 933rd meeting of the Ministers' deputies.* https://wcd.coe.int/ViewDoc.jsp?Ref=ResDH(2005)55&Language=lanEnglish&Site=CM&BackColorInternet=DBDCF2&BackColorIntranet=FDC864&BackColorLogged=FDC864 (last accessed 10.4.10).

Committee of Ministers (2004), Res(2004)3. *Resolution of the Committee of Ministers on judgments revealing an underlying systemic problem (adopted by the Committee of Ministers on 12 May 2004, at its 114th Session).* https://wcd.coe.int/ViewDoc.jsp?id=743257&Lang=fr.

Committee of Ministers (2004), RES (2004)3 *Resolution on judgments revealing an underlying systemic problem adopted by the Committee of Ministers on 12 May 2004 at its 114th Session.* https://wcd.coe.int/ViewDoc.jsp?id=743257&Lang=fr (last accessed 9.4.10).

Committee of Ministers (2009), *Supervision of the execution of judgments of the European Court of Human Rights, 2nd annual report 2008.* https://wcd.coe.int/com.instranet.InstraServlet?command=com.instranet.CmdBlobGet&InstranetImage=1221103&SecMode=1&DocId=1393816&Usage=2 (last accessed 8.4.10).

Directorate General of Human Rights and Legal Affairs (2009–2010), *Execution of the Judgments of the European Court of Human Rights. Pending Cases, Current State of Execution.* http://www.coe.int/t/dghl/monitoring/execution/Reports/Current_en.asp (last accessed 9.4.10).

European Commission for the Efficiency of Justice (CEPEJ), *Examination of problems related to the execution of decisions by national civil courts against the state and its entities in the Russian Federation (CEPEJ(2005)8*, 9.12.05.

European Court of Human Rights (2004), *'Bug River' Cases Adjourned*, European Court of Human Rights Press Release, 31.08.04. http://cmiskp.echr.coe.int/tkp197/view.asp?action=html&documentId=799850&portal=hbkm&source=externalbydocnumber&table=F69A27FD8FB86142BF01C1166DEA398649 (last accessed 8.4.10).

European Court of Human Rights (2010), *The European Court of Human Rights: Some facts and figures* http://www.echr.coe.int/NR/rdonlyres/E26094FC-46E7-41F4-91D2-32B1EC143721/0/Tableau_de_violations_19592009_ENG.pdf (last accessed 9.4.10).

European Court of Human Rights (2005), *Press release issued by the Registrar: Recent developments in Broniowski v Poland* 15.06.2005 http://cmiskp.echr.coe.int/tkp197/view.asp?item=1&portal=hbkm&action=html&highlight=recent%20%7C%20developments%20%7C%20in%20%7C%20Broniowski&sessionid=50884070&skin=hudoc-pr-en (last accessed 9.4.10).

European Court of Human Rights (2009), *The European Court of Human Rights, Country Fact Sheets, 1959–2009.*

European Court of Human Rights (2009), *The Pilot Judgment Procedure: information note issued by the Registrar.* http://www.echr.coe.int/NR/rdonlyres/DF4E8456-77B3-4E67-8944-B908143A7E2C/0/Information_Note_on_the_PJP_for_Website.pdf (last accessed 8.4.10).

European Court of Human Rights. President (2009), *Memorandum of the President of the European Court of Human Rights to the States with a view to preparing the Interlaken Conference, 3 July 2009.* http://www.coe.int/t/dc/files/themes/protocole14bis/03072009_Memo_Interlaken_anglais.pdf (last accessed 8.4.10).

Group of Wise Persons. *Report of the Group of Wise Persons to the Committee of Ministers,* SAGES(2006) 06 EN Def., Council of Europe, 10 November 2006, http://www.londonmet.ac.uk/londonmet/library/h26075_24.doc (last accessed 8.4.10).

Parliamentary Assembly of the Council of Europe. Committee on Legal Affairs and Human Rights (CLAHR) (2009), *Implementation of judgments of the European Court of Human Rights,* Christos Pourgourides, AS/Jur (2009) 36 31 August 2009. http://assembly.coe.int/CommitteeDocs/2009/ejdoc36ADD_2009.pdf (last accessed 8.4.10).

Parliamentary Assembly of the Council of Europe. Committee on Legal Affairs and Human Rights (CLAHR) (2008) *Implementation of judgments of the European Court of Human Rights: Introductory memorandum* Rapporteur: Mr Christos Pourgourides, Cyprus, AS/Jur (2008)24. http://assembly.coe.int/CommitteeDocs/2008/20080526_ajdoc24_2008.pdf.

Parliamentary Assembly of the Council of Europe. Committee on Legal Affairs and Human Rights (CLAHR) (2006), *Implementation of Judgments of the ECtHR, Report, Committee on Legal Affairs and Human Rights, Rapporteur: Mr Erik Jurgens, Netherlands, Socialist Group,* Doc. 11020, 18 September 2006. http://assembly.coe.int/Main.asp?link=/Documents/WorkingDocs/Doc06/EDOC11020.htm (last accessed 8.4.10).

Parliamentary Assembly of the Council of Europe. Committee on Legal Affairs and Human Rights (CLAHR) (2008), *The role of national parliaments in verifying state obligations to comply with the European Convention on Human Rights, including Strasbourg Court judgments: an overview,* in *Stockholm Colloquy: 'Towards stronger implementation of the European Convention on Human Rights at national level',* 9-10 June 2008, AS/Jur (2008) 32 rev, 23 June 2008.

Secretary General (2009), *Contribution of the Secretary General of the Council of Europe to the preparation of the Interlaken Ministerial Conference*, SG/Inf(2009)20 https://wcd.coe.int/ViewDoc.jsp?id=1571667&Site=COE (last accessed 8.4.10).

Steering Committee for Human Rights (CDDH). *Position paper of the European Court of Human Rights on proposals for reform of the European Convention on Human Rights and other measures as set out in the report of the Steering Committee for Human Rights of 4 April 2003* (CDDH(2003)006 final). http://www.coe.int/t/e/human_rights/cddh/3._committees/07.%20other%20committees%20and%20working%20groups/archives/06.%20guaranteeing%20human%20rights%20(cddh-gdr)/01.%20working%20documents/2003/2003_024_en.asp#TopOfPage (last accessed 8.4.10).

The Council of Europe's European Convention on Human Rights and the European Union's Charter of Fundamental Rights: Judges' Symposium – Luxembourg- 16 September 2002. Remarks by Ambassador Justin Harman, 16.09.02. http://www.coe.int/T/e/com/files/events/2002-09-Symposium-Judges/harman.asp.

JUDGMENTS AND PLEADINGS

Italy. Corte Costituzionale. Judgment 348 of 22 October 2007 http://www.cortecostituzionale.it/versioni_in_lingua/eng/attivitacorte/pronunceemassime/recent_judgments_2007.asp (last accessed 9.04.10).

Italy. Corte Costituzionale. Judgment 349 of 22 October 2007 http://www.cortecostituzionale.it/versioni_in_lingua/eng/attivitacorte/pronunceemassime/recent_judgments_2007.asp (last accessed 9.04.10).

Italy. Corte Costituzionale. Judgment 219 of 11 June 2008 http://www.cortecostituzionale.it/versioni_in_lingua/eng/attivitacorte/pronunceemassime/recent_judgments_2007.asp.

Moldova. Monitorul Oficial al Republicii Moldova (2006), *Acte ale Curţii Constituţionale a Republicii Moldova Hotărîre pentru controlul constituţionalităţii unor prevederi din Codul audiovizualului al Republicii Moldova nr.260-XVI din 27 iulie 2006 = Act of the Constitutional Court of the Republic of Moldova. Decision on the constitutionality of the Audiovisual Code of the Republic of Moldova.*

Poland. Trybunał Konstytucyjny. Judgment of 19 April 2005 K 4/05 Limitation of Rent Increases for living quarters http://www.trybunal.gov.pl/eng/summaries/documents/K_4_05_GB.pdf (last accessed 9.4.10).

R (On the application of Baiai and others) v Secretary of State for the Home Department [2008] UKHL 53. http://www.publications.parliament.uk/pa/ld200708/ldjudgmt/jd080730/rhome-1.htm (last accessed 11.4.10).

Russian Federation. Konstitutsionnyĭ Sud. *Postanovlenie Konstitutsionnogo Suda RF ot 14 iiulia 2005 g. N 8-P "Po delu o proverke konstitutsionnosti otdel'nykh polozheniĭ federal'nykh zakonov o federal'nom biudzhete na 2003 god, na 2004 god i na 2005 god i postanovleniia Pravitel'stva Rossiĭskoĭ Federatsii "O poriadke ispolneniia Ministerstvom finansov Rossiĭskoĭ Federatsii sudebnykh aktov po iskam k kazne Rossiĭskoĭ Federatsii na vozmeshchenie vreda, prichinennogo nezakonnymi deĭstviiami (bezdeĭstviem) organov gosudarstvennoĭ vlasti libo dolzhnostnykh lits organov gosudarstvennoĭ vlasti" v sviazi s zhalobami grazhdan Ė.D. Zhukovitskogo, I.G. Poĭma, A.V. Poniatovskogo, A.E. Cheslavskogo i OAO 'Khabarovskėnergo' = Decision of the Constitutional Court RF 14.07.05 g. N 8-P "On the matter of verifying the constitutionality of separate positions of the federal laws on the federal budget for 2003, 2004, 2005 and decisions of the Government of the Russian Federation "On the situation of how the Ministry of Finance of the Russian Federation is implementing court decisions against the Russian state to provide compensation for violations, unlawful acts (or failure to act) by state organs or authorities in connection with the complaints of citizens Ė.D. Zhukhovitskogo, I.G. Poĭma, A.V. Poniatovskogo, A.E. Cheslavskogo i OAO 'Khabarovskėnergo'.* http://ksportal.garant.ru:8081/SESSION/S__yUcOFK1X/PILOT/main.html (last accessed 11.4.10).

Russian Federation. Verkhovnyĭ Sud. *Postanovlenie Plenuma Verkhovnogo Suda Rossiĭskoĭ Federatsii No. 52 ot 27 dekabria 2007 g. "O srokakh rassmotreniia sudami Rossiĭskoĭ Federatsii ugolovnykh, grazhdanskikh del i del ob administrativnykh pravonarusheniiakh" = Resolution of the Plenary session of the Supreme Court of the Russian Federation, No.52, 27 December 2007 "On the length of judicial review of criminal, civil and administrative offences in the courts of the Russian Federation."* http://www.supcourt.ru/vscourt_detale.php?id=5121 (last accessed 11.4.10).

Russian Federation. Verkhovnyĭ Sud. *Postanovlenie Plenuma Verkhovnogo Suda Rossiĭskoĭ Federatsii No.16, O vnesenii v Gosudarstvennuiu Dumu Federal'nogo Sobraniia Rossiĭskoĭ Federatsii proektov federal'nogo konstitutsionnogo zakona "O vozmeshchenii gosudarstvom vreda, prichinennogo narusheniem prava na sudoproizvodstvo v razumnye sroki i prava na ispolnenie v razumnye sroki vstupivshikh v zakonnuiu silu sudebnykh aktov" i federal'nogo zakona "O vnesenii izmeneniĭ v otdel'nye zakonodatel'nye akty Rossiĭskoĭ Federatsii v sviazi s priniatiem Federal'nogo konstitutsionnogo prava na sudoproizvodstva v razumnye sroki i prava na ispolnenie v razumnye sroki vstupivshikh v zakonnuiu silu sudebnykh aktov"* 26.09.08. = *Resolution of the Plenary session of the Supreme Court of the Russian Federation No.16 to lay a federal constitutional bill with the State Duma of the Federal Assembly of the Russian Federation "On compensation for state violations of the right to trial within a reasonable time and the right to the execution of judgments that should have come into force" and the federal law "On amending individual legal acts of the Russian Federation in connection with the adoption of the Federal Constitutional law "On compensation for state violations of the right to trial within a reasonable time and the right to the execution of judgments that should have come into force""* 26.9.08. http://www.supcourt.ru/vscourt_detale.php?id=5491 or http://www.supcourt.ru/arxiv_out/TEXT.PHP?id_text=121232&i1text=разумные%20сроки (last accessed 11.4.10).

Slovenia. Ustavno Sodišče. *Odločba o ugotoviti, da bi odložitvijo uveljavite oziroma z zavrnitvijo zakona o spremembah in dopolnitvah zakona o odvetništvu lahko nastale protiustavne posledice = The decision to determine whether the proposed postponement with respect to the rejection of the amendments to the Attorney's law will have*

unconstitutional consequences, Uradni list RS, št. 35/2009, 08.05.09, http://www.uradni-list.si/1/content?id=92090 (last accessed 9.4.10).
Slovenia. Ustavno Sodišče. Judgment No. U-I-93/07, 22.10.09 http://odlocitve.us-rs.si/usrs/us-odl.nsf/o/3BA096F20C0B1BACC1257662004E4EA2 (last accessed 9.04.10).
Slovenia. Ustavno Sodišče. Judgment Up-2443/08-22, 07.10.09. http://odlocitve.us-rs.si/usrs/us-odl.nsf/o/C11D8876A72E2582C12576560043BF48 (last accessed 19.02.10).
United Kingdom. UK Government's Observations and annexes on the admissibility of the *O'Donoghue v United Kingdom* application (34848/07), Derek Walton, Agent for the Government of the UK, 28 April 2009.
United Kingdom. *O'Donoghue v UK.* Letter to European Court from Derek Walton, Foreign and Commonwealth Office, 12 November 2009.

ABOUT THE AUTHORS

Brad K. BLITZ is Professor of Human and Political Geography at Kingston University and former Jean Monnet Chair of the Political Geography of Europe at Oxford Brookes University. He received his Ph.D. in International Development from Stanford University and has published several studies on migration and comparative politics in the context of European integration, transitions to democracy and post-conflict development. He has also served as a consultant to several international agencies including the UN Office of the High Commissioner for Human Rights, the World Bank, Council of Europe, Organisation for Security and Cooperation in Europe, as well as several governments. His recent publications include *Statelessness and the Benefits of Citizenship* (2009), *War and Change in the Balkans: Nationalism, Conflict and Cooperation* (2006) and various journal articles (Journal of Ethnic and Migration Studies, Journal of European Social Policy, Human Rights Review, Journal of Refugee Studies etc). He is currently completing two books, one on statelessness in Europe (Cambridge University Press, 2010) and another on the benefits of nationality reform in a global context (Edward Elgar Publishing, 2010).

Helen HARDMAN was the primary researcher on the pilot judgments project at London Metropolitan University (2008-2010) and is currently editing her doctoral thesis for publication with Manchester University Press. She has a BA in Russian (Hertford College, Oxford), an MA in Slavonic & East European Studies (UCL, London) and a doctorate in Politics (St Antony's College, Oxford, 2007). Her doctoral thesis, on democratization in Central and Eastern Europe between 1988 and 1991, was supported by archival research in Russia and Hungary and interviews conducted in Moscow, Budapest and Belgrade. Between 2005 and 2007 Helen taught the graduate course on computer-assisted textual analysis software (QSR N6) for the Dept. of Politics and International Relations, University of Oxford. From 2007 to 2008 she taught courses on Russian and Central & East European Politics for the Political Science and EURUS departments at Carleton University, Ottawa. Her research interests include media freedom in Russia and Central and Eastern Europe. She has published with Stephen Coleman and Elizabeth Frazer: 'Democratic culture and the Internet' in *Krzysztof Piech (ed) The Knowledge Based Economy in Transition Countries*, SSEES-UCL Press, 2004.

Philip LEACH is Professor of Human Rights, a solicitor, and Director of the Human Rights and Social Justice Research Institute at London Metropolitan

University. He is Director of the European Human Rights Advocacy Centre (EHRAC) (also at London Metropolitan University) which assists Russian and Georgian NGOs in litigating before the European Court of Human Rights. He was formerly Legal Director of Liberty and of the Kurdish Human Rights Project and has extensive experience of representing applicants before the European Court. He has conducted human rights training for the Council of Europe, the OSCE, the British Council, the Foreign & Commonwealth Office, the Law Society of England and Wales, the Arab Lawyers' Union and for various NGOs. Recent human rights research projects have been commissioned, or supported, by the Equality and Human Rights Commission, the OSCE, Council of Europe and the Nuffield Foundation. He is the author of *Taking a Case to the European Court of Human Rights*, 2nd ed., Oxford University Press, 2005. He is a member of the Editorial Board of European Human Rights Law Review and in 2009 he was appointed to the Independent Advisory Panel on Deaths in Custody.

Svetlana STEPHENSON is a Senior Lecturer in International Comparative Sociology at London Metropolitan University. She has researched human rights and social justice in Russia and Eastern Europe, as well as disadvantaged social groups and youth violence in that region. Her consultancy work has included advising the Department of International Development on juvenile justice in Russia and the World Bank on poverty in Russia. She has also worked with the International Labour Organisation on child labour in Russia, and prepared a report on Youth and Violence in Moscow for the Council of Europe. She is a member of the Editorial Board of the European Journal of Homelessness. Her publications include *Crossing the Line. Vagrancy, Homelessness and Social Displacement in Russia*, Ashgate, 2006, and articles for Radical Philosophy, The Sociological Review, Europe-Asia Studies, Social Policy Review, International Journal of Comparative Sociology, Slavic Review, Social Justice Research and Work, Employment and Society, as well as many publications in edited volumes.

www.ingramcontent.com/pod-product-compliance
Ingram Content Group UK Ltd.
Pitfield, Milton Keynes, MK11 3LW, UK
UKHW051927100926
8556IPUK00022B/1414

9 789400 000414